Amber –
All the best.

Hope you enjoy
the stories & that
it inspires you in
your court-reporting
career.

All the best.

your court-reporting

S

GO FOR IT!

CROSS-EXAMINATION TO CLOSING: HOW TO WIN AN INTELLECTUAL PROPERTY TRIAL BEFORE A JURY

RAYMOND P. NIRO

authorHOUSE®

AuthorHouse™
1663 Liberty Drive
Bloomington, IN 47403
www.authorhouse.com
Phone: 1-800-839-8640

Published by AuthorHouse 6/05/2012

ISBN: 978-1-4490-3269-2
ISBN: 978-1-4490-3270-8
ISBN: 978-1-4490-3271-5

Library of Congress Control Number: 2009910798

I was inspired to write this book after reading some stories about cross-examination written by alleged masters at the art. Unfortunately, I found that some examples were good, a few exceptional and most merely adequate. That led me to think about my own cases, some of their defining moments (every case has at least one defining moment) and how we were fortunate enough to electrify a judge or jury with a winning cross-examination and closing argument. Let me share some of these moments with you in the hope they will provide guidance and inspiration for future cross-examinations and closings.

A special thanks to Judy for her unwavering support in nearly every one of these cases: I could not have done it without her.

Raymond P. Niro
October 2009/February 2012
©Raymond P. Niro 2009/2012

To My Sons,
Dean, Raymond, Brian and Sean

SPECIAL THANKS

I have so many people to thank: my parents for giving me the drive to succeed and the street smarts to relate to people, Paul Vickrey for editing the sections on the <u>C&F</u>, <u>TFD</u> and <u>Haas</u> cases, Chris Lee for his help on the <u>Coleman</u> case, Shanna Kwall for her editing and organization, Venita Berzina for her research, Donna Wartman for being there again and again (just like in most of the cases) and, of course, all the lawyers, paralegals and staff in every case discussed in this book, Tom Scavone, Tim Haller, Bill Niro, Joe Hosteny, John Janka, Bob Vitale, Paul Vickrey, my sons Dean and Raymond Niro, Pat Solon, Art Gasey, Chris Lee, Dave Sheikh, Bill Dossas, Sally Wiggins, Rich Megley, Matt McAndrews, Paul Gibbons, Brady Fulton, Greg Casimer, Doug Hall, Dina Hayes, Chris Laney, Dave Mahalek, Kara Szpondowski, Bob Conley, Laura Kenneally, Tahiti Arsulowicz, Brian Haan, Joe Culig, Anna Folgers, Nick and Dan Hey, Judy Niro, Katy Brennan, Ray Rzeszutko, Jenna Bayer, Erin Hobin, Cara Feinholz, Jane Zuckerman, Barb Baboian, Anne Marie Byrne, Tony Pichotta, Clare Sullivan, Barb Zylman, Susan Swierk, Lisa Esquivel, Angelica Regalado, Liz Vondrasek, Carol Koski, Mary Martin, Sue Burke, Marianne Mecyssne, Kim Nicks, Jim Koncz, Patrick Johnson, Dylan Brown, Judy Lockhart, Jorge Molina, Patrick Zanotti, Patrick Duggan, Jason Hicks, Jeff Lasley and Arnold Campbell.

CONTENTS

PART I
THREE OF THE BEST

<u>Frank Calabrese v. Square D Company</u>,

Civil Action No. 97 C 2199 (N.D. Ill., Jan. 2000)

<u>C&F Packing Co., Inc. v. IBP, Inc.</u>,

Civil Action No. 93 C 1601 (N.D. Ill., Nov. 1998)

<u>MuniAuction, Inc. v. Thomson Corp.</u>,

Civil Action No. 01-1003 (W.D. Penn., Sept. 2006)

HOW TO WIN WITH ONLY ADVERSE WITNESSES

<u>Frank Calabrese</u> v. <u>Square D Company</u>,
Civil Action No. 97 C 2199 (N.D. Ill., Jan. 2000)

Perhaps once in a lifetime, you get a chance to really make a difference in someone's life. I have been lucky enough to have been given multiple chances. This case is one example. The patent was poorly written. The case seemed dead and came back to life through an appeal no one in our office (except Chris Lee and me) was willing to take.

Frank Calabrese was an electrical engineer. Without the benefit of any research grant or big-company funding, he invented a new industrial control system called a data relay system. I explained Frank's invention in my opening by analogy to the rooms of a house where data from each room had to be monitored with minimal use of separate wires. ***First, the problem*** (the hand-written sketch I used in the Opening):

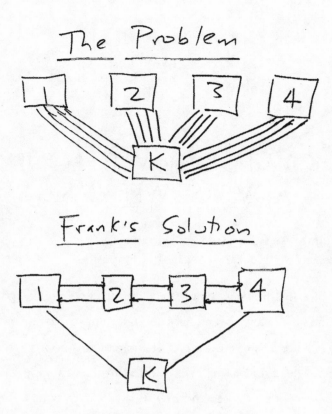

Now the patent; Frank Calabrese's patent, issued on an application that was filed almost 20 years ago. It's been said that necessity is the mother of invention, and I want to show you in the briefest form with a sketch. I apologize in advance because I'm not a very good sketcher.

If I had, say, a room in my home, a kitchen and four other rooms, calling them 1, 2, 3, and 4, and I wanted to determine from my kitchen what was going on in each of those rooms, what the temperature was, was the TV on, are the lights on, and in our house during the holidays with ten grandkids, what's the noise level? The way I would do that is to run four lines between room 1 and the kitchen, then four lines from the second room, then four lines from the third, then four lines from the fourth. As you can see, you've got a lot of wires to get that information to the kitchen.

That was the necessity, the problem that Frank Calabrese had to solve. It doesn't seem like much when you look at this, but if you imagine a hundred machines in a factory and imagine that you're trying to get 40 pieces of information, temperature, flow rate, this, that, who knows what, now you're talking about 4,000 wires. That's a lot, and that costs money to install. There are reliability problems and difficulties.

(Transcript, January 19, 2000, pp. 78-79). *Then the solution:*

What Mr. Calabrese did -- and you will hear him testify about this -- what he did is he came up with something called a Data Relay System. That's the title of his patent over here. You'll see his drawing. If we were to replicate what we just showed you, we now have the same four rooms. Only now, instead of running all those separate lines, we're going to put these little boxes in here which are data relays, and that's what the patent talks about.

You run the four lines, the 400 lines if it's in a factory, to the data relays, connect them up, connect them here, and what you have now instead of 4,000 lines or 16 lines, you have two (indicating). In some cases, it's four because you have what they call a ground and a shield. Then you send out, according to this invention, an address and say: I want to know what's happening in room number 2, and I want to know what the temperature is in room number 2 or how many grandkids are there making noise. If 2's number comes up, then you send it back to and through 1, then back to what we call the host.

(Transcript, January 19, 2000, p. 79). *Next, the words of the patent:*

You are going to hear words and language that

isn't going to make a lot of sense. Instead of calling
these things wires, which is what I would call them,
or conductors, they're going to be called a bus, not
the kind of bus you ride on, but a bus, and this will
be called a host, and these are data relays (indicating).
Square D may call them or has called them things like
I/O modules or data modules.

These words, data relay, address, data line, bus, serial,
parallel, they're words used in the patent to persons of
ordinary knowledge in the art. You'll hear Mr. Calabrese
testify about that, and you'll hear witnesses from Square
D testify about that.

(Transcript, January 19, 2000, pp. 79-80). *And last, but not least, the*
benefits of the invention, its value:

Now, the benefits of the Calabrese invention that
flow from what you will see and hear in the documents
of Square D, but in essence what you're going to hear
and see is that installation costs, labor and material
reduced 70 percent; cost of the basic unit, half the price
of the nearest competitor Allen-Bradley; reliability off
the charts; growth rate on the part of this company, 80
percent per year in this product area. That's the success
part of this story.

(Transcript, January 19, 2000, p. 80). That's how I start most of my
cases: invention, success and someone that decided to take something
rather than pay. Same story, different actors.

The <u>Calabrese</u> case was in for a rocky ride. Frank's patent was poorly
prepared, I would guess put together in just a few hours. It had two
drawings and two columns of text; one-half of one column constituted
the totality of both claims. The first trial judge found the patent invalid

on summary judgment for failure to disclose the best mode to practice the invention -- a requirement of 35 U.S.C. § 112.

We took an appeal; the Federal Circuit reversed. And suddenly, we had the opportunity for a new trial before a new judge. That was the good news. The bad news was that, in the five years of delay from filing through the first appeal, Frank's cancer had become terminal. He had only months to live.

We urged new Judge Harry D. Leinenweber to give us an early trial and to allow us to preserve Frank's testimony by videotape. He agreed, but Frank was so weak, he could only testify for an hour or so without total exhaustion.

So there we were: a trial with no live witnesses. No Frank, no experts -- technical or damage -- and no fact witnesses either. We would try the case with Frank's one-hour video and a series of adverse witnesses from Square D. Frank's son, David, sat at the plaintiff's table with Chris Lee and me. Frank's wife, Kathy, stayed home to care for Frank in his last days. It was the three of us -- Chris, Dave and me -- against the teams of lawyers that Square D had assembled for the defense.

I want to share some examples of the cross-examinations we did in the case to show that a lawsuit can be won solely on the basis of cross-examination. One examination uses the opposing side's misstatements in opening to destroy their credibility. Another shows how a simple background question taken from deposition testimony (I knew the answer had to be "yes" because he had said it in his deposition) exploded into the inescapable conclusion that the witness was simply not believable. Others show impeachment after impeachment of adverse witnesses. In the end, the giant fell.

USING AN OPPONENT'S OPENING ARGUMENT TO DESTROY CREDIBILITY

Four different lawyers were splitting trial responsibility for Square D (an acceptable approach, but one I do not prefer). Unfortunately, these guys must not have talked to each other. One lawyer didn't know what the other was saying. First, the representations made in the opening about Square D having what was called a "broadcast system":

> ... In essence, this isn't a complex case because what you need to learn, what you need to know to appreciate why Seriplex components and why Seriplex modules are completely and significantly different from the '849 patent is that you've got to know the difference between two concepts. One concept is called the concept of sequential transmission of data, and *the other concept is called the broadcast transmission of data.*

> Mr. Riley, though, in the Seriplex invention had a completely different way of doing it. You'll hear from the witnesses that Seriplex transmits its data *by broadcasting it, broadcasting* it down the line, much in the same way that a *radio signal is broadcast*.

(Transcript, January 10, 2000, pp. 91-92; emphasis added). Then came the cross-examination of the very first witness that exposed the lie about Seriplex being a broadcast system, just like a radio signal is broadcast:

Q.   You know how a radio wave works, right?

A.   Roughly.

Q.   I think when Marconi invented it they called it "wireless." Do you remember that or ever hear of that?

A.   It was before my time.

Q.   It was before my time, too.

In any event, when you have a radio wave, it goes through the air. A signal is sent from some place and it goes through the air and arrives at your radio, right? You can tune it in?

A.   Correct.

Q.   A *broadcast*, right?

A.   Correct.

Q.   The signal from the radio tower doesn't need a wire to get from the radio tower to my radio in my home, right?

A.   That's correct.

Q.   Now, the Seriplex system uses wires, doesn't it?

A.   To?

Q.   To take data from one point to another.

A.   Yes.

Q.   It doesn't send signals through the air, right?

A.   No.

Q.   It doesn't *broadcast* signals like a radio does, right?

A.   No.

Q.   So if somebody said this Seriplex System is like a radio; it *broadcasts* signals like a radio; it *broadcasts* over the air without wires, that wouldn't be correct, isn't that right?

A.   I'm sorry.

Q. If somebody said that the Seriplex system is like a radio; it **broadcasts** over the air without wires, that wouldn't be correct?

A. *That would not be correct.*

(Transcript, January 20, 2008, pp. 139-140; emphasis added). Who was that "someone" who misled the jury by suggesting that Seriplex was a broadcast system? I didn't have to say it was the Square D lawyer in his opening statement. The jury knew -- and down went Square D's credibility.

In his opening, Square D's lawyer gave me another opportunity to shake Square D's story. Back to the opening. Square D's lawyer also claimed Square D didn't sell any software and, hence, it shouldn't be held liable for contributory infringement:

> That's a fancy computer term for somebody who takes all the parts, Seriplex components and parts he buys from another source, puts them all together in to the kind of system that that customer wants, and **he's got to add to that software**, by the way. That system['] s integrator comes along, you'll hear, and **obtains computer software** that's programmed so that that system does what that customer wants.
> The evidence will show that how a customer is using the Seriplex components and the Seriplex parts way down the line, that down-the-line end user, **Square D doesn't know, and Square D doesn't control what that customer does**. So Square D isn't selling the data Relay System that's called for in this patent.

(Transcript, January 19, 2000, p. 93; emphasis added). That's right: Square D allegedly didn't provide any software; it was the system integrator. And it didn't know or control the customer's use. Right?

Here's my cross-examination based upon what we found on Square D's web site the night before:

Q. Do you recognize that?

A. Yes.

Q. Now, this relates to something called Seriplex Software Accessory Pak, right?

A. Yes.

Q. That is software that is offered and provided to users, potential users of the Seriplex system, right?

MR. STINE: Your Honor, I would like to object to the use of this in a presentation before the jury at this point. There is no foundation for it. He is apparently trying to just refresh recollection.

THE COURT: I do not know what the purpose of this is. Is this an exhibit in the case?

MR. NIRO: It is something we received last night, your Honor, and obtained from their web site. We will mark it as an exhibit. I am using it to refresh the witness' recollection as to the existence of software.

MR. STINE: I believe, your Honor, before it is published to the jury there should be a foundation.

MR. NIRO: That's fine.

THE COURT: Well, if it is just to refresh recollection, then it shouldn't be published.

BY MR. NIRO: Q. Let's see if we can refresh your recollection.

This Seriplex Software Accessory Pak has something called "windows NT utilities for the Seriplex CPU." That is part of the system, right?

A. Yes.

Q. You provide a seed programming library which contains routines and codes for software and drivers for the Seriplex system, isn't that right?

A. Yes.

Q. And you have a programmer's guide, correct?

Q. All of which is offered to customers and users of Seriplex systems, isn't that right?

A. Yes.

Q. *So, if somebody said to this jury that Square D didn't sell software related to its Seriplex systems, that wouldn't be correct, isn't that right?*

A. *Technically we don't sell the software. It's free.* It is downloaded from the Net. This is not software that one would use to make a complete system. This is simply a way to connect the Seriplex interface card into a PC. It still would not do anything with this software.

Q. Well, do you give it away?

A. This is given away, yes.

Q. *The purpose of giving it away is to encourage people to use this software on a Seriplex system, isn't that right?*

A. *Yes.*

⊹ ⊹ ⊹ ⊹ ⊹

Q. *Well, is it used, to your knowledge, for any purpose other than for use on Seriplex?*

A. *No.*

Q. *So, it is a specialty software in that sense, software designed and provided to customers free of charge for use on Seriplex systems, right?*

A. *That's correct.*

(Transcript, January 20, 2000, pp. 121-124; emphasis added).

So there you have it -- one promise made ("we have a broadcast system") that was proven to be false; another promise made ("we don't supply software") that was also proven to be false. Two examples in one case of destroying an opponent's credibility through misstatements made in the opening.

But in this case, it got even worse. In his opening, Square D's lawyer also said that Square D did not know anything about the components it sold or how they were made or used:

> So certainly we believe that by the time you hear all the evidence and hear all the testimony, you'll find that Square D could not be contributing to anybody's infringement because they had *no knowledge* that their products were so made, didn't know how the products were being *used*, and based on the care and investigation they took they certainly couldn't have been doing anything like that willfully.

(Transcript, January 19, 2000, pp. 97-98). Oh yeah?

On cross-examination, the same adverse witness admitted Square D set-up a company to train customers on how to use the Seriplex system, to set-up an industry standard and to promote Seriplex technology -- all for the purpose of selling more components. Notice the string of leading questions:

Q.   So, the goal here was to set up an organization, fund the organization and get the organization, STO, to help other people set this as an industry standard, Seriplex, right?

A.   That's right.

Q.   That way [you] can sell more of our components to those users, correct?

A.   That's correct.

Q.   That was part of the plan, right?

A.   Yes.

Q.   That was what was done, correct?

A.   We set it up, yes, sir.

Q.   Now, part of what you did at STO was give training classes to engineers, right?

A.   That's correct.

Q.   Did there come a time when you had a whole group of something called "Seriplex-compliant manufacturers"?

A.   Yes.

Q.   That was part of the goal of this STO entity, correct?

A.   That's correct.

Q.   Now, when you set up people to do this work, this promotional work, you provided them with kits, isn't that right, to help promote the Seriplex sales?

A. There was a kit available to make this an easy thing. We gave the Seriplex technology away but we would sell a kit that would contain the components needed to get started.

Q. When you say that you are giving the Seriplex technology away, what you are trying to do is get customers, end users to use Seriplex, to specify Seriplex so that you can sell more components, right?

A. The reason –

Q. Is that right or wrong?

A. Ultimately, correct.

(Transcript, January 20, 2000, pp. 126-128). So we had established through Square D's own witnesses that Square D not only knew how the products were being made and used, but it was telling customers exactly how to use them. Three lies in the opening statement, all exposed through the very first witness. We didn't need any witnesses. The defendant's witnesses (who we called in our case) were doing just fine for us.

IMPEACHMENT

Impeaching an adverse witness is about as much fun as you can have in a courtroom. It goes like this:

Q. X.

A. No.

Q. Let me read to you from your sworn testimony given on (date). Answer: Yes. Did you give that answer to that question at that time?

A.   Ugh.

What does any normal person think? Liar! I tell my witnesses never, ever get impeached. It's deadly.

Here is an example of impeachment of another Square D witness in the Calabrese trial (remember, we didn't have any witnesses of our own, except Frank's one-hour video).

First, some background on who he was. Notice how every question is leading and how I know what the answer has to be:

Q.   I'm sorry. I will start again. Would you state your full name.

BY WITNESS: A. Richard Karl Bazany.

Q.   You work for Square D, Mr. Bazany?

A.   Yes, sir.

Q.   The defendant in this case, right?

A.   Yes.

Q.   You are the product line manager for something called Network Products, is that right?

A.   That is correct.

Q.   That responsibility includes the Seriplex line of products, is that right?

A.   Yes, it does.

(Transcript, January 21, 2000, pp. 337-338). ***Then, the first impeachment -- what is Seriplex technology?***

Q.   The Seriplex technology is really a simple way of communicating signals over a signal wire to I/O devices out in the field, is that right?

A.   No, it's not.

＊ ＊ ＊ ＊ ＊

Q.   That's wrong?

A.   That's wrong.

Q.   Let me read to you from your deposition at Page 8. This was taken on November 10th, 1997. (Reading)

"Q   What is the Seriplex technology?

A   The Seriplex technology is a simple way of communicating signals over a single wire to I/O devices out in the field."

Did you give that answer to that question at that time?

A.   If I gave that answer, I misstated it. Sir, it is really over a single cable which includes four wires inside the cable.

Q.   So you gave the answer and you are going to change it now, right?

A.   I misspoke myself. Yes, sir.

(Transcript, January 21, 2000, pp. 338-339). Each time I impeached him, I used the exact language of his prior answer. ***Now, the second impeachment; he never used the word "shop overhead":***

Q.   The contribution margins are between forty and fifty percent, right?

A.   At the time of my deposition that was correct. That was based on the previous years' contribution margin.

Q. That number doesn't just include labor and materials. It includes some of your **shop overhead**, right?

A. No. It is labor and materials. *I guess you would have to define "shop overhead." We don't use that term. So, I am not sure what you mean by it.*

Q. *You don't use that term?*

A. *I don't use that term, no.*

(Transcript, January 21, 2000, p. 340; emphasis added). I had him:

Q. Let me read to you from your deposition, Page 6, where you were asked at that point to define contribution margin. This is Line 23. (Reading)

> "Q What do you understand it to mean?
>
> A. It's labor and materials, **some shop overhead.**"

Did you give that answer to that question at that time?

A. If it was in my deposition, I guess I did at that time. It has been quite a while ago.

Q. You understood what "**shop overhead**" meant when you gave that answer. That was a term that you used at that time, is that correct.

A. I used that term.

Q. But today you don't use that term, is that right?

A. I no longer use that term.

(Transcript, January 21, 2000, pp. 340-341; emphasis added). Think about that one for a moment. He never used the words "shop overhead";

he wasn't sure what that meant at trial. But, in his earlier deposition, he used those exact words. This witness was going down -- big time.

Remember the representation in the opening that Square D didn't sell software? Here it comes again:

Q. Am I correct, sir, that, as part of the Seriplex line, Square D sells input/output modules?

A. As part of the line we do sell input and output modules. That's correct.

Q. CPU interfaces?

A. Yes, sir.

Q. Accessory products?

A. Yes.

Q. Software, isn't that right?

A. No. We don't sell software, in the strict terms of the sense of "software," what most people would consider to be software. We don't sell software. We have something that we call software, a label, but it's not really software as you would normally purchase software commercially.

Q. Don't you sell some software?

A. Maybe I should understand what you mean by "software" and what does software do in terms of your question?

Q. Let me read to you from Page 8 of your deposition, Line 23. (Reading)

"Q And does Seriplex line -- does the Seriplex line, as you understand it, consist of the sales of input/output modules, CPU interfaces, accessory products and some software, is that right?

A   Yes.

Q   Anything else?

A   That's primarily it."

Did you give those answers to those questions at that time?

A.   I did give those answers to those questions at that time.

Q.   So, at least as of the time you gave your deposition you believed that, in addition to selling input/output modules, CPU interfaces and accessory products the company also sold some software as part of the Seriplex package, right?

A.   The software that we sold at that time was something we called C-libraries, which was just an instruction set for people who had real software to be able to use our product.

Q.   So, now today it's not real software that you sell, is that what you are saying?

A.   It's a software library. It's not useable by itself. It can only be used with somebody's additional software.

Q.   But there is no dispute here that it is part of what you sell?

A.   That is correct?

Q.   *You sell software, right*?

A.   *Absolutely*.

(Transcript, January 21, 2000, pp. 341-343; emphasis added). It keeps going. He didn't know what "install" meant but, in his deposition, he talked about the "install base":

Q. When you talk about an install base, there was a million installed, right?

A. What do you mean by "installed"?

Q. Well, maybe I will read to you, again. Page 52 of your deposition. (Reading)

> "Q On the next page it says, 'Seriplex currently has an install base of more than 150,000 points.' Was that correct as of 1995?"
>
> A That is I/O points, that's correct.
>
> Q What is the install base now?
>
> A Something in the area of a million I/O points."

Q Did you give those answers to those questions at that time?

A. Yes.

And "install base" is a term that is widely used in our industry to describe the number of I/O points that a company has sold.

Q. What is the install base now?

A. I really don't know. I haven't calculated the install base in a couple of years.

(Transcript, January 21, 2000, pp. 353-354). How about this one? Again, notice how I use the exact words of his prior testimony:

Q. Would you agree with me that the most significant part of the value of the Seriplex system has to do with the savings that are realized by an end user of the Seriplex system?

A. Would you restate that question? I'm not sure I followed it.

Q. Would you agree with me that the most significant part of the value of the Seriplex system has to do with the savings that are realized by an end user of the Seriplex system?

A. ***No, I wouldn't, not at all***.

Q. Let me read to you from Page 68 of your deposition. (Reading)

> "Q Would you agree with me that part of the value, maybe the most significant part of the value of the Seriplex system, has to do with the savings that are realized to the end user?
>
> A ***Yes, I would***."

That was your answer. Did you give that answer to that question at that time?

A. Yes, I did. But, I guess, I would want to know the context of the question and the discussion we were having. Because, if the system doesn't provide a value to the customer in terms of what it does for the customer, the automation it does for the customer, no matter how much in savings it is going to give him, it's not the single-most important thing. It's a combination of things. It has to get the job done as well as save them money.

(Transcript, January 21, 2000, pp. 361-362; emphasis added). He went from "no, I wouldn't, not at all" to "yes, I would." Nothing could save this guy; again, I use the exact words of his prior testimony "prime objective":

Q. Mr. Bazany, I'll ask you, again. Wasn't the *prime objective of the purchase* the acquisition of the Seriplex technology?

A. I'm not sure I know how to answer that. I think you're looking for a yes or no answer and I'm not sure I know how to answer that yes or no.

Q. Well, let me read from your deposition, again, given in this case on November 10, 1997, at Page 90, Line 13. (Reading)

"Q   The total purchase price was round $2.5 million?

A   Just under that, right.

Q   What Group Schneider and Square D acquired, essentially, was the Seriplex technology, right?

A   That's correct.

Q   That was the *prime objective of the purchase*, right?

A   Yes. It was an asset purchase."

Did you give those answers to those questions at that time?

A. Yes. I think the important thing was that it was an asset purchase because they purchased all of the assets, not just the bare technology. The Seriplex technology at that point included the product line, trademark and ASIC design as well.

Q.   Am I correct, sir, that the prime objective of the purchase was the acquisition of the Seriplex technology, which you testified to under oath?

A.   If you include all of those things in the "Seriplex technology," you are correct.

(Transcript, January 21, 2000, pp. 363-364; emphasis added). I started using his prior testimony even when it didn't impeach him:

Q.   As head of the business unit of the Seriplex product you were never given any analysis of the claims of Frank Calabrese's patent, isn't that right?

A.   That's correct.

Q.   You were given nothing that showed that there was no infringement correct?

A.   That's correct.

Q.   Let me read to you from Page 113 of your deposition, Line 11 (Reading)

"Q   Were you given any analysis of the prosecution history or the prior art or of the claims of the Calabrese patent, any analysis of those kinds of things?

A   Analysis from Mr. Femal?

Q   Right.

A   No.

Q   From any attorney did you get those analyses?

A   No, I did not get those analyses from any attorney."

Is that correct?

A.   That's what I said. That was different than the question you asked.

(Transcript, January 21, 2000, pp. 371-372). Square D could not even be saved by its own attorneys -- they admitted one thing in response to requests to admit and the witness said the admission was wrong:

Q.   Am I correct that all of the Seriplex I/O modules and products are designed to be multiplex or support and work with multiplexing?

A.   You are not correct. All of the Seriplex products are not designed for multiplexing.

Q.   So, the statement made in this Item No. 170, signed by Mr. Stine in this document filed with the Court, it is your view, is incorrect? I'll read it. (Reading)

> "All of the Seriplex I/O modules and products are designed to be multiplex or to support and work with multiplexing Seriplex modules" --

And then it identifies a bunch of things. (Reading)

> "Response: Admitted."

You say that should be denied?

A.   I think my answer -- was that my answer?

Q.   No. That's the answer of your company. Do you disagree with that?

A.   Yes, sir, I disagree with that.

Q.   That was an answer given to the Court as part of these proceedings in this case.

You disagree with that?

A.   I disagree with that.

(Transcript, January 21, 2000, pp. 386-387; emphasis added). Now, how could anyone believe these guys? Again, this was a case based solely upon adverse witnesses and a one-hour video.

In closing, I tied it all together. First, on contributory infringement:

> You heard the testimony early on from the first witness we called after Frank Calabrese, Mr. Newell. He was the sale marketing guy. He said, "We sell components to customers. I'm in charge of doing that." And we went through the stack of materials -- I have it here -- the stack of materials that they put out -- and this is just some of it -- through this SPO organization to tell people how to use it. Big manuals, white paper, product description, kits on how to put it all together, Design and Installation and Troubleshooting manual, data sheets, detailed specifications, lists of manufacturers on, and on, and on and on. They set up an organization, a special organization, called SPO, whose purpose it was to help sell these components.
>
> Now, they will tell you -- in fact, they have said it throughout this case -- we didn't know what these people were going to use these things for. I mean, come on. Let's use common sense here. They write these manuals to tell them what to do. They troubleshoot to tell them what to do. They have sales people to tell them what to do. They establish an organization in their office, this SPO, to tell them what to do. They suggest to you that they didn't know that their components were being designed for use in an infringing system? They even licensed people to use the infringing system, suggesting that without their permission you can't do it.

(Transcript, January 26, 2000, pp. 853-854).

I read the jury the testimony from another witness who admitted

Square D actively helped customers understand how to use the individual components it sold. Then, I hit hard on credibility (mining the gold I had developed in cross-examination):

> Ultimately, when you think about it, this case comes down to who are you going to believe, credibility. Judge Leinenweber will tell you that's your job. You look at the witnesses, you judge their demeanor, you look for discrepancies, you look at inconsistencies and in the end you decide who is telling it like it is, who is not, who do I believe and who do I not.
>
> Now, Frank Calabrese is too sick to be here. And you sa[w] him and you heard him and you could decide whether in his condition it was his mission to lie. You saw Mr. Riley on the video and Mr. Bazany here in person and Mr. Phillips. Were they straightforward or were they evasive?
>
> You heard Mr. Barry's opening and the six promises he made. I believe he said, the Calabrese design is like an old Christmas tree light system. Take out one bulb and they all go down. When the witnesses were confronted with their own documents, they said, hey, that's not so. Ours is the same way.
>
> He told you that the Seriplex system broadcasts signals like a radio signal. That's not true. They had to deny that as the case went forward.
>
> He said, "We sell only generic components. None of them were specially made for use in Seriplex." Not true. They had to admit that as the case went forward.
>
> He said, "Square D has nothing to do with these customers. They use whatever they want. We don't help them." But the stack of materials in Mr. Newell's testimony put the lie to that.
>
> He said, "We don't know what our customers are doing. We don't provide any software." Not so. We went on the Internet that night and we found that they are selling software. They want to draw a sharp distinction

now between application software and other software. They admit they sold software and they know why they did it. The patent doesn't talk about software, anyway.

(Transcript, January 26, 2000, pp. 856-857). I also hit hard on the "shop overhead" impeachment and the word games about "serial data":

> Credibility. Mr. Bazany. Remember Mr. Bazany when I called him as a witness? How many times did he deny testimony that he had given previously? We talked about Seriplex technology being defined. He denied the definition that he gave in his deposition under oath. He said, "I never used the word 'shop overhead.'" I read him his answer where he defined "shop overhead."
>
> I asked him whether savings were the most significant part of the product. He said, "No." In his deposition he said, "Yes." He said, "We never sold software. We give it away." Isn't that a nice word game?
>
> Ultimately -- and I want to read this to you, the ultimate word game. At page 380 of the transcript, this is Mr. Bazany at his best. Here is what he says: (Reading)

> "Q   It transmits serial data, right?
>
> A   It transmits data serially, that's correct.
>
> It's important --"

And this is his answer. (Reading)

> "A   It's important to understand that it is not transmitting serial data. It transmits data serially. It transmits pure serial data, as well."

Now, let me go back. He is saying here "I don't use the word 'serial data'." And then I asked him to look at his deposition and see what he said there. Right there he says: (Reading)

"It transmits pure serial data, as well. Not data serially."

And I asked him: (Reading)

"Q   You understood then what you meant then by 'serial data.'?

A   I understood then what I meant and it's no different than what I understand today."

Why the argument over whether it is serial data or data serially? Is this person credible? Is this honest, forthright, truthful testimony? And, if it is, you don't have to play those kinds of games.

(Transcript, January 26, 2000, pp. 859-860). I accused them of playing games:

So, what's the game here? Redefine the invention and then say we don't have it. That is what you have heard. You heard talk about Christmas tree lights. I don't see that in the claim. Pulses. I don't see that in the claim. Connections, computers, circuits, series circuit, parallel circuit, nice little diagrams by their patent attorney. Those don't have anything to do with the claims of the patent. Broadcast. You don't see "broadcast" in the claim. So, they want to redefine it and then they want to say, well, we don't do it. They say they broadcast like a radio signal. We know what happened there. They sell only parts. They don't tell anyone. We know what happened there. Parts aren't specially made. We know what happened there. And we don't know what our end users and customers are doing. But what are they doing with all this (indicating)? They say don't believe our documents; they can't be trusted.

(Transcript, January 26, 2000, p. 864). I hit hard on invention, success and taking and the fact that Frank Calabrese was ahead of his time:

> Was this invention a success? Eighty percent sales growth, seventy percent reduction in cost, one million I/O points sold by November of '97, a savings of two hundred-sixty to one billion dollars to the consuming public.
>
> Before the lawsuit it was important and a success and after the lawsuit it is suddenly a failure. It's almost like: You don't have an invention. If you had the invention, I didn't take it. If I took it, I didn't use it and, if I used it, it was of no value. Those are all of the defenses.
>
> You sa[w] Frank Calabrese explain his invention. He drew it. He showed you his prototype. He explained why they infringed. And I wish he could be here today to explain it to you.
>
> They belittled his contribution by saying you didn't build a manufacturing plant and you didn't sell thousands of these things. But you don't have to do that if you are the inventor[]. Inventors oftentimes are way ahead of their time. Chester Carlson invented xerography, the copying machine. We take it for granted today. He did it in 1938. Do you know when the first copying machine went to the market? 1960. He was ahead of his time.
>
> Maybe the most famous inventor[] of all, Robert Go[dd]ard, the inventor[] of the rocket. He got a patent on a rocket in 1914. There it is, 1914 (indicating). United States patent 1,102,653. The Saturn rocket came into existence in 1969 and took a man to the moon, fifty-five years after the invention. He was ahead of his time, too.
>
> So, the fact that Frank Calabrese created something before the market was ready for it isn't a penalty. It ought to be an award. He shouldn't be punished for being ahead of his time.

(Transcript, January 26, 2000, pp. 868-869). And, as always, I tried to save the fireworks for "the final five" rebuttal:

> Now, I showed you the patent, the original patent there in the frame, and I said it's one of a kind and, indeed, it is. There's been something that's been bothering me from the outset of this case. I don't know if you remember it. Mr. Barry said on behalf of Square D: Frank Calabrese didn't have any takers. He didn't have any takers.
>
> You know, that's been ringing in my ears: he didn't have any takers. What are we here today for if he didn't have any takers?
>
> The takers are right over there (indicating). They took it and used it, and they didn't pay him one cent for it. Now, only you folks, the six of you, can decide whether that taking was proper.
>
> But, you know, Mr. Goddard, the inventor of the rocket, had a wonderful thing to say. I put his patent up as a pioneer, and I think about it a lot. He said: I can't tell what's impossible because yesterday's dream is today's hope and tomorrow's reality. Dream, hope, reality.
>
> Well, Goddard's dream came true in '69, 1969, when a man went to the moon. But Frank Calabrese had a dream, too. He wanted to license his technology. He wanted to share it with someone. He wanted to see it commercialized, and he saw it commercialized. What he didn't see is anything in return. Square D crushed that dream, and it did so shamelessly.
>
> I keep a book on my desk. In fact, my wife gave it to me. It's good to read it. I find it helpful. It's called Life's Little Instruction Book, 511 Suggestions, Observations and Reminders on How to Live and be Happy -- a Happy and Rewarding Life. [by H. Jackson Brown, Jr.] There are three things in here that as I was thinking

about what to say to you at the end of the case I looked at. Number 59:

"Live so that when your children think of fairness, caring and integrity, they think of you."

I hope that David thinks of his dad when he thinks of that.

Number 158:

"Pray not for things, but for wisdom and courage."

I wrote Frank and Cathy Calabrese a letter before this trial started, and I prayed for that.

The last one is 130 -- I'm sorry -- 139:

"Never deprive someone of hope. It might be all they have."

They took his hope, they took his dream, and only you people have the power, the power to set it straight. If we didn't -- if they didn't infringe and this patent is invalid, we deserve nothing and rule against us. But if you conclude they did infringe and they didn't prove it's invalid, then give him back his dream. Give him back his hope. I know you'll do the right thing. Thank you.

(Transcript, January 26, 2000, pp. 921-923).

No witnesses except a one-hour video of a dying inventor. But, the jurors had seen enough of the adverse witnesses to give them what they needed to decide the case. The result: a verdict finding the Calabrese patent valid and infringed and awarding damages of $13,200,000 which the trial judge increased by $6,819,780 with prejudgment interest. After the trial, I got a call from the jury forewoman, Janet Owens. She asked if she could write a letter to our client, Frank Calabrese. On January 31, 2000, a few days before Frank died, she had this to say:

Hi! I was the foreman of the jury who deliberated your case against Square D Company. I wanted to write you to let you know that your attorney, Mr. Ray Niro, proved without a doubt that you deserved to win. He presented the facts, showed charts, explained in great detail about your patent. His knowledge was outstanding and I felt that he spent a good amount of time preparing, going over the facts and putting everything in order. He knew precisely where to look when Square D witnesses contradicted earlier testimonies. The people from his firm that were in the courtroom helping locate files, etc. were all in tune with him. Chris Lee was always ready with exhibits to be displayed on the easel and also have exhibits ready to be placed on the monitor so we could see them on the television. Never was there a delay in the presentation of facts. Mr. Niro should be commended for his dedication and the fine job that he did. His expertise, finesse, and even his closing statements to the jury had warm touches to the heart, which were overwhelming to say the least. Never did he talk down to the jury, nor did he insult our intelligence in any way. He was precise in what he told us and proved that you should win.

I didn't know if it was proper to write you, so I did contact Mr. Niro and he gave me your address. I feel that I know you to some degree, and wanted you to know that Mr. Niro is truly a wonderful person who believes in justice and goes all out to prove that someone is right.

I am proud to have served on the jury and even prouder to know that something I did in my life caused something good to happen to someone else's life.

As a final note, I want you to know that I am having prayers said for you and your family at my Church in the city.

With all my best wishes,
Janet Owens

That letter, to my dying client, means more to me than any amount of money I have won in any case. I had given a dying man his last wish; he was vindicated and his family had security for life. Frank's wife, Kathy, died a few years later, also of cancer. She said she wanted to see Frank again. Frank's son, David, and his sister are secure for life.

THE PROFESSOR GETS SCHOOLED

C&F Packing Co., Inc. v. IBP, Inc.,
Civil Action No. 93 C 1601 (N.D. Ill., Nov. 1998)

Every now and then, a trial turns on the cross-examination of a single witness. One such case was C&F Packing v. IBP. The case involved the misappropriation -- *theft* -- of trade secrets for making precooked Italian pizza sausage; the witness was Professor Robert Rust of Iowa State University, the top meat processing expert in the country, someone IBP's counsel called "the Michael Jordan of sausage-making."

The storyline is something I have seen countless times: little guy comes up with a great idea only to be run-over by an industry behemoth. Here, the little guy was my client, C&F Packing, a small Chicago meat-packing company owned by the Freda family. Joe Freda was my neighbor and friend. His children were about the same ages as mine. He left early for work (like me) and he worked with his father and brother in a family-owned business. I felt privileged when the day came to represent him and the family business.

C&F was run by Joe Freda, his brother Gerry and their brother-in-law Dennis Olson. The Fredas' father, Sam, started the company in a small shop on the west side of Chicago in 1933. Among its products, C&F made a great Italian pizza sausage, and by the mid-1970s, C&F was supplying that fresh, raw sausage to Chicago-area Pizza Hut franchises. Their sales of sausage pizzas were better than franchises who purchased sausage elsewhere. So C&F immediately caught the attention of Pizza Hut. Unfortunately, Pizza Hut and other major chains were shifting away from using raw, home-made sausage to frozen, precooked Italian sausage. But Pizza Hut still wanted its sausage to look like it was home-cooked Italian sausage.

The problem with the existing precooked Italian sausage was that it tasted bland and resembled rabbit droppings -- way too uniform and machine-like. So the Fredas set out to create a process for making a precooked Italian sausage that looked and tasted as good as their raw product after cooking. It took nearly ten years, and many failed experiments, but by 1984, C&F felt it had something really special. In fact, it was so special that, in 1985, Pizza Hut decided C&F's product was the answer; it had the look and feel and, best of all, the taste of home-cooked sausage. Pizza Hut's president allegedly said, "I want this stuff in every Pizza Hut restaurant in the country."

THE PLAN

At first, Pizza Hut had its major suppliers try to reverse-engineer C&F's product, but none of them could do it. Then Pizza Hut demanded C&F share its secret process with other suppliers under a confidentiality agreement; in exchange, C&F was promised it would get half of the Pizza Hut business.

And that's what happened for a few years. C&F taught other Pizza Hut suppliers its secret process under strict confidentiality agreements; in exchange, C&F became Pizza Hut's largest supplier. C&F expanded its facilities and, by 1990, its annual revenue exceeded $50 million. C&F had written a hit record. And the Fredas were rock stars taking a $3-million-per-year business and turning it into a $50-million-per-year success story overnight. But the end was coming: Pizza Hut's long-range plan was to cut C&F completely out of the picture by secretly giving C&F's trade secrets to a new low-cost supplier, IBP (Iowa Beef Packing), the largest meat-packing company in the world. Though IBP had never made a processed meat product before, Pizza Hut said, "Don't worry; we'll help you." And help they did. In fact the Pizza Hut employee who knew the most about C&F's process, Al Killian, helped IBP set up and test its process. The discovery process revealed that Killian made 10 different visits to IBP spanning 27 days during that period. To be sure it got everything it needed to duplicate the C&F product, IBP even hired C&F's former plant manager, Kevin McDaniel. IBP tracked him down in Florida, doubled his salary, made him plant superintendent for IBP's new plant in Waterloo, Iowa, and then put him in charge of ironing out the kinks in its precooked Italian sausage process. I asked the question early on: If everything was old (like IBP contended through its key witness, Professor Rust), why then did IBP have guards to protect its secret process?:

Q. Now, you do know that IBP considers all of its operating conditions as it relates to the manufacture of precooked Italian sausage, whether they're in writing or not, to be confidential and proprietary, right?

A. Yes, I assume they do.

Q. And that's not unusual, is it, in the meat industry?

A.   No, it is not unusual.

Q.   That's why people have guards and security and try to keep their process information secret, right?

A.   Well, that isn't the only reason for having guards and security.

Q.   Well, it's certainly one of them, isn't it?

A.   Certainly they don't want nonemployees or others to be present in the plant without their permission.

Q.   *If everything that you were doing to make this precooked Italian sausage was old and well known and obvious and easy, you wouldn't be worried about whether somebody came in and found out what you were doing, would you?*

A.   *I find people still worry about that even though it is commonly known technology.*

(Transcript, November 19, 1998, pp. 1948-1949; emphasis added). Right!

The Pizza Hut plan of getting into C&F's plant, learning its secrets and then giving them to the low-cost suppliers had worked. IBP used each one of the 11 individual process trade secrets created by C&F. But, most importantly, it used C&F's combination of the 11 secrets out of millions of other possible ways to do it. The secret process included different grinds, spices, cooking at a particular temperature, holding times, extruding the sausage through a beveled plate, the spacing between the plate and the blade, and even what kind of casing to use. And once IBP had its copy-cat process up and running smoothly, it promptly fired Kevin McDaniel. He had served his purpose.

C&F GETS THE AX

Almost immediately, IBP was able to significantly undercut C&F's price, and C&F saw its sales to Pizza Hut plummet. C&F wondered what was going on, and heard industry rumors that IBP was supplying Pizza Hut. That seemed odd, since IBP had no experience in the processed meat business, and C&F had never authorized Pizza Hut to give the C&F process to IBP.

In October 1992, C&F notified IBP of a possible legal problem. IBP responded that its process was secret and took years to independently develop. C&F asked to inspect IBP's plant. A simple request which suddenly caused Pizza Hut to start complaining about an alleged quality issue with C&F's product -- they asserted the meat was too pink and appeared under-cooked. We eventually learned that the pink coloration was the result of Pizza Hut's demand that phosphates be added to the meat. But that comes later. We also learned that the timing of Pizza Hut's complaints was no coincidence. It was a clear message to C&F to "back off; don't ask too many questions -- or else."

On March 2, 2003, my brother, Bill, inspected IBP's plant in Iowa and, on that very same day, Pizza Hut sent C&F a letter warning C&F it had 30 days to fix the pink problem or it would be terminated as a supplier. A day later, C&F responded that it had solved the problem. Pizza Hut reacted by terminating C&F as a supplier of precooked Italian sausage anyway, but not as a supplier of other products. On March 17, 1993, C&F sued IBP and, a day later, Pizza Hut retaliated by terminating C&F as a supplier of all products. Weeks later, C&F added Pizza Hut as a defendant in the lawsuit.

The Lawsuit

In my experience, trade secret misappropriation cases nearly always turn on circumstantial evidence. Seldom do you find a memo in the file saying, "Let's steal the trade secrets." In this case, however, we had something close. During pretrial discovery, we found what we believed to be compelling circumstantial evidence. We learned about Killian's numerous visits to IBP. We learned about Kevin McDaniel and the role that IBP had him play in creating a duplicate process. We discovered IBP had three times more quality complaints than C&F. We even found C&F's extrusion plate design in IBP's files. How did it get there? Killian had asked Gerry Freda for it under the ruse that a Pizza Hut franchisee in Russia needed some help.

We also came across a compelling internal document from Pizza Hut -- a secret memo that laid out its plan: "Let's get into their plant, learn what they are doing and then dial-up our low-cost suppliers to see if they can duplicate what C&F is doing." Not a smoking gun, but close.

Also in discovery, we learned IBP's defenses, which were like most trade secret case defenses: (1) you don't have any trade secrets; (2) if you had any trade secrets, we didn't take them; (3) if we took them, we didn't use them; (4) if we used them, they were of no value; and (5) regardless of all of that, we could have done it all ourselves in 30 days. Of all of those defenses, we were most concerned about the first one (C&F's process steps were not, in fact, trade secrets), and that was where IBP's expert, the preeminent Professor Rust, came in. Before trial, Pizza Hut was dismissed from the case on statute of limitations grounds, a ruling which was later reversed on appeal. So C&F headed to trial just against IBP in November 1998.

THE TRIAL

The actual trial took a little over three weeks and played out for the jury like a proverbial whodunit. Joe Freda was my first witness; he testified about the history of C&F and its dealings with Pizza Hut. We put on a videotape of Killian's deposition, because he refused to appear at the trial. Killian seemed shifty and evasive; he also didn't have a plausible explanation for Pizza Hut's internal documents which set out the plan to move the C&F process to a low-cost supplier. We put on the IBP executive in charge of dealing with Pizza Hut, David Layhee. Layhee admitted that, despite all of the fluctuations in the price of meat, IBP was always able to undercut C&F's price. Layhee also admitted to a serious bacteria problem at the Iowa plant, leading to a temporary shutdown of its operations. But, instead of terminating IBP, Pizza Hut rewarded it with more and more business.

Next up was Kevin McDaniel, who agreed to testify at the trial, even though he was then living in Madison, Wisconsin, and had no legal obligation to come to Chicago to testify. I walked Kevin through the various C&F trade secrets, and he admitted seeing IBP use all of them in combination in its plant. I used my last question to let Kevin explain how he had been used by IBP and why he felt a moral responsibility to tell the jury what had happened:

Q.   Mr. McDaniel, why did you take the time away from your work and your family to come down here from Madison, Wisconsin, without any pay, without any compensation, without any interest in this litigation, to tell the truth to this jury.

A.   Because I felt that while I was put in an unfair position where I had to draw on my experience at C&F to solve IBP's problem, I still feel that I was there, and I feel some responsibility for it, and I think it was important to come down and share that information I had.

(Transcript, November 19, 1998, p. 508).

Earlier, Gerry Freda had done a remarkable job explaining to the jury the years of trial and error C&F undertook in developing its new process. I laid out nearly twenty different devices, which C&F had made and tested during the development of its process, on a table before the jury. They included crude prototypes and metal plates with irregularly shaped, beveled holes. Gerry came down from the witness stand, picked up and explained how each device was made, how it fit into the process and why it was either abandoned or refined.

Judge Williams allowed me to hand the jury some of the plates for their examination. Gerry made this "show and tell" even more entertaining with anecdotes about the development process. For example, he told of his experiment of dropping a sausage chubb from the roof of the plant onto a shopping cart below to see whether a metal grid would work better than a plate. Gerry was a compelling witness, and the jury genuinely seemed to like him.

We finished our case with testimony from our technical expert, who confirmed that IBP had used C&F's trade secrets. As we moved into IBP's case, I was feeling pretty good about our chances, but I also knew enough not to dance in the end zone before the game clock showed no time was left. How true that turned out to be -- we had yet to hear from the Michael Jordan of sausage-making in the fourth quarter of the game. And we all know what Michael Jordan could do in the fourth quarter.

Before Professor Rust testified, IBP paraded several of its own executives to the stand, including Mr. Layhee (again). They denied that IBP used any of the C&F trade secrets and attempted to minimize the role that Kevin McDaniel played in refining the process. On cross-examination, I was able to contradict much of their testimony with internal documents, and Layhee didn't play any better the second time around. I was still confident about our chances. But then the Professor testified. He was great.

THE PROFESSOR TEACHES CLASS

Professor Rust was the King of sausage-making; the jury had been waiting for him. He looked every bit the distinguished, seventy-year-old Professor Emeritus that he was. He began by recounting his academic accomplishments in forty years of teaching meat science at Michigan State and Iowa State University. He had written over 200 articles and had received the highest possible awards from the American Meat Science Association, the American Society of Animal Science, the Institute of Food Technologists, the National Association of Meat Purveyors, and the American Association of Meat Processors. Professor Rust also had literally written the book on sausage making, a textbook titled "Sausage and Processed Meats Manufacturing." Maybe IBP had, indeed, found the Michael Jordan of sausage-making, and the jury seemed understandably impressed.

IBP's lawyer methodically walked Professor Rust through each of the 11 trade secrets, and he identified each and every item as generally known in the industry for decades, if not longer. He showed the individual trade secrets were trivial. He claimed that the use of a 1/1/8th inch sized plate for a final grind was identified in a 1975 chart used for home butchering. For maintaining optimum mixing vessel temperature between 28 to 33 degrees, he pointed to a lecture given at Iowa State in 1982. For holding the mixed product 12 to 24 hours before stuffing and cooking, he pointed to another 1982 lecture. Holding the sausage chubbs after chilling to equilibrate? That was in a 1973 textbook. And so on, for each and every one of the individual trade secrets. It was an impressive performance. It was also turning into a trial lawyer's nightmare: several of the jurors were starting to nod in agreement whenever the Professor made a point. I felt we were in serious trouble.

And he didn't stop there. Professor Rust next emphatically denied that IBP used many of the C&F trade secrets. He concluded that even if IBP was given no information on the 11 C&F trade secrets, it would have independently come up with the process in 30 to 90 days because "much of the information that IBP used here is publicly known information and would be well known to a skilled meat scientist familiar with sausage manufacture."

Rust had scored big with the jury, and I knew that, if I didn't immediately change that dynamic, we were done. It is a trial lawyer's greatest challenge and greatest thrill -- cross-examination to win or lose the case. As I stood to cross-examine Rust, I whispered to Paul Vickrey (who was working on the case with my brother, Bill, and me): "We win or lose right now."

CROSS-EXAMINATION

As devastating as his direct testimony was, I noticed that Professor Rust had carefully avoided the fact that the most important trade secret of all was the **combination** of the various steps that yielded the C&F product. I decided to use his own books against him and focus on the **combination** of the 11 trade secrets:

Q.   Oh, so you're not saying that the combination is something you could go find in a book, right?

A.   I assume that one could find this combination of steps or variations thereof in some book.

Q.   Well, you mentioned your sausage and processed meat short course. It's a big thick book. Is the recipe set forth in these steps explained anywhere in this book?

A.   As far as I know, it is not.

Q.   Right. In fact, you have a whole section on recipes. I have one of them right here that tells you what to do to make some liver sausage. It gives you the steps: to presoak the livers, chop the livers and cure them with spices, then add pork trim and grind it through a three-16ths-inch plate, then chop it and heat it to 55 degrees, then stuff it -- I'm sorry -- cool it to 55 degrees, stuff it, have an internal temperature or cook at an internal temperature of 155 degrees F, chill it in cold water, and then you have your product, right?

A.   That's right.

Q.   But nowhere in any book, any article, any text, any patent, any publication that you've been looking for the last four years is the recipe that's set forth in these items here called C&F's trade secrets, isn't that right?

A.   That is by no means a complete recipe.

Q.   Sir, am I correct that you have been unable to find in any book, any text, any patent, any recipe book, anywhere in the world, the **combination of steps** set forth in the claimed C&F trade secrets to make precooked Italian sausage? Isn't that right, sir?

A.   I have not looked for that specific recipe.

Q.   Have you found it?

A.   I haven't looked for it, so how would I have found it?

Q.   Wouldn't you think it important if you could find someplace the recipe to be able to come in and tell this jury: This is old. Somebody has done it before. Here's the book. I did it in 1945. I wrote a book about it, or somebody else wrote it down. Don't you think that would be important?

A.   I would disagree with that.

(Transcript, December 3, 1998, pp. 1941-1943; emphasis added). He was being cute and evasive, but I wasn't about to let up:

Q.   Well, you did write a book entitled "Sausage and Processing Meat Manufacturing." That's this red book?

A.   Yes.

Q.   Is the recipe in there?

A.   As far as I know, it is not.

Q.   In fact, you say things in here that tell you to do the exact opposite. For example, you suggest cooking to 155 to 165 degrees, not to 150 to 151, right?

A.   That is one alternative.

Q.   The section is "manufacturing processes, cooked and smoke sausage," Chapter 11. I'm going to focus you, if I can get it here, on the section called "blending." It says, quote: "The meat mixture is then unloaded and chopped or emulsified to a final temperature of 60 to 70 degrees F." Is that what you teach in this book?

A.   Yes, and that is a totally different process. That is a process for making a base emulsion into which a course ground material is incorporated.

Q.   There is no place in this book that you can point to that would show *the combination* of using a final grind of one-eighth inch, carbon dioxide injection, maintaining temperatures of 28 to 33 degrees, and so forth, all the way down through it. Not once in this book is that said, isn't that correct, sir?

A.   That's correct.

Q.   And your other book called "The Science of Meat and Meat Products, Third Edition," the same thing is true about that, right?

A.   That's correct.

Q.   In fact, the section you wrote on sausage products tells you: "Regardless of the method" -- Well, I'll put it up here so there's no confusion. It says: "Regardless of the method of commutation, it is important that the temperature of trimmings be minus 2 degrees C. 28 degrees F. or lower to ensure a clean cut. This prevents tearing of the lean meat and smearing of the fat. Dry ice is sometimes added during commutation to ensure that the meat remains cold." Aren't you suggesting there that you should be at temperatures below 28 degrees F?

A.   This specific reference does not apply to a product such as this. This is applied to small-diameter fresh pork sausage.

Q.   It says in your section on how to make sausage: "Final internal temperatures of at least 68 degrees C. 155 degrees F. and preferably 71 degrees C. 160 degrees F. are needed to ensure optimum microbial destruction and maximum subsequent shelf life." Is that right?

A.   Again, this is applying to a totally different product. This is a small-diameter frankfurter.

Q.   Sir, is this the section of the book entitled "Sausage Products"?

A.   Yes.

Q.   This is the section you wrote?

A.   Yes.

Q.   *Is there anything, again, in this book that gives you the recipe that's at issue in this case?*

A.   *None of these books are intended to be a complete compendium of all sausage recipes. We would probably need a rather large truck to haul it around if that were available.*

Q.   *All right. Is the answer to my question that there is nothing in this book, the third book we've looked at --*

A.   *For this specific product, no.*

(Transcript, December 3, 1998, pp. 1943-1946; emphasis added). I was starting to put some cracks in Rust's armor. He was shifty, but he kept looking at the IBP lawyers for help. Was he losing his confidence? I moved out of the academic world and into the real world:

Q. Do you know of anyone anywhere in the world besides IBP and C&F that use those process steps?

A. Like Dr. Leising, I'm not aware of anyone.

⫿ ⫿ ⫿ ⫿ ⫿

Q. And you've never designed a process from start to finish to make precooked Italian sausage, isn't that right?

A. Not to make precooked Italian sausage.

(Transcript, December 3, 1998, pp. 1947, 1950). Wow! He was folding. I emphasized how Rust had carefully avoided the combination of trade secrets, focusing only on the old individual components of the combination (the individual notes, not the song):

Q. Now, getting back to the methodology for a moment, I want to understand exactly how it is that you arrived at the conclusions that you did in the marked up chart relating to the trade secrets. If I understand what you did in terms of method, the first thing you did was look at, what I call, a piece of the puzzle. You looked at the specific trade secrets, right?

A. That's right.

Q. Then knowing what those trade secrets are you went to step two, you went out and you looked at the books and texts and articles to see if you could find those individual pieces, right?

A. That was part of what I did, yes.

Q.　And then step three was to put them all back together again to say, well, since all the pieces are there, the **combination** is there, right?

〰 〰 〰 〰 〰

A.　I did not really attest to the combination here.

Q.　*Would you agree that using your methodology nobody could ever have trade secrets in anything if all the steps or all the components were old?*

A.　*If all of the components were known and there was nothing unique about putting these steps together, I think that would be true.*

(Transcript, December 3, 1998, pp. 1957-1958; emphasis added). I switched to organic chemistry (remembered from my early days as a chemical engineer at Shell Chemical in Houston) and the fact that most organic compounds are simply combinations of a few basic elements -- carbon, hydrogen and oxygen:

Q.　You took courses in chemistry when you were in school, right?

A.　Yes.

Q.　And part of your understanding is, of course, organic chemistry, right?

A.　To some extent.

Q.　All right. You can, for example, understand that if I were to write C_2H_5OH that that represents a chemical compound?

A.　Yes.

Q.　Ethyl alcohol?

A.   Yes.

Q.   But I can take these same components: Carbon, hydrogen, and oxygen, mix them up in a little different way, and I could get a plastic or carpeting or synthetic wood or gasoline or any number of chemical compounds, right?

A.   This is outside my area of expertise.

Q.   I see. You don't understand that you can take the same elements that are old, mix them together in a different way, and create new things in combination?

A.   I assume one could do this in chemistry; however, this is sausage manufacture, which is much less complex.

Q.   Well, you talked about choices, and the choices that one could go through or have to make in coming up with a recipe, right?

A.   Yes.

Q.   And you heard the testimony of Dr. Clark that if you were to take the 10 or 11 trade secrets, plus some of the subcomponents, say, up to 17, and look at the possible combinations, it would be in the millions. You heard that testimony, right?

A.   I heard that testimony.

(Transcript, December 3, 1998, pp. 1958-1959).

I had set the stage earlier, by asking Dr. Rust about the Coca-Cola trade secret -- all the components were old, but no one knew how to put those old components together -- the combination was the secret:

Q.   Now, it was very interesting in your methodology on how you can figure out formulae and processes. You're familiar with Coca-Cola, aren't you, that recipe?

A.   No, I'm not. I know one exists, but I don't know what the recipe is.

Q.   In fact, nobody knows what the recipe is, do they?

A.   That's what I've been told.

Q.   It's a secret. It's been a secret for 80 years, right?

A.   That's what I've been told.

Q.   All right. I want you to assume that they have water, coca, sugar, carbonation, and some flavoring. Now, those ingredients are old and well known, aren't they?

A.   This is outside my area of food science.

Q.   Well, I understand it may be outside, but surely if I told you to go find a book about how to make a cola, you would be able to find out that water could be put in there, that coca might be put in there, and sugar, carbonation, and flavoring. You'd know that, wouldn't you?

A.   I would assume if it was documented in a book, yes.

Q.   *Tell us what the secret formula is for Coca-Cola.*

     MR. UNIKEL: Your Honor, objection, foundation. It's outside the scope here.

     THE COURT: Overruled.

BY THE WITNESS:

A.   *That is insufficient information.*

BY MR. R. NIRO:

Q.   *Because you don't know what percentages, you don't know what temperatures, you don't know what operating conditions, you don't know what sequence of steps, you don't know how they do it, right?*

A.   *As I mentioned before, this is not my area of expertise.*

(Transcript, December 3, 1998, pp. 1939-1941; emphasis added). Rust admitted he had knowingly avoided looking at the combination. Was it new? Was it known before?

Q.   Now, you testified that there wasn't a single, not one item on this list of 11 items that in combination you considered to be a trade secret, right?

MR. UNIKEL: Objection, Your Honor. I don't believe there was any testimony about combinations.

THE COURT: The objection is overruled. He may answer.

BY THE WITNESS:

A.   *I did not state an opinion on the combination.*

(Transcript, December 3, 1998, p. 1941; emphasis added). The theme for closing was now set. This case was not about the individual notes to a song (all of which were old and well known); it was about the combination -- a new song written from the same old notes.

THE EXPERIMENT

I later made the point again by conducting an experiment with Professor Rust to drive the point home that, even if IBP had only four different options to select from for each of the 10 process steps (the

11th secret had to do with pricing), it was no coincidence that IBP implemented the very same combination as C&F had created.

> Q. Now, did you do any independent analysis to determine how many possible combinations there might be of the variables that constitute the alleged trade secrets in this case?
>
> A. No, I did not.
>
> Q. Just as a matter of example, I'm going to show you 10 boxes that are blank, and I'll ask you, if you would, to take my pen and write in the numbers 1 through 4 in any random way that you want on those 10 boxes.

(Transcript, December 3, 1998, p. 1959).

> Q. Would you do that for me, the numbers 1, 2, 3, 4, in any combination you want, just four old numbers. Did you fill in all the boxes?
>
> A. Oh, you want all of the boxes filled?
>
> Q. Right. You can put a one in one a two in another and a three or a four or any combination you want. Okay. Do you want to initial that?
>
> Now, you've put in the numbers 1, 1, 3, 3, 4, 2, 4, 4, 3, 1. I did the same thing a few minutes ago. I put in the numbers 1, 2, 4, 1, 3, 3, 2, 4, 1, 2.
>
> Would you agree with me that taking something as simple as four numbers and 10 boxes, that is, 10 conditions and four numbers, that no two people independently are going to arrive at the same sequence of numbers? It's not likely to happen, is it?

(Transcript, December 3, 1998, p. 1960).

> A. I'm not an expert on statistics or probability.

BY MR. NIRO: Q. It would be relatively easy for you to put my combination down if the boxes weren't blank and you knew what I started with, right? That might take a matter of a minute or two, right?

A. I assume that would be very easy.

(Transcript, December 3, 1998, p. 1961). Try this experiment with a friend: draw 10 boxes and have him or her put in numbers 1 through 4 in any sequence and combination. See if it matches your combination. Not likely.

I finally showed that Professor Rust's deliberate avoidance of the combination of steps as a trade secret didn't even square with his marching orders from IBP's lawyers before the trial began:

Q. Mr. Rust, when you wrote the entry, "Trade secrets individual and combined," did you understand that the trade secrets were not only the individual items that are listed, but the combination of these items?

A. Yes, that's correct.

Q. That's what you were told by the lawyers in this case, isn't that right? The IBP lawyers, they told you that, right?

A. I was told that a combination of individual steps that were known could become a trade secret.

Q. But your testimony here today with this jury excluded that whole topic of the combination, didn't it?

A. Because these are no by -- by no means a complete set of steps for the manufacture of a product.

(Transcript, December 3, 1998, p. 1966). I would not let Professor Rust get away so easily:

Q. Did you understand, sir, that the combination of steps could be trade secrets, and despite that understanding you did not share with the jury your view of whether this combination was new and unique and different and something that hadn't been done or seen before?

A. I understand the question related to combination. I'm not sure I would classify this as new and unique.

Q. Well, whether you classify it as new or unique, the fact of the matter is you can't find a single piece of paper anywhere on the face of this [earth] or that's in a book, an article, a text, a publication, that has this combination in it, isn't that right?

A. As I say, I haven't looked through all the possible articles.

Q. Well, you've assembled hundreds of articles that are marked as exhibits in this case, isn't that right?

A. I don't believe, really, it's hundreds.

Q. How many?

A. I didn't make a count, sir.

Q. Well, in your book you have about seven or eight, and the fact of the matter is you went and did research, you went through the literature to try and find articles and materials that would describe or discuss the C&F trade secrets, isn't that right?

A. I by no means made an exhaustive search.

Q. Well, did somebody tell you not to make an exhaustive search?

A. No.

Q. So you were told go find these trade secrets, if you can, right, in combination?

A.   I was told to examine the trade secrets.

Q.   Well, Point 1 --

A.   The combination issue was peripheral.

Q.   Point 1 of the notes, again, dated 9-19, that's September 1996 says, "Point 1 steps 1 to 4" dash "prior art supporting materials."

     Weren't you being told by the lawyers to go out and find "prior art," things that were old that would show the trade secrets?

A.   I was looking for supporting materials to what I considered prior art.

Q.   Things that were old, publications, articles, books, right?

A.   That's right.

Q.   ***And whether your search was exhaustive or not, the fact of the matter is you didn't find the combination, right?***

A.   ***I didn't find this exact combination.***

(Transcript, December 3, 1998 at pp. 1967-1969). Amen! I had him. He ignored the single most important trade secret of all: the combination. The hit recording. The new song written from the same old eight notes. So I decided to go for the icing on the cake–get Professor Rust to admit that Pizza Hut's excuse for terminating C&F as a supplier (the pink color in its sausage) was also phony. Why was this important? Because the jury had learned that IBP had suggested Pizza Hut incorporate phosphates in its specification so the end product would have more water and more fat. Nice suggestion -- the customer gets less meat and more fat. But, as a by-product, phosphates cause the sausage to get a pink color. And it was allegedly because of a pink color in C&F's sausage (made to Pizza Hut's new specification) that C&F was terminated.

Q.   Let me show you your book, "Sausage and Processed Meat." Am I correct, sir, that you say in this book that the test work conducted indicated that elevated pH readings of the meat resulted in a pink color even when the meat is cooked to high temperatures above 155 degrees. I'll show it to you, if you have some question about it.

A.   I have no question about that; however, that says nothing about nitrous oxide.

Q.   I see. Then elsewhere it says the phosphates will also raise the natural pH of the meat. You say that in your quote, correct?

A.   Yes.

Q.   And that is your understanding of exactly what happens, right?

A.   The phosphates raise the pH of the meat, that is, lower the acidity, raise the alkalinity.

Q.   So that if you use something like sodium tripolyphosphate and alkaline phosphate that has the effect of raising the pH and creating the condition where you can have a pink coloration even if you cook it, right?

A.   That can result in a pink coloration - in a noncured product.

Q.   Right. In fact, that's what you said in the article, "Meat Color Explained." I'll give you a copy, again, if you have a question about it, Mr. Rust. This is your article "Meat Color Explained," Professor Robert

Rust, Iowa State University. Do you see that you do say here that the higher the pH the more likely it is that the pigment will not be converted to its oxidized state and will remain the pink color of native -- what is it, myoglobin?

A. Myoglobin, m-y-o-g-l-o-b-i-n.

Q. It says, "If oxygen is restricted, you might get a pink color which is nothing more than the native myoglobin color," right?

A. That's correct.

Q. And that pink color can be the result of elevated pHs, right, or elevated pH?

A. A pink color can develop as a result of elevated pH in a noncured product.

Q. All right. And adding sodium phosphate would have the effect of elevating the pH, right?

A. Adding sodium phosphate would elevate the pH.

Q. And that would cause, at elevated temperatures, the color -- the pink coloration of the meat, right?

A. It could.

(Transcript, December 3, 1998, pp. 1970-1973). It was IBP, not C&F, that wanted higher phosphate levels. So the pink color was just an excuse to punish C&F for fighting to protect its trade secrets and its business.

Rust was wrecked. In fact, before it was over, three jurors were actually glowering at the Professor. Jurors typically do not forgive a party for attempting to lead them down the wrong path, and this was one such instance. It's like someone you trust lying to you, which is far worse than a stranger lying to you.

IBP's damage expert was next, and she did nothing to help IBP's case. Her opinion was that, if IBP was found liable for misappropriating C&F's trade secrets, it should only have to pay $13,000 in damages of $70,000,000 in sales -- less than 1/50th of 1%. On cross, I stressed how preposterous that was, first by showing that what she charged IBP to testify in the case was ten times what she claimed the damages were. I returned to that $13,000 in my last question:

Q.   That's your idea of what's fair in sharing the benefits of the theft of trade secrets, $13,000 on 70 million in sales, right?

A.   If they could have done it themselves, that's correct.

(Transcript, December 4, 1998, p. 2047).

Not only did IBP take C&F's trade secrets, but they paid a damages expert more than $100,000 to say C&F was entitled to $13,000:

Q.   I see. Now, it's ... fair to say then that you've been paid over $100,000 to come in here and testify ... C&F ... is entitled to $13,000 if they win this case; is that what your -- the situation here?

A.   My firm bills for my time, and my time is applied to determine the nature of the damages and the appropriate amount. That happens to be the appropriate amount for a 30-day head-start period.

(Transcript, December 4, 1998, p. 2038).

CLOSING

In closing, I hit all these points, saving the passion for rebuttal -- the final five minutes. Pizza Hut was not a defendant, but it was the master mind of the scheme: get access to the C&F trade secrets and give them to the low-cost supplier, IBP.

PIZZA HUT'S AND IBP'S MEANNESS

It's been a long road, three weeks now going on four, and you've seen, I think, in the past three weeks a little bit, the tip of the iceberg of what life has been like for Joe and Gerry Freda at C&F in the past six years, the objections, the delays, the mean-spirited approach to this whole process that the defendants in this case have adopted.

◆ ◆ ◆ ◆ ◆

You've seen the evidence as to exactly what happened, the hardball tactics of Pizza Hut and IBP in this litigation for the privilege of going in to inspect that facility, the amazing coincidence happened that C&F was terminated on the same day allegedly for having "pink" problems with its sausage. And then a few days later -- in fact, after the supposed 30-day notice, 9 days later they were terminated on all products of everything that they made for Pizza Hut. And that was the punishment that [C&F was] given for having the audacity to go to these defendants and say, hey, we want to take a look at what you're doing. We think you may be using things that came from Kevin McDaniel or from Al Killian or from Pizza Hut.

(Transcript, December 8, 1998, p. 2172).

The Theme

I went back to our theme -- trust, betrayal and someone who decided to take something rather than pay:

> Now, at the outset of the case, I told you that this is a case about trust, about betrayal, and about two companies that decided to take something rather than pay for it. And that really sums up, in a sentence, what this case has been about: trust, betrayal, and two companies that decided to take something rather than pay for it.
>
> And you'll remember the notes of the Attorney Young. Now, this is George Young, an attorney in Washington, D.C., who is reporting on his conversations with Mr. Leising and some other person named Yokum who was employed by IBP. And what did he say? "It's too expensive to take a license." Too expensive to take a license. Why was it too expensive? It couldn't have been $25,000 that made it too expensive, because you heard the testimony of Arthur Andersen that they charged five times [$]25,000 just to come in here and tell you that we're entitled to $13,000 on 70 million in sales.
>
> It was too expensive because they knew that if C&F found out that IBP was coming into this business with their trade secrets, they would never, ever have agreed to that unless they had a commitment from Pizza Hut to keep buying some product from them, too.

(Transcript, December 8, 1998, pp. 2176-2177).

MOM'S RECIPE

I like to humanize my cases by telling stories about my childhood. Here is one about my mother's recipe for her wonderful tomato sauce and how, like C&F's sausage recipe, that combination was unique:

> Now, this case, in a sense, is about recipes. And I was thinking a little bit about recipes, and it reminded me, quite frankly, of growing up in Pittsburgh with two immigrant parents and what would happen on Sundays when my mother would cook this fantastic sauce that she had a knack of cooking.
>
> And it was truly a recipe, not too much unlike some of the things you've heard here. All the components were old: the tomatoes and the tomato sauce and the parsley and the onions and the other things that went into this process. And it was a process, believe me.
>
> I had that experience of watching the day and a half process with the meat being taken and put in the sauce and cooking it at low temperatures for a long period of time, the sugar -- or the salt and a little bit of wine and all the rest. It was an event, because eating a meal together was an event in our home.
>
> And my wife, who is here in the courtroom, and my sister, who is not, tried to duplicate that even with the assistance of my mother, and as hard as they tried, they never could quite get it. Maybe she didn't explain it quite the way she could have, and it was never written down, but that was the process. That was the recipe. And that's what food recipes are about.
>
> There was something else that happened with respect to the sauce. My older brother Joe, who is a bricklayer and worked with my father, he would come home on Thursdays -- and we would have the same sauce on Thursday, too. And he had the habit, which my mother didn't like very much, of taking the piece of bread and dipping it into the sauce and sort of testing and enjoying

that moment. And he would do it when my mother wasn't around, but she would find out ultimately what was going on.

Invariably, she'd say, Don't do that anymore. As I got older, I asked my mom, How did you always know that Joe was dipping in the sauce with the bread? She said it was easy. There were always a few crumbs around. There were footprints, footprints. He left footprints.

And there are footprints in this case, just like the little crumbs that were around that pot of sauce. And the footprints are left by IBP. Let's talk about some of those footprints for a moment.

(Transcript, December 8, 1998, pp. 2178-2180). I tracked each of the footprints.

THE MEMO

I also hit hard on the secret Pizza Hut internal memo:

And how did it start and where did it go? You know they started talking about how the product was superior in quality and appearance. And then they said in Exhibit 88 -- this is the one I showed you in opening, and I've shown some of the witnesses. This is right at the outset. "The C&F Arco product is clearly superior to our current product, yet more expensive." In fact, it was less -- more expensive than the raw, but 25 cents per pound less expensive than their precooked.

"It seems possible that we should be able to get into the process and formula, dial up our other suppliers, and get a better product for little or no extra cost.["] They never told C&F that, but that was the plan from the get-go. Get in there, find out what they're doing, dial up our other suppliers, and get rid of these guys. That's the way the hardball people do business.

(Transcript, December 8, 1998, pp. 2182-2183).

KEVIN McDANIEL

Why did they use Kevin McDaniel? I suggested they needed his experience at C&F to iron-out their problems and to be sure they got it right:

> And the second source for the information came because even with Killian's help they couldn't get it right, just -- God bless her -- the way they couldn't get my mom's recipe right. They couldn't get it right. So they needed something else.
>
> That something else was Kevin McDaniel. And you heard him testify in this case. He came down here from Milwaukee. He left his family. He wasn't promised anything. He didn't get anything to come here. And he said perhaps some of the most powerful things that were said in this case. I asked him on the last question, I think: "Kevin, why did you come down here? Why did you come down here to testify?" And he said, in a nutshell: "I was part of this. I feel responsible. They put me in a position I shouldn't have been in, and I wanted to tell these people about it."
>
> They needed Kevin to solve the problems, and indeed, Kevin solved the problems.

(Transcript, December 8, 1998, pp. 2184-2185).

COMBINATIONS

And combinations -- the theme of the case, which turned on the combination of 11 secrets, just like a new song written with the same old notes. I like to show the actual sheet music to the jury:

We've been talking about combinations, and you'll hear an instruction from the Court on the law that trade secrets are in fact combinations of old things.

And from time to time I've made reference to songs and music. And this season I want to show you one of my favorites, the Christmas song Chestnuts Roasting on an Open Fire, written by Mel Torme. Eight notes. Eight notes put in a combination, all old, all available to anyone. Rudolph the Red Nosed Reindeer. The same eight notes over and over again. Just different combinations for a different song.

And you can go through one after another. Wonderful World. Louie Armstrong recorded that. Same eight notes as the other songs. "Let it Be" by the Beatles, John Lennon, Paul McCartney. Same eight notes, different combinations, over and over again. That is what inventions are about, that's what trade secrets are about.

And you'll recall we talked about choices, the choices you have to go through. Professor Rust said: "Well, I didn't bother worrying about the combinations," even though that's what he was told to do. "I just looked at the pieces, and I showed that all the parts were old."

That's a little like saying Mel Torme didn't write a new song because he used the same eight notes that everybody else had. Or George Gershwin's Rhapsody in Blue isn't a new song because he used the same eight notes as Mel Torme. It doesn't make any sense. And it's not the law.

Remember the test that I did with Mr. Rust where I asked him, I said: "Look, I'm going to give you eight --" I'm sorry, "ten boxes. You write in the numbers." These are all old and well-known, been around from the beginning of time. 1 through 4. Put them in any arrangement you want. Create a new combination formula. I have a trade secret here. I get the same thing. Of course, mine is totally different than his.

And if you look at the chances of two people coming up with exactly the same combination, with 10 and 4, four variables, ten boxes, we could have been here for ten and a half years doing a hundred a day, and the odds of him coming up with the same one that I had would take that much time.

And these people suggest that it's old, obvious, and just a coincidence. It's a coincidence that C&F was terminated, it's a coincidence that they had a plate in their file, it's a coincidence they had our chubbs, it's a coincidence that they talked to Killian, it's a coincidence that they hired Kevin McDaniel, it's a coincidence that all our trade secrets are used in combination, despite the odds.

(Transcript, December 8, 1998, pp. 2189-2191). After the verdict, one juror told me he felt there were too many "coincidences" for the jury to believe IBP.

When we were done, the footprints pointed to IBP's liability. As for sharing, what did these guys know about sharing?

GREED

They come in and say $13,000 on 70 million in sales is fair. I'm blessed with nine grandkids, and I have to tell you, six of them are under the age of eight. And kids at that age I think we all probably can appreciate sometimes don't share too well. But there isn't one of them that knows less about sharing than these people over here. $13,000 on 70 million in sales for the best product they ever had, and that's their idea of being fair and sharing.

(Transcript, December 8, 1998, p. 2194).

THE FINAL FIVE

As always, I saved the fireworks for the final five -- rebuttal:

These aren't coincidences. And if they are, they're too many to be believed.

I want to conclude with this: There's really been something that bothers me about what Mr. Layhee said two or three times in his testimony. He said: "This isn't rocket science." Remember that? This isn't rocket science we're dealing with here. He demeans what these people did by saying this isn't rocket science.

Well, Gerry Freda told you about the ten years of his life that he worked trying to get this. And I have to tell you: Thomas Edison, the greatest inventor of our time with a third-grade education -- these guys aren't Ph.D.s in meat science. They're just regular guys trying to make a better product. But Thomas Edison had a third-grade education, and he created more inventions than any person on the face of the earth. And if they were in the light bulb business, they would be telling you that because a filament is old, and a fuse is old, and a bulb is old, that anybody could do it. And we'd be sitting in darkness today.

If it was old and easy, why didn't they do it? Why didn't they do it without Layhee, why didn't they do it without Kevin McDaniel?

And I looked back at rockets. And you know, I found that a guy named Goddard had a patent on a rocket -- I'm just going to share it with you for a moment -- way back in 1914. Robert Goddard. Rocket apparatus. And Goddard said -- I'm going to read it to you. Goddard said: "It's difficult to say what's impossible, for the dream of yesterday is the hope of today and the reality of tomorrow."

Dream, hope, reality. That's what Goddard said. And in 1914 he had a dream, and in 1969 that dream became reality when men went to the moon, and today space travel is just sort of an everyday thing. That was rocket science, I suppose.

But Joe and Gerry Freda had a dream, too. They didn't dream about putting a man on the moon. They dreamt about making a better product, carrying on the tradition of their father, and trying to share that with a big company. Maybe that was the beginning of their demise, sharing with Pizza Hut.

But they hoped they [could] build that business and share it with their kids and their grandkids and build their company. And these people over here shattered that dream. Shamelessly. Shamelessly. They shattered it. They drove Gerry Freda out of the business. They punished this company by taking what belonged to them and by using it.

Well, it may not be rocket science to Mr. Layhee, but it was all these guys had. And they took it. And the only people on the face of this earth that can make them pay for what they did to get back the benefits are you folks. The ten of you.

If you believe we didn't have any trade secrets, we didn't contribute anything, it's old, it's obvious, it's easy, anybody could do it, then don't award a cent. But if that's not the case, they ought to give back every benefit that they got.

And you're the only ones that can do it. You have the power to do it. You have the power to tell them that this community doesn't accept this kind of conduct as something that's appropriate and acceptable. That's the message you've got to send back to them. They don't believe in dreams. We do believe in dreams.

We thank you for your attention to this case, and we know you'll do the right thing.

Thank you.

(Transcript, December 8, 1998, pp. 2255-2257). I laid out the challenge and I empowered the jury. The result: a verdict of $10,939,391 increased to $16,070,656 by the judge. Later, Pizza Hut paid a little more than $15 million to settle the case against it. We had struck a blow for the little guy. A few months later, Joe Burlini (a famous artist friend to both Joe Freda and me) came into my office with some rocks and a sling. He said I was David slaying Goliath. Nice image for a trial lawyer. I keep the rocks and the sling on the table in my office.

STRIVING FOR PERFECTION

MuniAuction, Inc. v. Thomson Corp.,
Civil Action No. 01-1003 (W.D. Penn., Sept. 2006)

Perfection. That's the goal in every case. No one is perfect, of course; but if we try for it, well, who knows what can happen?

I was born and raised in Pittsburgh and met my wife, Judy, there in the summer before my last year in engineering school at Pitt. We left Pittsburgh in September 1964 after we were married. This trial was a return home 42 years later. The <u>MuniAuction</u> case gave me a chance to come home and prove who I was and what I could do. And some of my family members were there to see it. Judy was my advisor and super paralegal. My brother, Joe, was my informal jury consultant.

I mentioned my Pittsburgh roots in my opening:

> You know, I grew up in Pittsburgh and am the son of a bricklayer. My dad used to take me to work with him in the summers and I had the distinction of being a laborer. I mixed the mortar and carried the bricks, and my brother is here and he knows firsthand because he was laying the bricks beside my dad and I was carrying the mortar. He used to talk about goals. My dad told me the story about the three bricklayers and the visitor. The visitor came to the first bricklayer and said, what are you doing? He said, I am laying bricks. Went to the second bricklayer and said, what are you doing? He

said, I'm building a wall. He went to the third bricklayer and said, what are you doing? He said, I'm building a cathedral.

What is your goal? Do you want to lay bricks or do you want to build a cathedral? These guys decided to build a cathedral. I think the evidence will show they were successful at doing that.

They started a new business called MuniAuction. It was a huge success. They got the recognition for that success from around the country.

(Transcript, September 25, 2006, pp. 44-45).

MuniAuction (t/d/b/a Grant Street Group) had a patent on a system/ method for auctioning municipal bonds over the Internet. The inventor, Myles Harrington, explained how he experienced the problems with old bond auctioning systems first-hand:

A.   [B]y far and away the most popular means of submitting a bid prior to MuniAuction was to use a fax machine so that the bidder would compute their bid on their computer and then frequently they would either print it out or else they would transcribe onto a piece of paper that was given to them by the issuer the bid that they were submitting for each maturity of the bond issue, as well as the total purchase price that they were willing to pay. They would transcribe that onto a piece of paper, they would walk over and stick it into a fax machine and send it to a number that had been given them by the issuer, and then the issuer would stand by the fax, wait for these bids to come in, and then they'd look at them one after another and compare them to each other and try to determine who the winner was.

Q.   Any problems in terms of the fax machines having clocks that were set at times that were not accurate?

A.   Well, in almost every competitive auction that Dan and I were involved in prior --

Q.   Dan is Mr. Veres?

A.   Mr. Veres, the co-founder, and I were involved in almost every single auction. The bids would come in with a variety of mistakes, some of them very significant mistakes, and one of the things that issuers and bidders all took quite seriously was the time stamp that was shown on the fax. So that, for example, if the time stamp shown on the fax were one second after the published deadline for submission of bids, technically, it was an invalid bid. So, Dan and I had had the experience working with City of Pittsburgh and Pittsburgh Water and Sewer Authority and a number of other local issuers, like Presbyterian Association on Aging where the bids would come in and the time stamp on the bid was a minute, two minutes, three minutes late, and also the clocks that were being used on the fax machines by the bidders weren't set properly. They might be on daylight savings time and we might be on standard time, that type of thing.

Q.   Did that create any problems in terms of sorting out who was the winning bidder?

A.   Well, in fact, it made it impossible without the involvement of lawyers and telephone calls and some shouting back and forth. Often the issue of the bidder is, well, my clock is right, your clock is wrong. I had my bid in on time, somebody else's bid must have been in front of me and prevented mine from coming in by the deadline. So the faxes would get backed up on the fax machine, that type of thing.

Q.   So what if the municipality, for example, just had a single fax machine and there were multiple bids com[ing] in at the last minute, did that create any problems?

A.   It practically guaranteed there would not be timely submission of all the bids because, unlike faxes today, most issuers did not have faxes where the faxes would lineup and get time stamped in a queue before they got printed out. In the old days, the only time you'd get a time stamp on a fax was at the point in time at which it was actually printed by [the] fax machine.

Q.   So I might submit my bid on a timely basis, but because twelve people were in front of me, my bid didn't get in?

A.   Right.

Q.   What about this person hand delivering, were there actually people that would hand deliver bids to the municipality?

A.   There were. And, for example, in Tennessee [there] was a place where people used to deliver bids [by] hand delivery and other places actually like Georgia, it was very common to actually have to take your bid right at the courthouse steps and hand it to somebody, or try to find a room where you would deliver the bid, and often people were late showing up, they couldn't find the room, they got caught in traffic, that type of thing.

Q.   I have to confess in the sixth grade I was the only student that did not get a writing certificate, so my writing skills were very poor. Were there legibility problems of any kind in transmitting these bids where somebody like me that didn't write neat enough would say something or write something and then that would create a problem?

A.   Often. I don't notice it so much on the newer faxes, but on the older faxes, frequently you would get like print lines and the pages would be fuzzy, it would be difficult to read things, and because the bidders were in such a mad rush to get their bid transcribed onto a piece of paper and get it out on the fax machine before the deadline, they were often writing in a way that once you received it, you could not make out whether it was a 4 percent or 4.05 percent, that type of thing. And the problem with calling bids, which is shown on here as well, telephone bids, is that the person you were calling was not an employee of your company, it was somebody that was designated to receive bids over the phone. So the bidder would call in the bid and somebody that didn't know it was transcribing the bid onto a piece of paper, and if they should have happened to make a mistake, there -- it's not a situation where the bidder can say, well, whoever you had take my bid got the wrong number. So, because they were bidding millions of dollars at a time, it was a pretty significant problem if there was a transcription error, whether it came in by fax or whether it was a third party that was actually writing it down.

(Transcript, September 26, 2006, pp. 82-86).

Myles Harrington explained that the solution was a new electronic-auctioning system that addressed and solved the many problems with manual or fax bidding:

A.   ... [W]e began to focus on these problems that you just highlighted with some of the exhibits here and we were focused on how could we use the Internet to solve some of the problems that we had encountered in handling bids that were coming in in competitive sales. And there was an exchange of ideas about how would we deal with errors, how would we deal with a problem of bids not coming in on time, how would we deal with the problem of not being able to read the bids that we were getting, how would we deal with the problem that the calculations that the bidders were doing weren't consistent across firms that in fact were using the same software even.

(Transcript, September 26, 2006, p. 101). We created a simple chart to illustrate the MuniAuction invention and it became the centerpiece of our case:

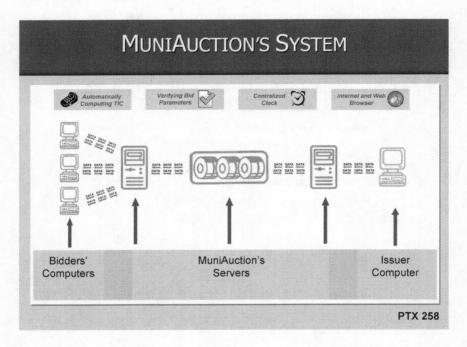

Creating pictures works, as was seen through the testimony of Myles Harrington:

Q. Mr. Harrington, I'm going to show you another illustration. This is Plaintiff's Exhibit 258. Tell us, if you would, what that illustrates?

A.   This shows the system that we had conceived of in detail in that on the far left, you have bidders' computers.

✳ ✳ ✳ ✳ ✳

Q.   Then the next thing is verifying bid parameters. Why did you want to do that?

A.   Well, the bidders often, as I mentioned earlier, would violate the parameters that were established by the issuer, so what we would do is make sure that the bid conformed when it was submitted to the specifications established by the issuer.

Q.   Now, up top you show a centralized clock. Why would you want a centralized clock?

A.   To address the problem we were having with conflicting time stamps between bidders' bids and what the issuer understood the time at which the bid was submitted.

Q.   If I'm running a marathon there is one clock that would decide the time everybody was measured by?

A.   When anybody crosses the finish line, you see the official time at which they cross the finish line.

Q.   Then you have to the far right issuer computer and then Internet and web browser. Explain what that is for.

A.   Well, as I mentioned earlier, one of the problems with the technology at the time that we conceived of this was that there was no mechanism for all of the participants in this process to communicate with each other freely and openly. And the closest thing to it was software, shrink wrap software on a disk that had to be loaded onto a computer to do a calculation, and then some other device, like a fax machine or the telephone had to be used to deliver the bid, that type of thing. So the combination of the Internet and the web browser enabled us to tie people together seamlessly so that we could eliminate the problems that we have encountered.

Q. Why did you want a single computer or server to automatically compute the true interest costs rather than have them done at different places at different times?

A. Well, at the time, there were several software programs which were in use by bidders, and even bidders who were using the same software weren't getting the same answer. In other words, the calculations that they were running weren't generating consistent answers in terms of a true interest cost, and the only way we could think to deal with that problem was to get everybody to use the same calculator and enable them to use it without bumping into each other. In other words, you didn't want to have to wait if somebody was using a calculator until they were finished so you could use it. So there had to be a calculator everybody could use simultaneously to do their calculations and that the issuer as well had to be willing to rely upon as the official calculator, and the issuer had to be satisfied with the calculations that that was performing as well.

(Transcript, September 26, 2006, pp. 102, 104-105).

We had a jury of seven women and one man (a truck driver): two school teachers with master's degrees, a petroleum engineer -- mostly college graduates. They paid close attention to everything.

The trial judge had a new high-tech courtroom and told us before trial how lawyers often miss an opportunity to persuade by using technology. That opened the door for us. Nicholas Hey, our animation specialist, created graphics for everything and they told our story. It was pure persuasion. One example: the defendant had a demonstrative exhibit to suggest it was unfair for our client to recover $38.4 million when its sales were only $3.2 million. That bothered me. After a "brainstorming" dinner session, Judy had an idea. We countered with our own exhibit. We showed a car hitting a tree that caused $3,840 in damage. The friend who borrowed it for his new business only made $320. The loss was $3,840, not $320. Who cares that the friend's business only made $320?

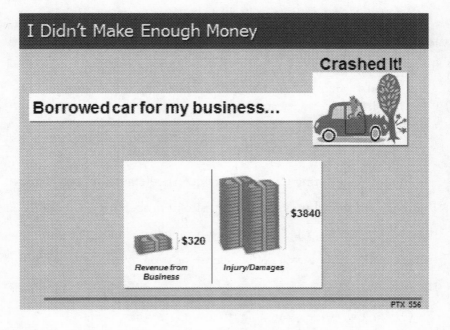

In closing, I used the analogy as follows:

> One thing I want to mention here because it bothered me when I heard it. I think we've got to address it. Remember they had a stack of things, dollar bills, 10 dollar bills, whatever it is, they said actually

PARITY/BIDCOMP, 3.2 million and these people have the audacity to ask for 38 million. That doesn't make any sense. Think about it this way for a minute. Judge Lancaster has already told you, you don't measure lost profits by what the defendant's sales were.

You measure it by what your profits were. Let's assume I have a car. I use it to get back and forth to work. Friend of mine comes in and says, hey, I got a business, can I borrow your car? And the friend, perhaps not being such a good friend, wrecks the car. Now you say, hey, you owe me $3,840. You wrecked my car. He says, you know what, my revenues from my business were only $320. That's it. You get $320. Doesn't make any sense. You don't measure injury by what you did and if you just change and add four zeros to this analogy. You got their chart. I made 3.2 million, you want 38 million. It's a question of how much the injury was, not how much they made. They were giving it away. Of course they didn't make much, but they were making it in some other ways.

(Transcript, October 4, 2006, p. 102).

In cross-examining Cheryl Horowitz, the defendant's star witness, I emphasized two things: (1) the statistic improbability that Thomson did not copy and (2) the fact that Thomson had a choice not to infringe -- Thompson could have taken a license or tried to design around. But they did neither:

Q.　Now, were you able to compare the similarities between this patent and the Thomson system? And I'll put before you Exhibit 270-A. Does that show similarities; that is, elements of the claims that are also present in the Thomson system?

SIMILARITIES BETWEEN THE MUNIAUCTION PATENT AND THOMSON SYSTEM

- Centralized Clock (18, 40)
- Central Server Acting as Web Server (1, 31)
- Automatic Calculator (1, 31)
- Confirmation Prior to Submitting Bid (9)
- Bidder Computer (1, 31)
- Issuer Computer (1, 31)
- Transmit Interest Cost (1, 31)
- Transmitting Time Indication (18)
- Displaying Bid Times (18, 40)

- Verify Bid Parameters (2)
- Web Browser Access to Internet (1, 31)
- Observer Computer (20)
- True Interest Cost (TIC) (24)
- Ranking Bids via (TIC) (32)
- Predetermined Time Period (36)
- Communicating Messages (1)
- Displaying Interest Cost Value on Issuers Computer (31)
- Submitting the Bid (1)

(Claim numbers shown in parentheses)

PTX 270(a)

A.   Yes, it does.

Q.   And in the parenthesis, the actual claim is indicated. For example, issuer's computer Claims 1 and 31, true interest cost, Claim 24, communicating messages, Claim 1 and so forth?

A.   Yes. …

Q   … Now, you're background is in mathematics?

A.   Yes, it is.

Q.   And you're familiar with statistics?

A.   Yes.

Q.   What is the probability, if you just had an "on/off" condition, you either have that centralized clock or don't have it, you either have the verification of bid parameters or you don't have, you either have a web browser or you don't have, you either have an issuer's computer or you don't have it, what is the probability of two people independently coming up with the same 18 features?

A. Very high.

Q. How high?

A. 1 in 262,000.

Q. How do you calculate that? I'll put up Exhibit 274.

Coincidence ..... or Copying?

18 of 18 Identical Features

$$2^{18} = 2x2x2x2x2x2x2x2x2x2x2x2x2x2x2x2x2x2$$

$$= 262,144$$

1 in 262,144 chance of getting all the same features...

PTX 274

A. It's basically taking, taking things two at a time and doing the, the multiplication that's shown there to, to reveal that there's one chance in 262,000 of getting the same features.

Q. That's two to the 18th power?

A. That's two to the 18th power. That means you take "two," and you write a "times sign," and write another "two," and keep doing that until you have 18 two's, and then you, you start doing two times two, two times two.

Q. Two times two is four, and four times two is eight, and four times eight is 16.

A. Is 32, is 64, is 128, is 256, and keep on going. It goes faster at the end.

Q. Now, and that represents the probability statistically of two people independently, with a choice of doing it or not doing it, coming up with the same 18 features set forth in the claims?

A. It does.

(Transcript, September 27, 2006, pp. 128-130). I hammered away at their choices because that would be my theme in closing:

Q. It's your representation that given the choice, you would rather go through that process and pay that money than paying $400,000 to design around, is that what you're saying?

A. Yeah, that's what I'm saying because I don't believe that everybody who approaches me and says I'll file a lawsuit that I should immediately react and change my software. More than that, I don't believe I infringed, and I don't believe the patent is valid. So in the case where every person who came up with a software that had features of mine and came to me and said I have a patent on it, I don't think it's rational to immediately say okay, I'm sorry. Let me change it.

Q. I see. So you had a choice, and you made that choice, right?

A.   We as a firm made that choice, sure.

Q.   I'd tell my children and my ten grandchildren life is about choices.

A.   Absolutely.

Q.   Sometimes you make good ones, sometimes you make bad ones. Hopefully, you make a lot of good ones and have a better life?

A.   I would agree with that philosophy.

Q.   You made a choice, and your choice was you could design around the patent or not design around the patent, right?

A.   Yes.

Q.   And you chose not to design around, right?

A.   That's correct.

Q.   Now, am I correct that it would cost you, you said $400,000 --

A.   A maximum of $400,000.

Q.   To design around?

A.   Yes.

Q.   And your choice was to simply proceed and pay nothing to MuniAuction, correct?

A.   No. My choice was to proceed with the lawsuit and let a jury decide that.

Q.   You have admitted that your client, that is your company that you represent, needed to have this electronic auctioning system in one way, shape or form, correct?

A.   What I believe my testimony was is that my clients needed a way to get their bids, to calculate their bids and get them to the issuer. In most of the PARITY eligible sales, they have PARITY, they have fax, they have phone. So, yeah, they need a way to do that in one way, shape or form, absolutely. That was my testimony.

Q.   Let me show it to you so there is no confusion about it. Did you say in response to the question that was asked:

> Let me say this. The fact is my clients need that product, so it's a product that they need to have in one way, shape or form; and additionally, the Bid Comp/PARITY revenue has grown over the last number of years.

Did you give that testimony in this case?

A.   Absolutely. Well, this was my deposition. That was my answer in my deposition, and what I said yesterday was, and I clarified that yesterday to, again, say that my clients need a way to do this. If they didn't have a way to do it and had to calculate by hand, I think we would all agree it would take a very long time.

Q.   And the choice you made was not to design around for $400,000, correct?

A.   That's correct.

(Transcript, October 4, 2006, pp. 91-94; see PTX-422).

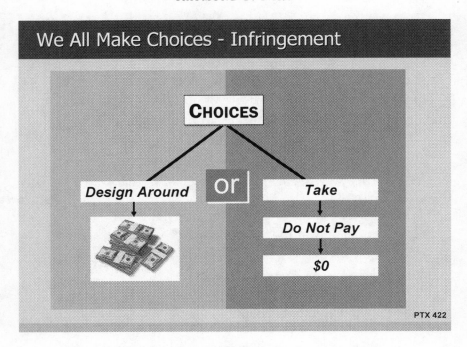

We All Make Choices - Infringement

CHOICES

Design Around **or** Take

Do Not Pay

$0

PTX 422

I continued to expose their poor choices, which ultimately led to the finding that Thomson's infringement was willful:

Q. Choices. You made a choice. Have you ever done this? I had this happen to me. You go to the parking meter to go run into the store. You don't have a quarter in your pocket. You go in and say I'll be right back out, and invariably, there's a $25 ticket there when you come out. That's a choice.

A. Yes.

Q. I made a little schematic of that choice. Pay 25 cents, pay $25. Now, the choice you made in this case was not to design around and to let this jury decide whether or not you infringed, correct?

A. That's correct.

Q. And if the jury finds that you infringed and you made the wrong choice, then you're certainly prepared to pay MuniAuction what's fair, right?

A.   If the jury finds that I have to pay MuniAuction, I'm not not going to pay them. That would be illegal.

Q.   So let's take the analogy one step further. You're prepared, like I'm prepared when I didn't put my quarter in the meter, to pay whatever this jury decides is an appropriate damage if they find there is infringement, correct?

A.   If the jury finds there's infringement and they provide a damage report, I'm either going to design around or pay or something.

Q.   Well, you haven't designed around?

A.   No, I haven't designed around yet.

(Transcript, October 4, 2006, pp. 96-97; see PTX-423).

Judy said my closing in the <u>MuniAuction</u> case was the best ever (and she heard most of them). Almost everything I said was keyed off a demonstrative. I started with my mom telling me that "a picture is worth 1,000 words":

> ... I think my mom used to say a picture is worth 1,000 words, and indeed it is. Sometimes you can put it in a picture; it illustrates what is being said. The technology in this wonderful courtroom lets us do that. ...

(Transcript, October 4, 2006, p. 78). Then I moved to the cover page of the patent:

> Right on the cover of the patent it says, the requirements of law have been complied with and it has been determined that a patent on the invention shall be granted under the law.
>
> The examiner in examining this application set forth in the written record what are the reasons that I find that this is a patentable invention complying with the patent law. He said it about as succinctly as you can. You invented a combination, some pieces that were out there and you put it together in a different way. It was novel, unobvious, unique, and distinctive over the prior art.

(Transcript, October 4, 2006, p. 80). I ridiculed their non-infringement arguments:

> The second argument is even more interesting than the first. I think I said if you get your hand caught in the cookie jar, sometimes you have to come up with some bizarre excuses for your conduct, and there are some bizarre excuses here. This one is really, I think, first prize.
>
> People only use the electronic submissions part of the time. You heard Mrs. Horowitz say, I think this is

right, 55 percent of the time you do it electronically, 45 percent of the time they do it by fax, by mail, by telephone. That makes no sense. It's a little like saying we come to this beautiful courtroom with the electronics we have here, the televisions, with the Elmo, with the ability to present instantaneously evidence to you, photographs, whatever, and we shut them all off. Shut them down. Let's go back to the old system we did 20 years ago.

(Transcript, October 4, 2006, pp. 86-87). I emphasized common sense:

> They say that there were 12,000 auctions to give the users the option. Think about that for a minute. Apply common sense. If there are 12,000 options where people would prefer to go back into time and use a fax or the mail, why wouldn't one of them come here and testify? You heard evidence from two users. They're paying experts, $300, $500, $450 an hour. You couldn't afford to have one user out of those 12,000 sit on the witness stand, say, by the way, I like all the errors that are made when we get it by fax and mail and I don't want it electronically. There was no testimony because there is no testimony.

(Transcript, October 4, 2006, p. 88). Then I hammered away at their silence -- what didn't they say?

> It's been said the cruelest lies are told in silence. It's not what you say but sometimes what you don't say. Where is [the] silen[ce] here? Where is the real PARITY disk, not a demo? Where are the users, the issuers, these people that they have done business with? Silence. Where is the legal opinion on validity? Silence. Where is the actual working, operating scissors method? Silence. Doesn't exist. Where are

the claim charts showing they don't infringe? Silence. You didn't hear a word from Mr. Bradner. Where is the lawyer from Hale & Dorr that wrote the 73-page opinion? Silence.

(Transcript, October 4, 2006, p. 94).

Make-believe. That was their game on the prior art. I argued the land of make-believe was for Mr. Rogers, a Pittsburgh native (another idea from Judy), not for a trial:

> We've had a lot of make-believe, and I have to say, I'm blessed, I have ten grandchildren, three sons, two of whom work with me, and as they were growing up, like most kids, they watched Mr. Rogers who was a legend not only in Pittsburgh but nationally. And I don't know if you remember this, he had this little train that would go into the Land of Make Believe. It was good for kids to use their imagination. To go into make-believe and to be in that world. But that's not the world you should be in in a federal courtroom trying a patent infringement case. This is not about make-believe and let's pretend and maybe ifs and buts and it could have been. This is about a United States patent and some people that put their life on the line, literally, inventing and creating new business. That's what it's about. It's demeaning to talk about make-believe, let's pretend. This is not Mr. Rogers' Neighborhood. This is a federal courthouse and scissors methods and demos that don't work, and design-arounds that never happen are the world of make-believe.

(Transcript, October 4, 2006, pp. 95-96). The Mr. Rogers chart was great (see PTX-440) and helped push the point.

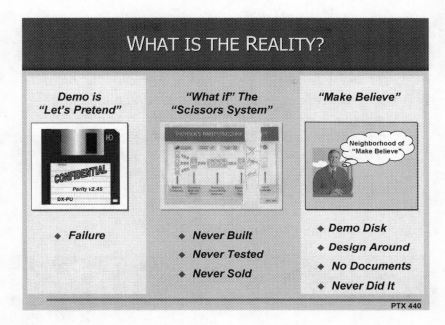

I also touched on obviousness and looking at the combinations. Apparently, opposing counsel had studied my other closings, so I switched from musical notes to a combination lock:

> This case should not be about make-believe, hypothetical designs and all the rest. There's only one defense in this case they really tried to make and that is this obvious defense, that the invention would have been obvious at the time the invention was made. You have to look at the combination. Inventions of combinations.
>
> It's like this lock. There's a combination here, I don't know if I can even do this. If I know the numbers and I know the sequence, I have to look on the back to get it, I can open the lock. If I don't know the combination, I can play with this from now until the end of time, you're not going to open it.

(Transcript, October 4, 2006, pp. 96-97). I introduced the puzzle:

> What is the best evidence here of what was happening

in the real world? Assume this is a little puzzle, a novel, an unobvious system. I asked Mr. Landes this and I asked Mr. Bradner this and I think the answer was, did you invent it? No. Did Mr. Miller invent it? No. Did Amazon.com invent it? We know they didn't. Mr. LaRoche? No -- Ms. LaRoche. Did Mr. Bradner invent it? No. How about Microsoft, they're one of the owners? No. Merrill Lynch? No. Mr. Brown? You heard about Brown and Fisher, did they invent it? No. Citibank? No.

(Transcript, October 4, 2006, p. 97; see PTX-535).

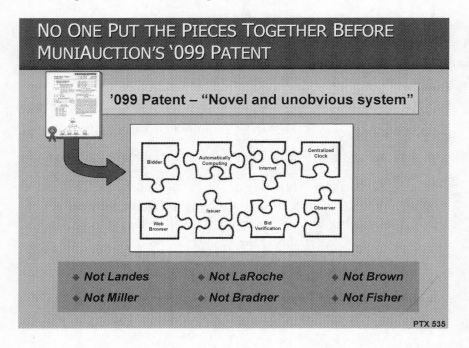

The puzzle provides the pieces, but the invention was knowing how to put the puzzle together:

> Who put the puzzle together? MuniAuction. Mr. Harrington, Mr. Veres, they figured it out and nobody else did. And they demeaned the process by saying it's

easy, it's old, it's simple, anyone can do it. If you use that rationale -- I went back and I looked at a beautiful story, we all know about the light bulb. The inventor of that light bulb is a guy named Thomas Edison. He had an assistant named Louis Lattimer. Edison had a third grade education. Lattimer was the son of a slave, and together they invented a great invention. Look at how simple it is. You have a fuse, you have a glass, you have some wires, it's easy. It's obvious. It's all old. Anybody can do it. You know what? We'd be sitting in darkness if they hadn't figured out the combination. If there were a case here with Thomson Edison and Mr. Lattimer suing Thomson for infringement, you would have these guys saying to you, that's easy, that's old, that's obvious. Anybody can do it. But nobody did. That's invention, doing something in combination that nobody had before.

(Transcript, October 4, 2006, pp. 97-98). I went to my favorite book for the "final five" minutes in closing -- a little book written by a father for his son on the important things in life just before his son leaves for college:

No. 59. Live so that when your children think of fairness, caring and integrity, they think of you. 359. Don't let anyone talk you out of pursuing what you know to be a great idea.

Nobody talked these guys out of pursuing what they thought was their idea.

Here's one that I thought really was right on the money. Never deprive someone of hope -- it might be all they have.

That's what they had. Hope. Dreams. And these folks over here crushed it shamelessly, without remorse, without concern. Take it, we don't care. Maybe we'll pay later. Just like Wimpy said, maybe we'll never pay, but at worst, we're going to pay later.

Ms. Horowitz said, there's no big deal. No big deal, we'll design around it and we'll pay.

(Transcript, October 4, 2006, pp. 104-105). I challenged the jury not to let innovation die in our country:

> And if they can do this, you think about it, if they can do this here, they can do it anywhere. And invention, innovation ends today, right here because there isn't anyone that's going to invent anything if some big bully on the block can take it and not pay anything. That's what this is about. There won't be any more light bulbs, there won't be any more Internet auctions, there won't be anything.

(Transcript, October 4, 2006, p. 105).

Then, back to my roots and the comment opposing counsel made about Wimpy:

> I'm the son of an immigrant. Third grade education, just like Thomas Edison. And I remember when he got a certificate to become a citizen. On the side there was a ribbon. Made him accepted. Made him part of this country. Just like he was proud of that, they're proud of what they did. That was the last question I asked Mr. Harrington, I think the Judge said, what did you expect him to say? That's the truth. Sure he's proud of it. He got a reward for an invention that was found patentable by the United States Patent [and] Trademark Office. It wasn't old and obvious, it wasn't easy. It wasn't like what these guys say now. It's not okay to end a patent.

(Transcript, October 4, 2006, p. 106). I then do what I like to do at the end of every case -- empower the jury to do what is right:

> This case is not about who is big and who is small, who is rich and who is poor, it's about right and wrong. If we're wrong, if this patent is invalid, this patent is not infringed, then give us nothing because we deserve nothing. But if this patent is infringed and this patent

is valid, then give us what is right, tell these guys it's not okay to infringe a patent, it's not okay to run somebody over. It's not okay to say, you know what, I'm like Wimpy, I'll pay you later because I know what I did is wrong. And I'm going to force you through the process to get there. I know you'll do the right thing.

(Transcript, October 4, 2006, pp. 106-107). We even had charts for Wimpy:

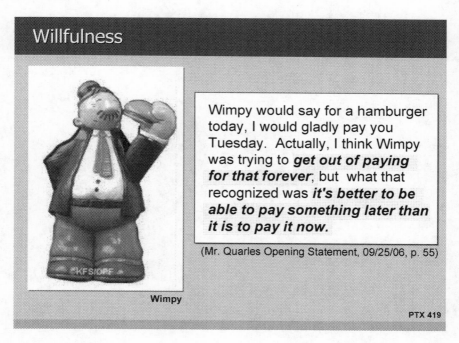

Willfulness

Wimpy would say for a hamburger today, I would gladly pay you Tuesday. Actually, I think Wimpy was trying to *get out of paying for that forever*, but what that recognized was *it's better to be able to pay something later than it is to pay it now.*

(Mr. Quarles Opening Statement, 09/25/06, p. 55)

Wimpy

PTX 419

The defendant's response was that I had engaged in theatrics:

But this case, there's been an awful lot of theatrics. There's been an awful lot of cartoon graphics that have been shown to you. There's been an awful lot of emotion in the courtroom, but that's not what this case is about. It's not about Buck Rogers or any of that stuff. When you retire to the jury room in just a few minutes to deliberate what happens to my client, you will have to decide two issues. Do [they] infringe the claims of this patent? Is this patent valid?

(Transcript, October 4, 2006, p. 107). Using visualization is not theatrics; it is persuasion in its purest form. The jury decided all right: patent valid and willfully infringed; damages of $38.4 million, later increased by the trial judge to $84.6 million.

PART II
LESSONS LEARNED

<u>Famolare, Inc.</u> v. **<u>Edison Brothers Stores, Inc., et al.</u>**,
Civil Action No. 75 C 2708 (N.D. Ill. 1978)

<u>FMC Corp.</u> v. **<u>H&K Machine</u>**,
Civil Action No. 88 C 0365 (E.D. Wis. 1989)

<u>Johnson</u> v. **<u>FMC Corp.</u>**,
Civil Action No. CIV-S-92 062 GEB (E.D. Cal. 1994)

<u>Black & Decker</u> v. **<u>Coleman</u>**,
Civil Action No. CA 96-656-A (E.D. Va. 1996)

<u>Wolens</u> v. **<u>Wear-Ever Aluminum, Inc., et al.</u>**,
Civil Action No. 79 C 4291 (N.D. Ill. 1980)

EARLY LESSONS

Experience -- the product of an accumulation of one's mistakes. Some of the greatest trial lawyers -- Edward Bennett Williams (five years representing local streetcar companies, insurance companies and other corporate interests), Gerry Spence (years working as an insurance defense lawyer), Abraham Lincoln (travelled twice a year with the presiding judge and fellow lawyers to the county seats of Illinois' Eighth Circuit to try as many as eight cases per day) to name a few -- honed their skills as trial lawyers from early experiences.

In his book, The Outliers, Malcom Gladwell identifies some of the components of success: opportunity, timing, hard work, practice, luck, help, ambition, personality. Under "hard work," he includes a chapter called "The 10,000-Hour Rule." Gladwell explains how ability alone is not enough. It takes work: "... ten thousand hours of practice to achieve the level of mastery associated with a world-class expert -- in anything" (quoting Daniel Levitin; The Outliers, Malcolm Gladwell at 40). And so successful people from Harold Schonberg to Bill Joy to Bill Gates to the Beatles all put in their 10,000 hours of practice before opportunity eventually came their way.

These five cases represent a few early experiences (some actually not too early) that made me a better trial lawyer, as I, too, put in my 10,000 hours of practice.

DON'T LET THE JUDGE BULLY YOU

Famolare, Inc. v. **Edison Brothers Stores, Inc., et al.**,
Civil Action No. 75 C 2708 (N.D. Ill. 1978)

In this case, we represented the big guys in a string of patent infringement suits brought by inventor Joe Famolare against the volume shoe retailers. Our client, Edison Brothers Stores, owned hundreds of shoe stores across the United States that sold lower-priced knock-offs of designer shoes, including those created by Joe Famolare. Our other client, USM Corporation, made the infringing shoe soles initially simply by purchasing the original Famolare shoes and then copying the wavy-bottom sole design.

In the early 70s, Joe Famolare was as close to a rock star as one could be: Italian, artistic, offices in Florence and New York. He created a wavy-bottom shoe design called the "Get There" that was a huge hit:

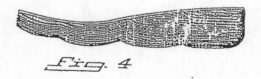

Nearly fifty percent of the young women in Hawaii wore his wavy-bottom "Get There" or "Hi There" shoes (see below); hence, one lawsuit was brought there. California was big too. Another lawsuit was filed in Sacramento, one in Minneapolis, another in Portland, Maine and one, of course, in Chicago. Famolare had utility patents, design patents, copyrights and even a trademark on his product configuration. We joked that he probably would have filed for a plant patent if his shoes could be asexually reproduced. His "Hi There" sole looks very much like the wedge shoes that are so popular today:

Fig. 1

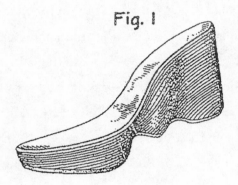

The first case went to trial in Chicago in December 1978 before one of the very best judges on our federal bench, Judge Hubert L. Will. Juries in patent cases were not in vogue then, so Famolare opted for a bench trial and we agreed. Trial counsel for Famolare was C. Fredrick Leydig -- tall, handsome and smooth as silk. The industry paper *Footwear News* covered the trial and reported on developments daily. Judge Will (as was his practice) let you know where you stood at all times:

THE COURT: That is what you patent lawyers do all
the time. A tree is a tree is a tree. I have said many

times, Gertrude Stein would have been a good patent lawyer.

(Transcript, December 19, 1978, p. 243).

Our client insisted that a seasoned patent litigator sit with Jerry Hosier and me at counsel's table. And Jim Hume -- a legendary patent trial lawyer -- was the choice. Jim was the Senior Partner at Hume, Clement, Hume & Lee, the firm where Jerry and I started. He listened and advised, met with us as we prepared witnesses and was involved in most phases of our strategy and the trial itself.

Here are some excerpts from Judge Will at his finest:

> THE COURT: No way. You read the question and you read the answer. I don't want the Niro interpretation of anybody's previous testimony, or the Leydig interpretation, or anybody else's.
> I want the question read and the answer read, and I will decide whether or not there was prior testimony that is inconsistent with what he says here.

(Transcript, December 18, 1978, p. 132). He was right. ***Impeach by reading the deposition and answer.*** See how I did it correctly in the Calabrese case (p. 16). Lesson learned. Thank you Judge Will.

He accused us of fooling around:

> THE COURT: So obviously it isn't a production model. You don't make a production model in one size, Mr. Niro. At least, I don't think you do. Let us quit fooling around with the problem of semantics and interpretation.

(Transcript, December 20, 1978, p. 383). He believed our clients copied (really not so inaccurate):

THE COURT: Is there any serious dispute the number of shoes made by Edison are almost exact, if not exact copies of the Famolare sole?

MR. LEYDIG: They have yet to stipulate that, your Honor. I don't know what their position is other than they deny it.

THE COURT: Let us find out.

I haven't looked at them all and maybe there are some that aren't, but it is my impression that a substantial number, at least, are deliberate copies. Isn't that true?

MR. NIRO: I don't think we can concede that they are deliberate copies, your Honor.

(Transcript, December 20, 1978, p. 496). He scolded me for trying to put words in a witness's mouth:

THE COURT: He didn't say he knew. He said he had an idea.

Mr. Niro, do not convert having an idea into knowing something. Now, that is not fair. That is an unfair question to ask him.

You read a statement which he says he had an idea, and it turns out the idea was right, and then you say, "Is it true, Mr. Famolare, that you knew it would work out and it turned out that your knowledge was correct?

Not so. That isn't what he said. I suggest to you that you don't make any points with me with that kind of examination.

MR. NIRO: Nothing further, your Honor.

THE COURT: Okay.

(Transcript, December 19, 1978, p. 267).

Down and out. After the "you don't make any points with me"

comment, I hung my head in shame, really wanting to ask, "Is there a rock out here, Judge, that I can hide under?" I was defeated. Jim Hume then took me aside to give me some advice I follow to this day. He said, "Always respect the Judge. But don't let him bully you. Don't let him change your game plan. Put in your evidence whether the Judge likes it or not." And so it was.

When I was accused of wasting the Court's time, it was time to stand up:

> THE COURT: ... If the patent is no good, it is not no good because it could also be done rigidly. If the patent is no good, it is no good because of prior art or other reasons, but it certainly isn't no good because a rigid sole would accomplish the same physiological results. You are wasting my time.

⸭ ⸭ ⸭ ⸭ ⸭

> MR. NIRO: The question, your Honor, is can a person of ordinary skill in the art, the shoe sole art, looking at that claim be able to determine what are its bounds; when are you resilient; when are you sufficiently resilient.

⸭ ⸭ ⸭ ⸭ ⸭

> MR. NIRO: Your Honor, the United States Supreme Court, the cases we cite, Seventh Circuit Court of Appeals consistently said the claims of a patent must be understood by a person of ordinary skill in the art.
>
> THE COURT: Sure.
>
> MR. NIRO: And these must be described in such a way so you can tell what the bounds are; when am I inside the scope of the claims.

THE COURT: No question.

MR. NIRO: When am I outside the scope of the claims.

THE COURT: No question.

(Transcript, December 21, 1978, pp. 539-42). This was classic Judge Will -- smart as can be and he now was beginning to understand that the Famolare utility patent had to clearly define the limits of the invention. So, at a critical point, he actually took over cross-examination of Famolare's expert himself:

> THE COURT: But, you are being asked for an opinion as to whether or not if, in fact, based on your knowledge of the way the foot works, there was a difference in the depth of troughs, and therefore, necessarily a difference in the height of the crests, or the thickness of the crests, whether that would change the functioning of the sole and at some point would it become nonfunctioning; or, could you vary this a great deal and still have it function effectively, in your opinion? Do you know?

⸾ ⸾ ⸾ ⸾ ⸾

> THE COURT: Can you tell from this patent, how high the crests and how deep the troughs should be?

> THE WITNESS: No, I really can't, your Honor. I just know that at the present time, in my opinion, it functions well.

⸾ ⸾ ⸾ ⸾ ⸾

> THE COURT: In fact, I don't really understand how that determines what the height of the crest and the trough is going to be.

❖ ❖ ❖ ❖ ❖

THE COURT: But, the patent sure doesn't say that, does it? It doesn't tell you where to put those crests, does it? You know where to put them --

❖ ❖ ❖ ❖ ❖

THE COURT: But, this patent says you can have as little as three crests, and you can have as many as who knows what. It isn't limited to four crests. It doesn't tell you how high the crests and how deep the troughs should be except it says that the crests shall be at least six times the trough. Isn't that right?

THE WITNESS: It doesn't say that.

THE COURT: That means it could be 10, 11, 12, 14, 18, 26, 35, whatever it is.

(Transcript, December 21, 1978, pp. 548, 549, 552, 554). Unbelievable. The Judge's own cross-examination was going to win the case for us. We had gotten off the floor by standing tall when we had to:

THE COURT: I am talking about that. That isn't covered by the patent. You want now to design a sole which will have four weight-bearing crests and troughs between, three troughs between, and you want to design one which will not be within the scope of the patent.

How high would those crests have to be, how deep those troughs or how low would those crests have to be and how shallow those troughs.

THE WITNESS: I don't believe I could do it on that basis.

THE COURT: You can't do it from the patent?

THE WITNESS: It's not --

MR. LEYDIG: May I add to that question --

THE COURT: Let him finish. You can't do it from the patent?

THE WITNESS: It's not that specific.

THE COURT: Right.

(Transcript, December 21, 1978, p. 583). Wow! The judge had turned on the other side. Just like Jim Hume told me -- don't be bullied. Stay with your game plan.

THE COURT: You missed my point, Mr. Leydig. How do you tell where these four ridges are supposed to be from this patent? How do you tell how high or narrow -- I mean how thick or how narrow they are supposed to be? How do you tell how deep the troughs are supposed to be and how high the crests?

(Transcript, December 21, 1978, p. 587). Judge Will now clearly understood that the Famolare utility patent had no limits:

MR. NIRO: First of all, your Honor, Mr. Cornman sent letters out to the trade and you have seen them, I think, already --

THE COURT: Yes.

MR. NIRO: -- where this utility patent covers the three, four, and five-crested versions. Number two, I think that the point your Honor treated at Page 4, of our brief, the United States Supreme Court said, "The inventor must inform the public during the life of the patent the limits of the monopoly asserted so that it may be known which featured may be safely used by manufacturers without a license and which may not.

THE COURT: That's what I said earlier.

⊕ ⊕ ⊕ ⊕ ⊕

THE COURT: No, Mr. Leydig, it is not an issue so far as the allegedly infringing devices are concerned, but it is a problem so far as the validity of the patent is concerned.

⊕ ⊕ ⊕ ⊕ ⊕

THE COURT: But, the fact that you have Chinese copies, or USM copies which are identical, it doesn't help me with respect to the question of whether or not you have got a valid patent.

(Transcript, December 21, 1978, pp. 591, 614-15). And so it was: the utility patent was infringed, but invalid.

In the end, Judge Will (who was teaching me to be a better trial lawyer) also had to tell the inventor, Joe Famolare (almost apologetically), that his design patent was invalid too. Fashion is cyclical; the old gets revisited as the new and that's all the Famolare design was (look at the "Hi There" design 35 years later -- it's back):

> THE COURT: I don't mean that there is nothing new in the sense that it is somewhat different from what has been done before. I mean because -- obviously every dress style is different in some respects than what has been done before, but I don't think anyone thinks you can get a design patent on a dress. The reason for that is that the variations are not significant over what has been done before; even some rather remarkable variations, but I'm not aware of anybody getting a design patent on a dress and I am not sure that it is possible to develop

a design which is sufficiently different -- not that it isn't somewhat different. Of course, it is different.

Your design is different than any other shoe design that -- of the sole that's ever been put together, but it has to be sufficiently different so that it is in fact a patentable, unique, inventive creation.

And that's what I am having trouble with. ...

(Transcript, December 28, 1978, p. 1485).

Judge Will found both Famolare patents infringed but, in the case of the design patent, obvious (and, thus, invalid) and, in the case of the utility patent, invalid because the patent claims were indefinite. Quoting the Court's March 30, 1979 Opinion:

Historically, fashions are cyclical whether in clothes, shoes or other fashion items. They come, go and return to repeat the cycle. The most common examples are the length and style of ladies fashion dresses. The duration of the cycles varies depending on a number of factors and the dispute as to whether the fashion designers or the consumers determine changes in fashions will undoubtedly never be resolved since, apparently, the former regularly propose new designs, some of which are accepted by consumers while the majority are rejected.

(Memorandum Opinion, March 30, 1979, p. 33). As for the Famolare design patent:

Given the present state of the patent law, the relevant prior art and the relative variation thereof reflected in plaintiff's patent, we conclude that, while the plaintiff's four wave "Get There" sole is the best wavy shoe sole design developed to date, has been an outstanding commercial success, and has been widely copied by a number of competitors including defendants, it does not represent such an inventive contribution to the public or such a meaningful advance in the shoe design art that it constitutes invention.

(Opinion, p. 40). As for the utility patent:

> It seems clear that the claims are not specific enough to define the invention so that a knowledgeable person could either build a sole embodying the invention or know its bounds in order to design around it. The best evidence of the latter fact is that, until very recently, the plaintiff and its patent counsel, Mr. Cornman, were contending that the patent covered three and five wave soles as well as four wave versions and without regard to where the crests were located or how shallow or deep they were.

(Opinion, pp. 52-53).

> We conclude as to the validity that both patents are invalid for the reasons heretofore stated. The design patent lacks invention and it would have been obvious to any designer of ordinary skill to design soles with three, four, five or more waves. The utility patent involves a structure which functions very well but apparently not significantly better than a number of other soles. In addition, the claims are not sufficiently definite to meet the requirements of 35 U.S.C. § 112 in that they fail to inform either the specific structure or the limits of the claimed invention.

(Opinion, pp. 56-57).

We had won a huge victory for the copyists -- people I would later sue with regularity. But the lesson was learned: ***stand tall when you have to, but always with respect, not arrogance***.

NEVER UNDERESTIMATE THE OPPOSITION AND NEVER BE TOO OVERWHELMING

FMC Corp. v. **H&K Machine**,
Civil Action No. 88 C 0365 (E.D. Wis. 1989)

We represented the plaintiff, FMC Corporation, in this case on a patent for a pea harvester. (That's right, a pea harvester.) The good news: a less-than-impressive lawyer on the other side. The bad news: we were suing in the defendant's home town and you really had to become a pea bouncing around inside the harvester to prove infringement.

Opposing counsel actually read his opening and it was pathetic. I blasted several witnesses. We overwhelmed the other side with charts and data. Lesson No. 1: ***don't be too good, too slick, too overwhelming***. Our jury instructions were pretty much adopted by the Court, but they were way too complex. Lesson No. 2: ***keep the instructions simple***. The trial judge read the instructions on a Friday before a three-day holiday weekend, but would not give the jury a written copy of the instructions without agreement.

Initially, it was agreed that the jury would get a written copy of the instructions:

MR. NIRO: Yes, Your Honor. The instructions, I agree, quite lengthy, complex, difficult even for attorneys, I think, to comprehend in many respects. And for that I guess we have to blame ourselves. But by the same token we wanted to have a complete set of instructions. I think both sides wanted that. Given the fact that we are facing a holiday weekend, three days between the time of the instructions, which were read rapidly, I think, and --

THE COURT: Only took an hour. Let's see. Quarter to four until quarter after five, only an hour and a half with a break, I admit.

MR. NIRO: Right.

THE COURT: Hour and 15 minutes worth of instructions. I call that rather long, yeah.

MR. NIRO: I think at least there's a strong possibility that the jurors may not have gathered and understood everything that was said. Reading along was even difficult to follow. Would it be possible to submit to the jury the written form of the instructions as well so that they could read them as well as having just heard them? And I'm particularly concerned about it because of the long break between the giving of the instructions and the beginning of deliberations?

THE COURT: Mr. Wheeler?

MR. WHEELER: I have no objection to that, Your Honor.

⊕ ⊕ ⊕ ⊕ ⊕

THE COURT: If you can produce it, I have no objection to them having it. I think they were long and they are complex and --

MR. NIRO: Do you have --

THE COURT: Excuse me. They were long and complex. But as far as the long weekend, I disavow that as a factor totally. Are they going to forget the evidence which is every bit, if not more, important? Are they going to forget the compelling remarks of counsel in summation, which were brilliant? Shame not to have them go out and deliberate immediately. No, I can't get concerned over the lapse of a three-day holiday. But, again, if you can produce the -- I can't assist you with it -- but there's a record and if you think you can give me a transcript that will be accurate to the point where you and Mr. Wheeler are both satisfied to have it represent what the Court said and what the instructions were, I'm not going to quarrel with giving it to the jury.

(Transcript, May 26, 1989, pp. 716-18). After thinking about it over the weekend, opposing counsel knew what was best for his client; why give the jury help. If they were lost, he might win:

THE COURT: ... I will not submit it absent a stipulation. I think I told you that the other day. If you both agreed upon it, it would go in. If you don't agree on it, I'm not going to bear the responsibility for examining this what was an hour and 15 or 20 minutes of instructions to see that it is correct. I gave the jurors [instructions] which I think were appropriate, and I'm satisfied that they have "been properly instructed." Plaintiff asked on Friday to have the jurors have the benefit of the transcript of it, and I had no objection to that provided it was stipulated. So Mr. Wheeler, bypassing the problem of number 43, I toss the ball to you. Unless you say, "Ay," the answer of the Court is "Nay."

MR. WHEELER: I am not in a position to so stipulate at this time.

(Transcript, May 30, 1989, pp. 3-4). One juror brought a dictionary into the deliberations for help; it was removed. The judge told the jury he would try to get them a written copy of the instructions (but it never happened):

> THE COURT: Good morning. I've invited you back into the courtroom to cover just a couple of matters that may be of concern to you. The first is that the Marshall tells me that one of you brought along a dictionary, and I'm sorry to tell you that that is inappropriate, not a horrendous violation of our procedures, but I ask that you set it aside and not use it for the same reason I tried to explain earlier why we can't supply you with one. So again I'll tell you to use the -- consider the evidence that you heard, the exhibits in the case and your common sense, and I'm afraid that's about all that we can provide you. I think counsel agree that you have all the tools you need in matters I just touched upon to reach a verdict in the case.
>
> That brings me to the second matter I want to touch with you on, and that is that the instructions in this case were somewhat lengthy and somewhat complex, and the Court and counsel have been endeavoring to assist you by providing you with a copy of what was said and in part read to you. At this juncture we have not succeeded in arriving at a bundle, a package of those instructions. We're not through. We'll continue to try. If we can do it, we'll send it in. If we can't, you won't have it, but I'm sure counsel will make an earnest effort to assist you in that regard, but I can tell that in almost I would say 90 percent of the cases that are tried before a jury in this Court, in 90 percent, there is no submission of the instructions as such, or for that matter, the evidence. If this case were a case that lasted for six months, it'd be darn hard for you to remember everything, but it's a relatively short trial. You heard all the evidence and the Court's instructions, and I hope it's recent enough in

your memory so that you can sift out all the facts, and apply the law as the Court tried to explain it to you. So far as the complexity of the instructions go, I'm afraid it's inherent, irresistibly involved in the explanation of the law to give you the detailed instructions that I did. I don't apologize for them because that's what the law required me to do, to give them in the form that I did, and while it may be a burden to you to apply those legalistic expressions, that's just part of the job of being a juror.

I think that's all I wanted to take up with you. Do any of you ladies and gentlemen have any questions about what I've said?

(Transcript, May 30, 1989, pp. 7-8). Lesson No. 3: **know the trial judge's idiosyncrasies**. The instructions took 1125 lines and 46 pages of transcript. They were incomprehensible if read one time quickly. Our English expert said they were equivalent to a first-year college chemistry class. Can you imagine taking a chemistry class with no book, based on just what you heard? We should have had a written version ready and known that the trial judge would not force the other side to allow written instructions to go back with the jury.

In the end, after deliberating for two days, the jury rendered a defense verdict of no infringement:

THE CLERK: The United States District Court, Eastern District of Wisconsin, FMC Corporation, plaintiff, versus H & K Machine, Incorporated, defendant, case number 88-C-365. Special Verdict. We, the Jury in the above entitled case find as follows:

Question No. 1: Did the defendant, H & K Machine, infringe claim number 1 of the FMC patent? Answer, no. If your answer to Question No. 1 is "No," do not answer any of the remaining questions.

(Transcript, May 31, 1989, p. 2). Devastating. We thought we had won -- overwhelmingly. But we didn't.

We objected, of course, to the absence of written instructions, but to no avail:

> THE COURT: Mr. Niro, you wanted to put something on the record?
>
> MR. NIRO: Yes, Your Honor, very briefly. Dealing with the question of the jury instructions and written jury instructions, on Friday at the conclusion of the closings we believe it was agreed that if we could get an accurate transcript of the jury instructions, the jury would be given those written instructions. We asked the reporter to work over the weekend in the hopes that we would have a transcript, and we were provided with a transcript on Monday, Memorial Day.
>
> We verified the accuracy of the transcript at that time, provided a copy to Mr. Wheeler which he received the next morning. He had an opportunity to review it, called me at eleven-fifteen yesterday, indicated that he found no material discrepancies in the transcript but that he had changed his mind and indicated he would not agree to have the written instructions transmitted, given to the jury. So we had a situation which there were no objections on Friday but an objection Tuesday.
>
> Because of the length and complexity of the jury instructions, we believe that the jury effectively was without instruction on the law and we objected to that and so object at this time.

(Transcript, May 31, 1989, pp. 4-5).

On appeal, we complained about the absence of written instructions again to no avail. Here is an excerpt from the appeal brief, pointing out that an actual test done with first-year college students showed less than 15% comprehension without written instructions:

> The only objective evidence bearing on the jury's understanding of the instructions comes from an independent study conducted at Loyola University by Dr. Stephen J. Spear; Dr. Spear actually tested a group of college students and staff on the very jury instructions used by the trial court. The group that heard the instructions once and could discuss them (as the jury could) remembered less than 15% of what they had heard two days later. In contrast, those that heard the instructions, and then could read them, correctly understood and applied 80% of what they had heard and read. A significant difference -- more than five times the understanding level when the written form of instructions were given -- the difference between a high level of understanding and no understanding at all.

(FMC Corp. v. H&K Machine, Inc., Appeal No. 89-1683 at pp. 14-15; citation omitted).

Isn't the goal of a jury trial to have jury comprehension? And is 15% a passing grade? In the end, we were done in by a marginal lawyer, some bad luck and our own overwhelming presentation. Lesson learned: ***don't be too good and never underestimate your opponent.***

SOMETIMES YOU CAN'T OVERCOME BAD FACTS NO MATTER WHAT

Johnson v. **FMC Corp.**,
Civil Action No. CIV-S-92 062 GEB (E.D. Cal. 1994)

We tried cases on pea harvesters and grape harvesters, so why not tomato harvesters? The Johnson case involved a patent on a tomato harvester invented by a Professor from the University of California. The key language in the patent was that the vines and tomatoes moved in an arcuate path through the harvester. Arcuate means circular. As opposing counsel so correctly pointed out in his closing, if a vine gets caught in the spokes of a bicycle wheel, will it move in a circular or linear path?

> ... And in this situation, I think all of you have paid an inordinate amount of attention to a case where sometimes you were not too sure or did not know where we were going. And to say we were going around in circles is probably not an over statement in this particular case, which must have seemed to you like three weeks of discussion of what happens to a bush when it gets stuck in a bicycle wheel.

(Transcript, May 16, 1994, pp. 2459-60).

Our client tried to get a license under the patent from the University of California, but was too late -- the plaintiff, Johnson, got there first and bought it before our client could get a license. The University lawyer testified as follows:

A. Yes, this is a memo that I wrote to Martin Simpson. Martin Simpson is resident counsel for the University of California and this memo was addressed to him to memorialize my conversation with Michael Lee [an FMC lawyer] because in this memo -- or in the conversation and I have subsequently memorialized it, in this memo Michael Lee had asked -- inquired about a license to the Studer patent and I had told him a license was no longer available and the reason that I wrote this letter to Martin Simpson is because during those discussions I had told Michael Lee had -- I had told Michael Lee that the University was aware that FMC was making a shaker kit and I believed that this was infringing our patent and I am letting our counsel know that I think there's a dispute between FMC and the University of California for patent infringement.

(Transcript, May 3, 1994, pp. 895-96). They hit it hard in closing:

And FMC, realizing that to stay competitive, decided that they were going to build a very similar harvester. And they thought at the time that they could get a license from the University of California, because as far as they knew, Johnson only had a non-exclusive license. And they tried to get one first of all by buying Blackwelders, but that didn't work.

And then after they had placed this machine on the market they, then, actually went to U.C. for the first time to inquire into the availability of a license and found out at that time that Johnson now had an exclusive license, that U.C. had given them an exclusive license because of what he had done in terms of developing this technology. And they realized that they either had to go ahead without any right to operate under the patent or go back to their old harvester, which was becoming very, very difficult to sell.

And at that point, FMC made its decision to continue selling the harvester that's at issue [in] this case, the 5700.

(Transcript, May 16, 1994, pp. 2459-60). I remember thinking after I heard the testimony from the licensing executive at the University of California: How do we overcome the argument that if our client really didn't infringe, why would it try to get a license in the first place? Bad facts make bad cases.

I started as I do in most defense cases with my analogy to seeing my hand -- you can't see all of my hand unless you see the both sides:

This is the first trial that my son, Dean, has attended. He graduated from law school a couple years ago. He is my oldest son. I have a younger son as well, who has chosen the path of becoming an artist instead of an attorney, to his credit. I have told my boys a story over the years. And I have told this story many times.

And it really demonstrates the difficulty of being a defendant, the accused, the infringer in this case. And it goes back to something that happened to me when I was practicing law about Dean's age, and lawyers debate issues back and forth.

An older lawyer in our firm, a distinguished gentleman, we disagreed about an issue. And he said to me, "Let me ask you a question. Can you see my hand?"

And I said, "Of course, I can see your hand." [I hold up the back-side of my hand for the jury to see.]

And he said, "You're wrong. You can't see my hand

until you see the other side." [I show them the other side of my hand.]

And that's what a defendant's dilemma is. You will see the plaintiff's side first, but you can't see the hand until you see the other side.

And we're going to tell you in this case about the other side, the FMC side, the side of the company that doesn't go around the country stealing inventions. A company that itself is filled with inventors, including Mr. Schultz, who has been issued patents in this very field.

The defense in this case is very simple. It comes down to a very simple proposition.

Johnson didn't invent anything, and when it attempted to make the patented product -- and it was very interesting in the opening statement, not one drawing did you see from the patent, not one. I'm going to show some drawings from the patent that illustrate what this invention was.

What Johnson did is to attempt to make something from the patent that didn't work. And it's not going to be FMC presenting testimony that it didn't work. It's going to be testimony in this case that you will hear from Johnson's witnesses, from Johnson's lawyer, from Mr. Johnson himself, and from employees of Johnson. They will testify that it didn't work.

(Transcript, April 26, 1994, pp. 29-31). During trial, we presented the other side -- hard. But to no avail.

We hammered away on Johnson Farm Machinery's owner -- he copied FMC:

Q. And did you, at any time, tell Mr. Maker at the University of California that what you did in this redesign was to copy the FMC machine?

A.   Definitely not.

Q.   Let me show you the handwritten notes of Mr. Maker, dated May 15, 1988.

MR. SCHWAB: I'd like to object to this as hearsay.

THE COURT: For what purpose are you using this document?

MR. NIRO: To refresh the witness' recollection.

〽 〽 〽 〽 〽

Q.   BY MR. NIRO: Take a look at what Mr. Maker says in paragraph 8 about his conversation with you concerning your redesign.

A.   "Johnson's next machine was a copy of the FMC." Well, it's not true.

Q.   You didn't say that to Mr. Maker; is that right?

A.   Of course I didn't.

Q.   And that doesn't refresh your recollection that you did, correct?

A.   I did not ever say that I was copying FMC, because I wasn't.

(Transcript, April 27, 1994, pp. 141-42). But the thought was there: they were copying FMC.

As for the University of California patent, it was useless in building a workable product:

Q.   BY MR. NIRO: Am I correct, Mr. Johnson, that in your redesign of the tomato harvester shaker portion, that the only thing you used from the University of

California patent was the vine rods, and you designed them yourself?

A.   The vine rods are in the Studer patent in every, almost every figure in that patent. I made it similar to the Studer vine rods. I designed them, but it follows the Studer patent.

You say the only thing I used?

Q.   Yes. Is it correct that the only thing Johnson used from the University of California patent was the vine rods, and you designed them?

A.   That's not true.

Q.   That statement is incorrect, right?

A.   When you say "the only thing," that's incorrect.

※ ※ ※ ※ ※

Q.   BY MR. NIRO: Now, I'd like you to look at the blowups. I want to show you the second page of this document that comes from Townsend and Townsend files. You have it there?

A.   I have it.

※ ※ ※ ※ ※

Q.   And paragraph 4 says, "The only thing," and underlines the word "only," "The only thing we are using from the U.C. patent are the vine rods, and we designed them."

And it's your testimony that that statement is incorrect, right?

A.   That's incorrect.

(Transcript, April 27, 1994, pp. 144-45, 149-50). This kind of stuff might win a normal case, but our facts were really bad.

To add a little humor to an otherwise dull process, I agreed to opposing counsel's suggestion that he was a tomato:

Q.   Now I want you to assume I'm a [tomato] vine.

MR. NIRO: I'll stipulate to that.

(Transcript, May 5, 1994, p. 1528). *Laughter!*

All to no avail. The jury loved us. But we couldn't overcome the fact that our client infringed.

After the verdict, a juror ran down the street after my co-counsel, Bob Vitale; she said: "We really like you guys. We wanted you to win. But your facts were so bad, we had no choice. We are really sorry." Lesson learned: *sometimes you can't overcome bad facts*. *(Then, again, as you will see later, sometimes you can.)*

TAKE A CHANCE TO DO THE WRONG THING AT THE RIGHT TIME

Black & Decker v. **Coleman**,
Civil Action No. CA 96-656-A (E.D. Va. 1996)

There is a great line by Edward G. Robinson in the movie *Cincinnati Kid*. The "Kid," played by Steve McQueen, is a high-stakes, five-card-stud poker player. He eventually gets a game "head to head" with the "Man," played by Edward G. Robinson -- the best of the best. In the last scene, McQueen goes "all in" as the cards are dealt one by one. McQueen thinks Robinson is going for a full house, then a flush, then a straight. Each time, Robinson should fold based on the statistics of having a winning hand. He stays in, as the bets are made, taking another card each time. Up comes the last card and then Robinson shows his "hole card" -- he filled an inside straight with a Queen; he had the unbeatable hand: a royal straight flush.

McQueen is devastated; he says to Robinson, "You should have dropped out on any one of the last three cards. The odds were against you every time." And Robinson responds as he picks up his money, "Well, Kid, that's what it's all about, doing the wrong thing at the right time. You're good, but until I'm done playing stud poker, I'm the Man."

So, too, with trials. As my first boss at Shell Chemical, Virdin Wilson, told me: "If you always play the odds, the best you can hope to be is mediocre. And if you always buck the odds, you will fail." So the key in life (and in trials) is to know exactly when you should buck the odds and when you should not.

Now to the <u>Coleman</u> case (discussed in detail later). The SnakeLight® flashlight was a huge commercial success and Black & Decker was getting patents on it as fast as it possibly could, trying to stop the Chinese copycats. The problem was that the SnakeLight® product was so successful, it spawned different forms of knock-offs faster than the Patent Office could examine, grant and issue Black & Decker's patents. I was quoted in a trade magazine as saying these Chinese copies were like bacteria mutating into different forms when treated with an antibiotic (our patents). One of the copycat products was the Coleman Coil Lite flashlight.

In February 1996, Black & Decker received a Notice of Allowance on two patent applications with broad claims. Coleman was already in litigation with Black & Decker in the Eastern District of Virginia, but Black & Decker's infringement claim based on the yet-to-be-issued patents would not be part of that case. Unless we bucked the odds, that is.

We first told Coleman of the Patent Office's notice to issue the patents in the future. We voluntarily provided discovery. I then asked my law partner, Chris Lee (then, a third-year associate), to file an Amended Complaint, bringing a declaratory judgment claim charging Coleman with infringement of the yet-to-issue patent "upon issuance." Chris said, "No way the judge is going to grant the motion to add a claim based on patents that do not even exist yet." Why was he right? Because a patentee has no standing to bring a lawsuit based on a patent that has not issued. I made Chris do it anyway and the trial judge predictably denied our motion. In doing so, however, the judge recognized that Coleman had already been put on notice of Black & Decker's intention to sue once the patents issued and that Black & Decker had voluntarily provided Coleman with discovery. Rather than forcing us to file a separate lawsuit, the trial judge held that the parties should act as if the patents had issued and that a claim for infringement would be added to the existing case once the patents issued. In May 1996, we added the newly issued patents to the case.

This is part of the verdict:

Infringement
Do you find that Black & Decker has proven by a preponderance of the evidence that Coleman has induced others to infringe the '803 patent by actively aiding and abetting its customers to resell version one JOB PROs after May 28, 1996?

Yes: _____ X _____   No: _____

◦ ◦ ◦ ◦ ◦

Invalidity
Considering each of the claims of the '803 patent, has Coleman proven, by a clear and convincing evidence, that the claims of this patent are invalid, in accordance with the Court's instructions concerning validity?

Yes: _____   No: ____X_____

Damages
If you find that Coleman infringed or induced others to infringe either of the Black & Decker patents, what

amount of damages do you find Black & Decker has proved by a preponderance of the evidence is adequate to compensate Black & Decker for the infringement that has occurred?

$ 3,723,575

(Verdict, August 23, 1996).

Now look at these dates: one patent issued May 14, 1996 and the '803 patent on May 28, 1996; trial began on August 19, 1996; the verdict came down on August 23, 1996. Judgment finding the patents valid and infringed was entered on the same day. A possible record from issuance to judgment that may never be broken (like Wilt Chamberlain's 100 points) -- three months from grant to verdict. Lesson learned: **when the time is right, do the wrong thing to win the war, even if you may lose a battle along the way.**

IF YOU CHEAT, YOU MIGHT GET CAUGHT

<u>Wolens</u> v. **<u>Wear-Ever Aluminum, Inc., et al.</u>**,
Civil Action No. 79 C 4291 (N.D. Ill. 1980)

This case involved a patent on the famous hot-air popcorn popper. The inventor, John Wolens, put a hair-dryer over a bowl to cause hot air to be charged downwardly into a popping chamber:

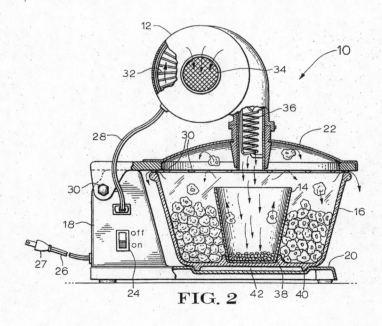

PATENTED SEP 4 1973

3,756,139

FIG. 2

We opted for a bench trial, which turned out to be a big mistake. The patent claims required that the hot air be directed vertically downward (like in the picture) and we had a real challenge proving that air coming in sideways in the infringing Wear-Ever poppers had a vertically downward air component like in the patent claim:

> means for charging a stream of hot air *vertically downward* into said popping vessel, said stream of hot air heating kernels of popcorn to be popped in said popping vessel to popping temperature and directing corn which has been popped upward out of said popping vessel into said receptacle.

(U.S. Patent No. 3,756,139, Col. 4, lines 27-32; emphasis added).

Wear-Ever did a demonstration with a flame showing that air entering horizontally from the side and swirling upward in its popper:

> THE WITNESS: I am going to turn this on. You see the flame deflected and blown upward.
>
> If you watch, your Honor, as I turn this on and then off, as you overcome the inertia of the fan first, and then as it slows down again, it's very graphically demonstrated what is happening to the tip of the flame.
>
> MR. BRINKMAN:
>
> Q   You indicated that it was graphically demonstrated. What was demonstrated.
>
> A   That the flow is horizontal in a swirling fashion, mainly upward.

(Transcript, October 2, 1980, p. 576).

Nonetheless, we felt downward air was necessary to clear popped corn from the popping chamber, effectively forcing it upward and out. Without that, the popped corn could get trapped in the popping chamber and burn as more and more hot air was delivered into the chamber.

To invalidate the patent, defendants' expert recreated a prior art popcorn popper (the Pritchard patent), claiming it would work just like the patented popper. The problem: it had no vertical flow component and the popped popcorn would not be forced out of the popping chamber. It would burn.

So here comes the live experiment. Frankly, I'm generally afraid to do live experiments because they almost never work. But this one (done by the other side) seemed to work. I sensed (based upon some input from my expert) that the replica of the 1921 prior art would not work with a full load of corn, so I asked that the witness tell us how much corn was going into the unit before the demonstration began:

> MR. NIRO: Please, before we put that in, are we putting in a normal load as compared to the Wear-Ever? I think we should have some indication how much corn is being put in.
>
> THE WITNESS: I think the amount of corn that we use is that amount that we found to work well with the unit that we produced from the concept, and I don't think that there was any attempt made to define what normal loads were. It was just that amount that we found would work.
>
> MR. NIRO: Your Honor, would it be all right if we had a measure as to how much corn is going into this demonstration?

THE COURT: All right. Do you have a measuring cup of some kind?

MR. BRINKMAN: Approximately half a paper cup, was it, Mr. Williams?

MR. WILLIAMS: Right.

(Transcript, October 6, 1980, p. 781). And, of course, it worked perfectly:

THE COURT: This specific one that you built, was there one on the market like it?

MR. BRINKMAN: Not to our knowledge.

THE WITNESS: This was a 1921 patent.

THE COURT: Yes, I know.

THE WITNESS: As a non-expert, I would say there were not very many houses that could support that kind of current in 1921. In fact, the courtroom barely can support his kind of popper.

THE COURT: That is not surprising.

MR. BRINKMAN: The first kernel has popped.

Several kernels have now popped, and I think your Honor can see that as they pop they rise upwardly and hit the lid and drop back down into the annular receptacle which is mounted around the popping chamber.

(Transcript, October 6, 1980, p. 784).

My fluidics expert, George Richards, told me after that testimony that the experiment would not work with a full load of corn. I said, "Are you sure?" His reply: "I'm sure; have him do it again with a full load."

RAYMOND P. NIRO

Transcripts don't always capture the moment -- but imagine this: we are in a courtroom on the 23rd floor of the Federal Courthouse in Chicago. There are smoke detectors everywhere. The only reason a partial load worked on the replica of the old prior art popper is there was not enough popped corn to seal the popping chamber. The popped corn simply flew out from the explosive force of being popped without any upward component of air. But would it work with a full load?

First, I set the stage:

Q   I would like to return very briefly to the Pritchard patent. I noticed when you were demonstrating the Pritchard model that you built, that -- and I can't estimate the volume, but maybe you could help me here.

Some of the corn stayed in the housing 56 above the popping vessel, and didn't go into the receptacle that you built around the thing, is that right?

A   Yes, I think that may be true.

(Transcript, October 6, 1980, p. 835). Then, I attack the model's accuracy -- is it like the patent or has it been modified:

In making your model did you keep those distances in the same proportion as shown in the drawing of the Pritchard patent?

A   I believe an effort was made to do that, and no effort was made to adjust those dimensions.

⸭ ⸭ ⸭ ⸭ ⸭

Q   Now, in the Pritchard patent, as you have read it, the air is introduced, is it not, below the bed of popcorn?

A Air is discharged below the bed, yes.

Q And that air as you indicated moves downwardly, goes through screen 116, does it not?

A Yes.

Q And then it is returned to the fan inlet and recirculated again and again?

A Some of it is, yes.

(Transcript, October 6, 1980, pp. 836, 839).

Now, I ask him to do the demonstration again with a full load of corn:

> MR. NIRO: Your Honor, perhaps the witness can step down and we can demonstrate the unit with two-thirds of a cup, which is the amount of popcorn that the Wolens prototype was demonstrated with.
>
> THE COURT: Yes.
>
> MR. NIRO: Mr. Lipinski, I think I will let you do this.
>
> THE WITNESS: You would like to add two-thirds of a cup of popcorn to this design?
>
> MR. NIRO: That's right, and I want to observe the action.
>
> I will let you put the top on. [Remember, the experiment was done with one-half of a paper cup, not two-thirds of a real cup.]
>
> BY MR. NIRO:
>
> Q By the way, I notice -- and correct me if I am wrong -- there is a switch that turns the heating element on

and off, and when the heater goes on the fan speed goes down, is that correct?

A   That's correct.

Q   Is that the way the unit that Wear-Ever has designed would operate, such that as the heat element is connected, the fan speed would go down?

A   Yes.

Q   Okay, why don't we turn it on and go through the demonstration?

(Transcript, October 6, 1980, pp. 839-40).

Look at this: the guy is cheating! He didn't turn the heat on:

BY MR. NIRO:

Q   Excuse me, is the heat on?

A   No, the first thing is the action here appears to be pretty good.

Q   What I would like you to do is turn the heat on.

A   Okay.

Q   Now, the fan slowed down, did it not?

A   Oh, yes. You would expect that.

You are getting a charring of the corn.

Q   You say the corn is charring?

A   Yes, you have insufficient air velocity.

(Transcript, October 6, 1980, p. 841).

And when he turns on the heat with a full load of corn, disaster strikes:

Q   All right, I notice some of the kernels are burning. You say that's a consequence of insufficient air velocity?

A   The blower -- the corn is beginning to pop now. The blower and the heating element, there's an adjustment that's on the side of that blower that allows you to vary the air flow. None of those things have been designed to handle this much corn. Whether it works or not, I can't say. It appears to be working pretty well.

Q   All right. Now, would you estimate how much of the corn has now exited from the upper housing?

     Is the corn being driven out of there in some way?

A   Yes, if you're asking whether I think there's more on the outside or the inside, I think right now there's probably more popped corn on the inside.

Q   Now, is the air taking the corn -- driving the corn out or is it just exploding out, those kernels coming out?

A   There's probably a combination of both. I think he makes that pretty clear in his disclosures.

Q   I notice some the unpopped kernels of corn are coming out as well. Is that a consequence of the explosions that are taking place?

A   I would think so. I think --

MR. SCAVONE: *It's burning*.

THE COURT: *You'd better shut it off, I think*.

MR. NIRO: Why don't we shut the entire unit off.

⚓ ⚓ ⚓ ⚓ ⚓

Q   *At the end of this cycle, I noticed some smoke coming up. What is that all about? Is that the corn that's in there burning?*

A   *Probably.*

MR. NIRO: *Thank you, Mr. Lipinski.*

(Transcript, October 6, 1980, pp. 843-44; emphasis added).

Judge Rostenkowski finally said "shut it off." I still wanted to keep going, even though there was enough smoke to make it hard to see people in the back of the courtroom. We had made our point. The so-called prior art Pritchard patent had nearly burned down the courthouse.

The good news: the trial judge found the invention revolutionary (in part, based upon the failed experiment) and upheld the patent's validity. The bad news: he found no infringement. Split decision. But, when you are the plaintiff, a split decision is still a loss. I got the bad news when I was in Hawaii with Judy. I remember looking out at the ocean, seeing a beautiful boat bobbing in the waves and telling her "When we win the hot air popcorn popper case, Judy, I'm going to buy a boat just like that one." And as I heard the result from my colleagues in Chicago, in my dream, at least, my beautiful boat sank slowly away. But I still learned a valuable lesson about cheaters getting caught. ***Don't cheat.***

PART III
SOME FUN ALONG THE WAY

Trimless-Flashless Design, Inc. v. Thomas & Betts Corp., et al.,
Civil Action No. 00-245-A (E.D. Va., June 2001)

TeleCommunication Systems, Inc. v. Mobile 365, Inc.,
Civil Action No. 3:06-CV-485 (JRS) (E.D. Vir., May 2007)

Injection Research Specialists, Inc. v. Polaris Industries, L.P.,
Civil Action Nos. 90-Z-1143 and 91-Z-663 (D. Col., April 1997)

Dastgheib v. Genentech,
Civil Action No. 2:04cv1283 (E.D. Pa., Nov. 2006)

Sakharam D. Mahurkar v. C.R. Bard, Inc.,
Civil Action No. 92 C 4803 (N.D. Ill., Aug. 1994)

Westinghouse v. Southwestern Engineering,
Civil Action No. 82 Civ. 681 (D. Del., Oct. 1986)

Black & Decker (U.S.) Inc., et al. v. The Coleman Company, et al.,
Civil Action Nos. 96-656-A, 96-216-A and 96-1512-A (E.D. Va., Aug. 1996)

Sufrin v. Hosier,
Civil Action No. 94 C 608 (N.D. Ill., Dec. 1996)

Black & Decker Inc., et al. v. **Robert Bosch Tool Corp.**,
Civil Action No. 04 C 7955 (N.D. Ill., Sept. 2006)

IMS Technology, Inc. v. **Haas Automation, Inc., et al.**,
Civil Action No. 97-1043-A (E.D. Va., Aug. 2000)

Black & Decker Inc., et al. v. **Porter Cable Corp.**,
Civil Action No. 98-436A (E.D. Vir., Feb. 1999)

Flint Ink Corporation v. **Sharen E. Brower**,
Civil Action No. 93-CV-73761-DT (E.D. Mich., March 1996)

USM Corporation v. **Detroit Plastic Molding Company**,
Civil Action No. 6-72536 (E.D. Mich., Dec. 1980)

National Business Systems, Inc. v. **AM International, Inc.**,
Civil Action Nos. 80 C 4915 and 81 C 6227 (N.D. Ill., April 1986)

In The Matter Of Mahurkar Double
Lumen Hemodialysis Catheter Patent Litigation,
Civil Action No. MDL-853 (N.D. Ill., Aug. 1993)

A HOSTILE JUDGE AND THE VIETNAM WAR HERO

Trimless-Flashless Design, Inc. v. Thomas & Betts Corp., et al.,
Civil Action No. 00-245-A (E.D. Va., June 2001)

Trimless-Flashless Design (TFD) was a company created by two brothers, John and Robert Walker, who knew a lot about injection molding, especially making molds for small pieces.

John Walker's story was compelling. After graduating from high school, John trained extensively in tool and die manufacturing methods. His career took a four-year detour to Vietnam, where he served on a Special Forces team that rescued downed pilots in enemy territory -- very dangerous work. When he returned home, he continued his technical training and eventually focused on trimless flashless design -- a special way to make small elastomeric parts. He named his company after the technique.

The defendant in the case, Thomas & Betts (eventually acquired by the notorious Tyco, whose former CEO and CFO were sentenced to 28 years in jail for stealing the company's money), knocked on the Walkers' door because it had a problem that nobody else could solve. Thomas & Betts had invented a new metalized particle interconnect device (MPI), which connected chips to the rest of the circuitry in computers and other products. The new MPI used hundreds of miniature molded bubbles, instead of pin and socket technology (which was more prone to fail). The problem was that Thomas & Betts didn't know how to make a device with such tiny and delicate features. Nobody else did either: Thomas & Betts tried nine different manufacturing sources and various techniques, but they all failed.

Along the way, someone suggested turning to TFD and the Walkers. Sure enough, John Walker solved the problem and created working prototypes. Though he couldn't afford a lawyer, John Walker still required Thomas & Betts to sign a non-disclosure agreement, hoping to hold Thomas & Betts to its assurances that TFD would remain involved in the manufacture of the MPIs if its technology solved the problem. What happened next is the same thing that happens all too often: Thomas & Betts took TFD's prototypes to another supplier for duplication; it cut TFD out of the project and stopped returning TFD's calls. When TFD finally did get through, a Thomas & Betts executive falsely assured John Walker that his technology was being held "under lock and key." The product was a huge success and, when TFD sued, Thomas & Betts claimed that the technology was old and obvious and that it had paid TFD for the technology in any event.

I had history with the trial judge. She had dismissed an earlier case of mine and, after the Federal Circuit reversed the ruling, we won big at the subsequent trial. She said this ("off the record," of course) at the outset of the TFD trial: "Mr. Niro, you're not going to hit a home run in this case." And she did her best throughout the trial to fulfill that prophecy. Later, she even reminded us that, if we were lucky enough to win, she would take it all away:

THE COURT: I think there can't realistically be pie in the sky because, number one, I would take pie away if that happened. All right. That doesn't mean there might not be tarts or cookies in the sky. All right.

MR. GRAHAM: Or fudge brownies.

THE COURT: Or fudge brownies. Look, I urge you now to try to work this one out.

(Transcript, Civil Action No. 00-245-A (E.D. Va.), June 19, 2001, p. 1495).

The jury sensed it too. At times, it almost appeared that she had become an advocate for the defense. They could do no wrong. We could do no right.

It reached a boiling point during my cross-examination of the defense damages expert:

BY MR. NIRO:

Q.   Mr. Jarosz, you spent did you say 85 percent of your time as an expert witness?

A.   I think what I said is over the past ten years or so about 85 percent of my work has been in the context of litigation.

Q.   So, you are a professional -- Your profession is to give testimony as an expert, correct?

A.   No. My profession --

Q.   Is that correct or not? You can just tell me it is not correct?

A.   It is not correct.

Q. Am I correct that you were paid or your firm was paid between 70 and $120,000 before you even gave deposition testimony in this case?

A. That sounds roughly correct, yes.

Q. And then based upon the additional work you have done, you have spent at least another 100,000, right?

A. I don't believe it would be that high, no.

Q. How high would it be?

A. I haven't calculated it out, but it would be in the tens of thousands of dollars.

Q. So, you are between 90 and 140 or $150,000 to give testimony in this case, is that right?

⸙ ⸙ ⸙ ⸙ ⸙

A. Probably after all our work is completed, my expectation is that we will bill something in the range of 90 to $140,000.

Q. All right. That is more money than was paid to TFD, is that right?

A. Yes, as I understand it.

(Transcript, June 21, 2001, pp. 1769-1770).

Q. Did you do a calculation on what the loss would be in terms of TFD's business if it had been given, for example, the opportunity to do one-half of the MPI sales?

MR. HERRINGTON: Your Honor, that's beyond the scope. His expert gave an opinion about that, great. My expert did not. And it is beyond the scope of the exam.

THE COURT: You can ask him more general questions what he did not do, but it needs to be relevant to the actual final opinions that he gave.

MR. NIRO: Yes. That's all I want to know.

BY MR. NIRO: (Continuing)

Q.   Did you give an opinion on what the loss would be to TFD if it got one-half of the MPI business? That is it made one-half of the MPI devices?

THE COURT: Don't object. The answer is either yes or no. It is straightforward.

MR. HERRINGTON: I would just like that the question would be clear as to whether that was on the misappropriation count or the breach of contract count.

MR. NIRO: We are only talking about breach of contract, Your Honor. All of my questions are dealing with that.

THE COURT: Breach of contract.

BY MR. NIRO: (Continuing)

Q.   Did you give such an opinion?

A.   No, not here and not in my report.

Q.   Okay. So, you have nothing that you can offer this jury that rebuts Mr. Gemini's testimony that the loss of the MPI business would result in a loss of $12 million to TFD, right?

A.   I am not quite sure how to answer that question. I have not provided testimony on the quantification of lost MPI part business.

Q.   Fine. So, you have nothing that you can offer the jury to rebut what Mr. Gemini said, correct?

A.   No, I do have things that I could offer the jury, but I have not been asked for that opinion.

Q.   All right. And you have not given them and I am not going to ask you to give them.

The answer to my question is, you don't have anything to offer the jury based upon your report and your testimony that would rebut what he said, correct?

THE COURT: That is repetitive.

MR. HERRINGTON: That's the type of question--

THE COURT: That's cumulative. So, the objection is sustained.

MR. NIRO: I would like to have one answer, if I could, Your Honor, yes or no.

THE COURT: Mr. Niro, we don't need those comments. Let's move on.

(Transcript, June 21, 2001, pp. 1773-1775).

Q.   Where does this contingent right come from? That's what I am trying to find out.

A.   Sections 3.2 and 3.4.

THE COURT: Don't argue with the witness. He said what he said. You can make your closing argument based on that.

Let's move on.

⫷ ⫷ ⫷ ⫷ ⫷

Q. Okay. You have not offered and done any opinion, have no opinion economic or otherwise to offer on the subject of a royalty applicable to one-half of the MPI business

THE COURT: He has already answered that he didn't --

MR. NIRO: He didn't do that.

THE COURT: He answered the generic question that he didn't give any opinion about MPIs. And this is a version of that.

Mr. Niro, you have to stop doing that. All right.

BY MR. NIRO: (Continuing)

Q. Sir, you talked about lost profits and then you talked about royalty. I would like to focus just on royalty. Okay.

A. Yes.

Q. Did you offer any opinion on a royalty applicable to the MPI business?

THE COURT: *You are almost in contempt, Mr. Niro.*

(Transcript, June 21, 2001, pp. 1787-1788; emphasis added). ***Contempt!*** I would gladly have spent a night in the lock-up if it meant my Vietnam Veteran, War Hero client got a fair shake from our judicial system. The trial judge saw to it that it never happened. ***Shame on her.***

THE CLOSING

In closing, I had to appeal to the jury's sense of fairness: Do the right thing. And I came as close to contempt as you can in final argument.

I suggested the jury do what the jury did in Paul Newman's famous movie "The Verdict" -- ignore the seeming bias of the trial judge and do what was right. But I couldn't say that. Fortunately, I found the answer in the Judge's own words uttered at the outset of the case -- the jurors wore the black robes:

> THE COURT: All right. Mr. Niro, your closing argument.
>
> MR. NIRO: Thank you, Your Honor.
>
> You know, I was watching a movie the other night when I went home in the break in this case, and it is one of my favorites, I was flipping through the channels, it is The Verdict with Paul Newman. And he is fighting against the big firm and doesn't quite have the resources and the power that they do. And a young nurse is testifying in this case about how she changed the number from 1 to 9 in an admittance form and then the patient died and the doctors made her do it. All that evidence was excluded [by the trial judge].
>
> But the amazing beauty of that case in that movie is that the jury came back and said, are we limited by what the plaintiff asked for damages? [They ignored the trial judge.]

(Transcript, June 21, 2001, p. 1800). Wow! I had gotten this far and the trial judge hadn't yet started yelling at me or holding me in contempt. But I had my safety net -- what the Judge herself told the jurors at the outset of the case:

> And I was reflecting on what Judge Brinkema told you at the beginning of this case, [they were] beautiful words I have to say. She said, you wear the black robes like I do. You come to this court with an open mind,

like I do. You have to be fair and impartial, like I am. And that is your duty, that is your obligation.

And that's what our client asks for. Take a look at this evidence. Consider what is fair. Consider what is reasonable. And do what is right. That's the only hope these two guys have is what's right, what's fair.

What did they do to deserve all this? What did they do? They succeeded where everybody else failed. Somebody came to them and said, hey, can you do this? And they did it.

They wrote an agreement, not as experts in writing agreements, but they did their best. Went to a library, figured it out. These guys signed it. There is no question there was an agreement there.

And it said, you can't do certain things, folks. You can't take what we are giving you and duplicate it. You can't take what we are giving you and measure it and making drawings and taking it out and giving it to somebody else.

You know, in this alternative universe, this hypothetical universe, and I know economists like to think that way, and there is nothing wrong with it, but in that hypothetical world, it is an interesting conclusion to say this is going to happen.

But this is the real world with real people and real dynamics and real expectations and real goals and real opportunities that were lost here.

Now, contracts are sacred documents. They indeed are. That's how we operate. You make a promise to somebody, you put it in writing, you abide by that promise. And these defendants did not, as you have found.

If you don't respect the contracts, or contracts period, then the society really breaks down. Now, if somebody wants to enter a contract knowing that they are going to disrespect it, then what are we doing? What is the sense of even having them?

(Transcript, June 21, 2001, pp. 1800-1802). I had to get back to fairness. Was it fair and reasonable to let them violate an agreement and pay nothing?

SUBTLE OUTRAGE. BACK TO THE THEME --LET'S BE FAIR

Now, what are the defendants saying here? They are saying, you get zero.

You know, I am blessed with ten grandchildren. I love them dearly. I have to tell you, they are a breath of fresh air in my life, but sometimes these little guys don't share too well. They operate on what's mine is mine and what's yours is mine.

And I think about that and I have to say, there isn't one of those kids that knows less about sharing than these people over here.

They say, for your work, your effort and our violation of that oath, that contract, those promises, you get zero. Nothing. We walk away from here, we are found guilty of mis-- Not misappropriating. Guilty of breach of contract. Two contracts. And you know what we get? We get a pat on the back, you wasted your time, you get nothing.

Is that fair? Is that reasonable? Is that right? I don't think so.

Mr. Gemini tried to quantify this. And think about some of those numbers. They came fast and furious. But let's think about them.

(Transcript, June 21, 2001, p. 1803). Again, I wanted to emphasize fairness -- to challenge and empower the jury. I wanted to remind them they wore the black robe and had the power:

REPEAT THE THEME -- DO WHAT'S RIGHT

I will write these numbers down for you, but basically there are three. 12 million for the lost MPI business. 20 million for the fee used, for the mold technology. And 26.2 million as a percentage of the sales price of Thomas & Betts.

We think that's what is fair. We think that is what is right. You have to decide what's right and what's fair. But I have to tell you, zero doesn't sound fair to me. And that's what they offered you, zero.

There is no testimony, no opinion to counter the testimony of Mr. Gemini, at least in trying to quantify what these expectations are on the subject of MPI sales or a royalty on MPI sales or a fee on MPI sales or a profit on MPI sales. And that's, that's one of the numbers, that's the $12 million number. Nothing to rebut that.

There is no dispute that they made the 202 million. You didn't hear their expert dispute that because he doesn't dispute that. He doesn't dispute the profit numbers. He doesn't dispute anything. He just drops to the bottom line and says, you know what, zero is the name of the game.

I submit that's wrong and that these fellow[s] deserve[] a little more respect than that.

And most importantly, more importantly, if contracts mean something, if they have some significance to the way we run our lives, then zero is not the answer. That's not fair, that's not right.

Thank you.

(Transcript, June 21, 2001, pp. 1805-1806).

THE VERDICT

The jury decided what was fair: a verdict of $10.4 million. But the trial judge had the last word. She took the verdict away a few months later, just as she promised. And, she did so on the finding that she had made a mistake in allowing us to put the second contract into evidence -- the one the jury found T&B had violated. Incredible. What were we doing, engaging in a practice trial?

Frankly, I was never more troubled about the outcome of a case in my life as a trial lawyer. I wanted to tell the judge: "This guy was a war hero. He was in a Special Forces Unit that saved downed pilots in Vietnam. He served our country proudly. You have an American flag behind the bench. We all stand each day and say, 'God save the United States and this Honorable Court.' And all he ever wanted was a fair shake, and he never got it." My colleagues talked me out of saying it.

But, I've said it after all these years. It's off my chest. Shame on the system for failing the "little guy." ***Shame. Shame. Shame.***

THE TEXT MESSAGING CASE -- DON'T GIVE THE VERBATIM TESTIMONY OF ANOTHER WITNESS

TeleCommunication Systems, Inc. v. Mobile 365, Inc.,
Civil Action No. 3:06-CV-485 (JRS) (E.D. Vir., May 2007)

My client, TeleCommunication Systems (TCS), created an invention that we all take for granted today. It allowed a user to send a text message to another person using a phone number only, even if the sender and recipient used different wireless carriers. Before TCS, someone could not send a text message using just a phone number to a person with a different wireless carrier. Wireless carriers in the United States at the time operated with different protocols and required more information than just a phone number to receive messages. The TCS invention effectively caused an explosion of text messaging usage in the United States (perhaps to the chagrin of many parents with teenagers). TCS made it possible so you didn't have to know anything except the phone number of the person to whom you were sending messages.

The defendant in the case, Mobile 365 (now Sybase), argued that their employees had come up with the invention first, saying that they had implemented a similar system in Europe that allowed sending text messages by a phone number only. In his opening statement, Mobile 365's lawyer even accused the TCS inventor, Chris Knotts, of "plagiarizing" the defendant's invention. But, because of the differences in the types of carriers (Europe used only GPS, so it did not have the inter-carrier problem), what worked in Europe did not work in the United States, and Mobile 365 could point to no documents showing that it had anything close to a workable system for the U.S. prior to TCS's invention. Instead, Mobile 365 contended that it had disclosed its invention during a key meeting with the inventor, Chris Knotts, before he applied for the patent. Since no documents described what actually occurred during that meeting, cross-examination would ultimately show which side was telling the truth.

I like to involve my family in my cases (it helps the jury understand who I am) so, in my opening, I sent a text message to my wife, Judy, who was in the courtroom:

> This case in a nutshell is about invention, success in a company that decided to take something rather than pay for it. The invention here, as Judge Spencer indicated, has to do with something called text messaging. My wife and I are blessed to have 10 grandkids. Five of them are 14 and older and text messaging is what they introduced me to because they spend a lot of their time texting, as they call it, their friends. They sort of live on text messaging. These are short messages. I think many of you have already used text messaging in one form or another. It is a short message that you can send from one cell phone to another. A personalized message of some kind that you can type in and they can then respond to you.
>
> I am going to try to show you, since most of you already know how this sort of thing works. As you know, you're not allowed to bring your cell phone here

to the courtroom. Judge Spencer was nice enough for this opening to let me bring mine.

If I was going to send a text message, I am not going to bore you with my typing skills, but I create a message of some kind that might look like this. ***Will call you later.*** And I would send that message to someone, send, by pushing the send button. New text message, will call you later. Now I have to put in a telephone number, an address. And I don't know the cell phone address or the carrier that this is going to because ***I'm going to send it to my wife and she has a cell phone that I frankly don't know what her carrier is.*** I think it is T-Mobile. This is Cingular. Will call you later, send. And it is off, it's gone. In a matter of seconds that message has gone from this phone to her phone hopefully back here. And in that process some very interesting things happen.

The invention here has to do with sending a message with only the phone number as the address. And the reason that's important is, in the United States, unlike the system in Europe, you have multiple carriers, T-Mobile, Sprint, Cingular, AT&T Wireless, a whole array of people, each of whom uses their own protocol so they can't talk to each other. In Europe they can do that. And the way you had to do this before, if you wanted to send a text message from one phone to another, was to add something more than the phone number. You had to put an identifier at the back that would tell you the routing information that you need to get it to, whomever you're sending it to, be it Cingular to Verizon or Verizon to Sprint or whatever. You can imagine how difficult it would be to not only know who you're sending it to, but what cell phone carrier they happen to be using at any point in time. That was an impediment to using text messaging as we know it today.

(Transcript, May 15, 2007, pp. 64-68; emphasis added).

My experiment worked and it did two things: (1) it demonstrated the invention, (2) it told the jury the lovely lady in the back of the courtroom was my wife. In another case, Glenayre Electronics v. Jackson, Civil Action No. 02 C 256 (N.D. Ill., March 2003), I used a voice message from my granddaughter, Nicole, in the opening using the Judge's speakerphone. This is how I did it (against the advice of my law partners who said, "You can't do that"):

> Although I don't have a Glenayre -- access to a Glenayre -- system right here, although they have one in the courtroom, with the Court's permission, I will try it right now and give you an idea of how it works on our own voicemail that I have in our office here.
>
> If I were to call our phone number, hopefully, I will get an answer.
>
> (Brief pause.)
>
> "OPERATOR: This is the phonemail message system. If you would like to leave a message, you may either enter your extension or --"
>
> MR. NIRO: I put my extension in.
>
> "OPERATOR: Raymond Niro at Extension 227. If this is correct, dial your password and then push enter or pound."
>
> MR. NIRO: Now, I have to put the password in. If I put the wrong password, it will hang up. But if I put the right password in:
>
> "OPERATOR: You may listen to your messages, record a message, change your answering options.["]
>
> "You have no new message. Message 1 was received at 6:20 p.m."
>
> MR. NIRO: This is my favorite message.

"Hi, Grandpa, this is Nicole, call me."

MR. NIRO: *That's a keeper.*

(Transcript, March 24, 2003, p. 81; emphasis added). The point was made: you need a password to get your voice messages, even from your granddaughter.

If it works, why not do it. ***Personalize and humanize.***

USING PRIOR TESTIMONY FROM A DECLARATION

In the TCS case, a key defense witness was completely undone by the fact that his prior testimony was a verbatim version of another trial witness's testimony. Here is a chart we prepared to drive home the point.

Similar Declarations		
18 *Identical* Paragraphs	**Zimmern Declaration**	**Hsiao Declaration**
	¶ 24 ← Identical →	¶ 26
	¶ 25 ← Identical →	¶ 27
	¶ 26 ← Identical →	¶ 28
	¶ 27 ← Identical →	¶ 29
	¶ 28 ← Identical →	¶ 31
	¶ 29 ← Identical →	¶ 32
	¶ 30 ← Identical →	¶ 33
	¶ 31 ← Identical →	¶ 35
	¶ 34 ← Identical →	¶ 37
	¶ 35 ← Identical →	¶ 38
	¶ 38 ← Identical →	¶ 40
	¶ 39 ← Identical →	¶ 41
	¶ 40 ← Identical →	¶ 42
	¶ 41 ← Identical →	¶42
	¶ 42 ← Identical →	¶ 44
	¶ 43 ← Identical →	¶ 45
	¶ 44 ← Identical →	¶ 46
	¶ 45 ← Identical →	¶ 47

PDX-111

How often are the lawyer-prepared declarations that are used for summary judgment motions fuel for the unraveling of a witness at trial?

ALWAYS LOOK AT PRIOR TESTIMONY GIVEN BY DECLARATION

Here, two trial witnesses gave identical testimony in declarations filed before the trial. This is how it was used in cross-examination:

Q. When you did your Declaration, Mr. Zimmern, did you understand that you were giving testimony just as you have now under oath, swearing to tell the truth?

A. To the best of my knowledge, yes.

Q. In fact, you said that in the last paragraph of the Declaration, correct? "I declare under penalty of perjury that the following is true and correct to the best of my knowledge and belief." That is your signature?

A. Yes, that is.

Q. You did sign it on April 3rd, 2007?

A. That's correct.

Q. And you wrote this, correct?

A. I worked with this document with Elizabeth Roesel, yes. I provided Elizabeth with all the input and the final, we had several iterations of reviewing the document, and then I finally signed the document.

Q. Were these your words, your words that you chose? Or did somebody write this for you?

A. Elizabeth Roesel wrote it based on what I told her.

Q. Well, my question is, are these your words that you testified to or did somebody put these words in your mouth, so to speak?

A. I testified to it and reviewed the document and made several changes to it.

(Transcript, May 18, 2007, pp. 967-968). Now I set the hook. Did he talk to the other witnesses before he gave his testimony?

Q. Did you talk to Mr. Hsiao before you wrote this?

A. No, I didn't.

Q. Did you meet with him?

A. No, I didn't.

Q. Did you discuss your testimony with him?

A. No, I didn't. I just said that.

(Transcript, May 18, 2007, pp. 968-969). Now I had him. How could his testimony be identical -- word for word -- to Mr. Hsiao's testimony?

Q. And one of the things that you swore to under oath and now admit that was wrong is that one of those meetings was with Chris Knotts and Tim Lorello of Telecommunication Services on July 26th, 2000, correct?

A. That's correct.

Q. That was a mistake.

A. That's correct.

Q. That testimony was wrong.

A. That was a mistake. That's correct.

(Transcript, May 18, 2007, p. 969).

The Words Were All The Same

He was beginning to unravel. His declaration had mistaken testimony (a nice way of saying he lied). Now for the clincher:

Q. And did you at any point in time see the Declaration of Mr. Hsiao that was given?

A. No, I didn't.

Q. On the same day.

A. No, I didn't.

Q. Let me show it to you. It is Plaintiff's Exhibit 287. And in it, he signs this document on the same day that you signed your Declaration swearing that he is telling the truth to the best of his knowledge and belief. Do you recognize his signature?

A. I don't recognize his signature. But that's what it states.

Q. Now, just by way of comparison, you say something in Paragraph 24 that begins with "In August, 2000 ..." and goes to the "... foreign operators." And you go on and use a lot of words to describe your testimony on that subject of August, 2000.

A. Yes. This was based, I believe, on a set of e-mails passing back and forth between me and Terry Hsiao.

Q. You even say, "An unsigned but otherwise complete and accurate copy of this contract is attached as Exhibit 7."

A . That's correct.

Q. Mr. Hsiao says in his Paragraph 26 in August, 2000, and he winds up with an attached Exhibit 6 instead of 7. But every word, every word of testimony that he gave is identical to your testimony. Can you explain that?

A. No, I can't.

Q. And Paragraph 25 of your testimony, under oath, begins with "At least as early as Mr. Hsiao's August 3rd, 2000 e-mail ..." and Paragraph 27 says, of Mr. Hsiao's Declaration, "... at least as of my August 3rd e-mail." And it uses exactly the same words, word for word as your Paragraph 25. Can you explain why that happened, sir?

A. No, I can't.

Q. I won't go through all of it. But I would suggest to you that the following paragraphs of these two Declarations are identical word for word for word. You and Mr. Hsiao. Your Paragraph 24 is his Paragraph 26. Your Paragraph 25 is his Paragraph 27. And on and on and on. Can you explain to this jury how you gave testimony under oath that is identical to the testimony of Mr. Hsiao word for word for word without ever talking to him?

A. I can't tell you and I didn't talk to him.

Q. And you have no explanation.

A. The only explanation I can see that this was done, I mean, the documentation was written and established by Elizabeth Roesel and it is my understanding that that is common practice.

Q. I ask you again, did you write this document or did somebody write it for you?

A.   I told you before, this was written together with counsel based on all the information I provided to this issue. And everything in it is correct.

(Transcript, May 18, 2007, pp. 969-971). Elizabeth Roesel was Mobile 365's counsel. And the unmistakable conclusion was that she wrote the sworn testimony of both witnesses and that the defendant's two star witnesses were mere puppets on a string, saying what the lawyers told them to say.

I was not quite finished. At the outset of the TCS case, opposing counsel made a big deal about not having our client hear the opening statement:

> MR. NIRO: Yes, sir. I hope a minor issue. We've agreed to the exclusion of fact witnesses. Experts can stay. Fact witnesses can't. During the opening statement I would like to introduce the inventor who is going to be the first witness. And I understand there is an objection to that.

> MR. GOTTS: I don't think it's appropriate to have the witness here for opening statement. We're going to be talking about the case, the theories of the case. And I think it is proper to exclude the witness.

> THE COURT: Well, we can exclude him in your opening about your theories. But, there is no problem with him introducing the inventor and he can leave after your opening.

> MR. GOTTS: That's fine.

(Transcript, May 15, 2007, p. 64). So we had an exclusion rule -- no fact witness could hear the testimony of another fact witness. But who broke the rule? The defendants. Here is how we caught them:

Q. You said you learned since you wrote your Declaration in April of this year that Tim Lorello said he was [not] at the dinner meeting with you on July 26th, 2000.

A. That's correct.

Q. Did you talk to Mr. Lorello about that?

A. No, I didn't.

Q. Who told you that?

A. I believe that came up in one of the discussions with my lawyers.

Q. With your lawyers?

A. Yes.

Q. These lawyers here?

A. Yes.

Q. Did you understand there was an order in this case that witnesses were excluded such that one witness couldn't listen to what another witness said?

A. No.

Q. Nobody told you that?

A. We might have talked about that, I don't know.

Q. I see. So if some of the lawyers or one of the lawyers told you that Mr. Lorello testified in this proceeding that he was not present at that meeting?

A. I don't think that was the case.

Q. What was the case?

A. I think it was mentioned that people were -- that my Declaration was questioned in terms of who was in the meeting, which made me dig deeper into my files to find out what really happened.

Q.   Who was it that told you that?

A.   I believe it was Elizabeth Roesel.

Q.   I see. One of the lawyers here in this case?

A.   Yes, sir.

Q.   That's why you now have refreshed your recollection and are correcting your sworn testimony in that Declaration; is that right?

A.   That is correct.

(Transcript, May 18, 2007, pp. 962-963).

In his opening argument, Mobile 365's trial counsel made three points. First, TCS was like a troll hiding under a bridge trying to tax the public by increasing the cost of text messaging. Second, our inventor, Chris Knotts, got his inventive ideas from someone else -- he had engaged in a form of plagiarism. Third, our client, TCS, didn't play by the rules. He pledged to prove all of this at the trial:

> It is like the old troll under the bridge. You have to pay a tax now to pass. They want to tax the business. I am going lay those facts [out] in detail.

⁂ ⁂ ⁂ ⁂ ⁂

Well, going in and trying to claim that's in the prior art, it is just like plagiarism. It is like taking something in the public domain and claiming it as their own. It is worse yet because TCS knew it was prior art. So it is not surprising TCS received a patent.

(Transcript, May 15, 2007, pp. 87, 92). He continued:

> And our job during the course of the week is to convey to you, ladies of the jury, all the evidence you will need to arm you with the tools to decide fair to decide, who plays by the rules and who did not, who was the successful person here and who took from him.

(Transcript, May 15, 2007, p. 86).

> And I'm going to point out what I said today, and if I haven't proven it, I'll tell you. That's my pledge. And then the case will be yours. But, I pledge, when we come back, we will talk about what we have proven. And if we haven't proven it, we'll let you know that, too.

(Transcript, May 15, 2007, p. 114).

In closing, I brought up all the promises made in the opening that were not kept. It is very dangerous to make promises to a jury and not keep them. First, the charge that we were trolls trying to unfairly tax the public:

> Now we're talking about, instead of trolls and taxing, we're talking about moving fenceposts to take something away. Inventors don't take something away from the public. If they did, they wouldn't get a patent. Invention is giving something to the public that wasn't there before that's new, different and non-obvious. And that's what Mr. Knotts did, that's what the evidence shows.

(Transcript, May 23, 2007, pp. 1678-79).

Then, to the point about plagiarism -- remember the verbatim testimony of two defense witnesses? Who was the plagiarist?

What about plagiarism? Remember that? He said in the opening statement Mr. Lorello and their wives were at dinner, so on and so forth, at the Macaroni Grill. Of course, we learned Mr. Lorello he wasn't there and neither were the wives. Not correct.

But then we heard about plagiarism. Going in and trying to claim [w]hat's in the prior art is just like plagiarism. That's what the defendants said in their opening statement. And what did we find? Two witnesses' declarations under oath that said exactly the same thing. Exactly, not once, not twice, paragraph after paragraph after paragraph, repeatedly; 3, 7, 11, 15, 18 times. Not short paragraphs, long paragraphs. Take a look at those declarations. Go back there and look at Hsiao's declaration sworn under oath and Zimmern's declaration, sworn under oath, and decide whether that's plagiarism. If one were teaching a class, and two students turned in papers that were identical, I think you could suspect that somebody was plagiarizing somebody. And it wasn't on our side of this case. These are the paragraphs, they are identical, switching names here and there, but basically identical.

And I asked Mr. Zimmern and, quite frankly, I think he was a little embarrassed by the fact that that had happened. I said to him, do you think it likely that each of you, that's him and Mr. Hsiao, if you come in here to testify live as a witness, would you use the exact same words for 90 percent of your time verbatim. Answer, probably not. I think that's being generous, probably not. I would say it is statistically impossible. I don't think you could get two people to say exactly the same thing on a witness stand in a court at any point in time whether they had to answer yes questions or no questions or anything on the face of the earth. And Mr. Zimmern said I changed my declaration. Did Mr. Hsiao make the same changes?

I would submit that that testimony wasn't the

testimony of any witness, and it is testimony just like sworn testimony when the witness goes on the witness stand, that's testimony of the lawyers. Let's play by the rules.

(Transcript, May 23, 2007, pp. 1582-84).

And, of course, who was playing by the rules and who was not?

I think you can see from what happened in this courtroom in the last week who was playing by the rules and who wasn't. And that's a microcosm of what was going on out in the marketplace. Mr. Tosé testified you put yourself in the other guy's shoes and you offer him an opportunity to take a license. And that's what he did. And he had Mr. Hamilton meet, and he had the opportunity, gave them the opportunity to take a license, and they said no. And you can search this record for evidence of their good faith, evidence of their investigation, evidence of their due care, evidence of their efforts to design around, evidence of anything that would show that they acted in good faith, and we submit you won't find it because it's not there. Who's playing by the rules here?

Remember the declaration of Mr. Zimmern written by one of the attorneys? And he said, unequivocally, one of those meetings was with Chris Knotts and Tim Lorello of Telecommunications Services on July 26, 2000. Mr. Lorello showed that he wasn't even there in Virginia, he was in Birmingham, Michigan. And Mr. Zimmern said I didn't disclose anything technically to Chris Knotts. In fact, I had to hire Mr. Rusche in January 2001 to solve the problem. Who's playing by the rules? They are quick to accuse, but fast to retreat. I think you saw it. You heard them say we're going to show you, we're going to prove to you that Mr. Zimmern took his idea and he gave it and disclosed it to Chris Knotts. And then he got on this witness stand and he said, you know what, I didn't do that, I don't know anything technical, I didn't disclose the idea to him, I didn't have the technology, and if I had it I wasn't going to give it to him. Quick to accuse, fast to retreat.

Remember, I felt a little bad about it, that you might get the wrong impression, that Mr. Knotts left the courtroom after my opening statement and wasn't sitting here. I thought you, jurors, might think he doesn't care about the case or he is afraid to hear what's going to be said. He had to leave because the defendants, consistent with the order of the Court, agreed that and insisted that witnesses were not going to hear what other witnesses had to say. That was a rule. We live by that rule. Mr. Knotts left the courtroom. And he didn't hear things they said about him. Troll, tax, taking from the public, increasing your bills. But, who was it that broke the rules? Who was it that took information on the witness stand about Mr. Lorello, knowing about American Express and where he was, and told another witness hey, by the way, you better, before you get on the witness stand, fix that. He might as well have invited him in here to listen to Mr. Lorello who said I wasn't there. Mr. Zimmern got on the witness stand and said yeah, I was told about it, one of the lawyers told me. Who's playing by the rules? They insisted Mr. Knotts leave the room, then they tell their witness what's going on here. Might seem trivial, might not seem important, but you know what, those are the rules we live by. And you obey them or you don't.

(Transcript, May 23, 2007, pp. 1580-82).

And what about the pledge?

Remember in his opening, defendant's counsel said I am going to make you a pledge. I'm going to come back and I'm going to tell you if I haven't proven what I have told you I am going to prove, I am going to point that out and I pledge this to you. Hold them to their pledge. He said you have to pay a tax now to pass. They want to tax a business. Since when is invention a tax? Is that what we're talking about? Thomas Edison was taxing us by creating something new? They said we're taking it from the public domain. In fact, what they took from the public domain, from the prior art that you heard in the video, they took it from all of us.

Chris Knotts didn't take anything from anybody. He invented something by putting it together just like a new song. They talked about plagiarism, we're going in and trying to claim that's in the prior art, it is just like plagiarism. You saw where the plagiarism was. It wasn't on this side of the room.

⊪ ⊪ ⊪ ⊪ ⊪

So before the defendant gets up and tells you all the things they proved, we ask you to hold them to those promises and think about what they said they were going to do and think about what they did.

⊪ ⊪ ⊪ ⊪ ⊪

I'm sorry it took so long to go through this. It has been a long case. We have tried to make it interesting. I will be talking to you briefly after the defendants get their say. Thank you.

(Transcript, May 23, 2007, pp. 1607-12).

What about the other defenses -- Chris Knotts stole the invention and, in any case, the invention was obvious:

And what did the independent voices say about all of this, the people that had no axe to grind? The patent examiner. He doesn't get paid extra for issuing patents. He issues the ones that he believes are new and non-obvious. Patent is valid, it is new and useful invention.

That's on the cover. Mr. Kiswani, Deutsche Telecom, these are contemporaneous statements, not when people think they are going to be in a lawsuit. He did not know of another company that was as far ahead of the game than TCS. John Frozadel, Verizon, TCS Technologies is the first company to come to the table with inter-carrier messaging.

And all of this prior art we contend is a little like the wastebaskets, put it in there and get rid of it, it was either considered by the examiner, wasn't early enough, missing the claim elements or it is evidence of prior failure.

The defendants we believe have not tilted the scales decidedly in their favor. If anything, they tilt decidedly the other way. But, in order to prove their case, this has got to be way down here. And we submit that didn't happen.

Who was first? Who was first? And what's the evidence show about who was first? You have TCS Technologies with a working system in March, Mobile 365 in November, eight months earlier. You have Chris Knotts introducing a system in 2001, files a patent application in September and getting a patent. You have Mr. Hsiao and InphoAlert filing a patent application for something else and abandoning it. And you have Mr. Lovell and Zimmern and Hsiao introducing a patent in November 2001 and not filing a patent application until February of 2003.

So who was first? Who was first? Enterprise to wireless, they filed a patent application in three months and then abandoned it later. If they really had inter-carrier wireless to wireless, why did they wait until February of 2003? If they had it in December of 2003 or February of 2002 or February of 2001, why didn't they do the same thing that they did with enterprise to wireless? Same lawyers.

So who was first here? First to build something and

put it out publicly at a show, albeit, it didn't take off like a rocket, but they had it, was TCS Technologies. Who was the first to file a patent application? TCS Technologies.

(Transcript, May 23, 2007, pp. 1609-11).

This was the final result: a verdict of $12.1 million plus a 12% royalty going forward and an injunction. In the end, our client was paid $23 million.

It is hard to say we won because Mobile 365's star witness (Zimmern) was undone by a declaration identical to another witness's (Hasiao). But they both testified they did it first. So why did they have identical, verbatim testimony prepared by their lawyer? When I proved the declarations were identical, I saw one of the jurors put her face in her hands as if to say, "I don't believe these guys." She later said I reminded her of the Andy Griffith character, Matlock. How nice: I was a movie star.

HOW TO MINE NUGGETS OBTAINED IN DISCOVERY

Injection Research Specialists, Inc. v. Polaris Industries, L.P.,
Civil Action Nos. 90-Z-1143 and 91-Z-663 (D. Col., April 1997)

Ron Chasteen may be the very best witness I ever had at a trial. He was deeply religious, humble, honest and knew what he was talking about. And for good reason: Ron was the son of a professor of Mechanical Engineering at the University of Colorado. When he was eight years old, his father gave him a small engine for his birthday. From that point forward, engines became his passion. While the other kids were playing football and baseball, Ron was working with engines. He built go-carts and, later, hot rods. He worked on his friends' cars. By the time he was ready for college, he told his father he wanted to be a mechanic, not an engineer.

After graduation from trade school, Ron went to the White Mountains of Arizona and worked in a snowmobile repair shop. He testified that he spent hours rescuing people who had snowmobiles that worked fine at lower altitudes and cold, morning weather, but failed at higher altitudes and warm, afternoon temperatures. In chemistry, they call it the ideal gas law: $pV = nRT$. Higher altitudes are lower pressure; higher temperatures at the same volume create more pressure. That is the reason airplanes do not perform well at high altitudes, like Aspen, in the summer and why, mechanically, fuel-injected snowmobiles do not work so well in the mountains.

Ron found the answer: an electronically fuel-injected two-cycle engine for use in a snowmobile. He built a prototype, took it to Polaris and they promptly stole his ideas from him. Within days of Ron's disclosure, the head of Polaris's engineering department was on a plane to Japan to meet with its engine supplier and co-defendant, Fuji. Why?

We were retained to try the case after five different law firms wasted $3 million of our client's money on meaningless discovery. There was one (and only one) nugget, however, and it proved good enough to undo a key witness. The witness answered this question in a deposition:

Q   Was it Baxter's suggestion that IRS be misled, or was it your -- did you generate that notion?

A   When you say "misled" what do you mean?

Q   Told false statement. Was that your idea [or] was that Mr. Baxter's?

A   I think it was my idea.

(Transcript, April 16, 1997, p. 903). I mined this gold nugget at trial. The result: a $57 million jury verdict increased to $75 million on appeal -- the biggest collected jury verdict in Colorado up to that time. I was named by the National Law Journal as one of the Top 10 litigators in the United States the next year (1998) because of the case (which is quite an honor since, in 20 years, only 200 lawyers had been given the award previously). I may have even been the first or, perhaps, second intellectual property trial lawyer to make the list.

In my examination of Jan Hedlund, Vice President of Engineering for Polaris (who was present at the first meeting between Polaris and Ron's assignee, Injection Research), we accused Polaris of stringing Ron along, while getting information about Ron's invention to send to Fuji. I got Hedlund to confirm that the tests on Ron's system had been positive and the result was devastating. You could hear a pin drop in that courtroom when this testimony was given:

Q. But you decided IRS's price was too high, correct?

A. That's correct.

Q. But you also decided and knew that the system, the idea of having a fuel-injected snowmobile was a good idea, had merit, and you didn't want the competition to have it, right?

A. That's correct.

Q. So what you decided to do at that point in time was to misrepresent to Ron Chasteen what your intentions were; isn't that right?

A. Yeah, I did.

Q. *You misled him?*

A. *Yes, I did.*

Q. *You lied to him, right?*

A. *That's correct.*

Q. *And you did that for a purpose; isn't that right, sir?*

A. *Yes, I did.*

Q. *And the purpose was that you wanted to tell him, We dropped this project, we put the brakes on it so that he might not go on to a competitor, right?*

A. *I was worried he was going to go to the competition and tell him that we were working on fuel injection.*

Q. *You were worried that he was going to go to the competition, right?*

A. *Right.*

Q. *And that's why you told him at that point in time what you agree was a lie, namely that you put the brakes on the project, right?*

A. *That's correct.*

(Transcript, April 16, 1997, pp. 899-900; emphasis added). I then confronted Hedlund with his own note written early in the negotiations, which said Polaris had two options: they could pay royalties to IRS and, thus, pay for the technology, but that would be expensive. Then the document ended. It was blank. There was no second option. Nonetheless, I asked Hedlund what the second option was:

Q. Do you recall now that you realized that it was blank below the second of the two options?

A. Yeah, there is not a second option on there.

(Transcript, April 16, 1997, p. 931). I asked for the original in front of the jury (impliedly suggesting someone removed the second option) and, of course, it was unavailable. The clear implication was that the second option was to take the technology and not pay. I didn't make that accusation in the cross-examination, because sometimes things left unsaid are the most powerful. Let the jury decide.

THE CLOSING

In closing, I hit hard on two things developed on cross -- the Hedlund lie that Polaris had dropped the project and the Polaris internal document that had on it two options: pay for a license or ... the blank for the second option:

> MR. NIRO: When we started this case two weeks ago, I think it's about two weeks now, I said that it was a case about trust, about betrayal of that trust, and about two companies that decided that they would just take something rather than pay for it.
>
> You will recall Mr. Hedlund's testimony here when we called him as an adverse witness, and he said -- he admitted, in fact, that he had lied to Ron Chasteen. He told him that we were dropping the project, those were his words, dropping the project, because he didn't want him to take it to any of the competitors.
>
> He said it was wrong to do that, indeed it was. But it raises a lot of questions as to why at that point in time Polaris would find it necessary to lie about the importance of an idea if it was unimportant, worthless, old, in the public domain. Why would you want at that point in time to discourage Ron Chasteen from talking to a competitor?

(Transcript, April 24, 1997, p. 1742). Now for the document:

> Now, Mr. Hedlund had another very important document in this case, his notes. Don't know if you recall them. They were marked as Exhibit 123, and I will show them to you again because they become so important in the context of this case.

Right at the very end of his handwritten notes, and I asked him about these, and I asked him where the originals were, and he didn't have them, he says, Based on my and David Thompson's estimate regarding dollars required to develop fuel injection, I recommend we do one of two things, negotiate with IRS to license these -- their system for snowmobiles and ATVs. That's option No. 1. And beneath it is nothing, blank, no answer. No revelation of what option No. 2 was.

Option No. 2 we would suggest was what they did, betrayal. Take it. Don't pay. Use it. Don't pay.

(Transcript, April 24, 1997, pp. 1743-1744).

THE MUSICAL NOTES

Invention is like music, creating new combinations from what is old. I love this analogy and use it in many of my closings:

You know, we would be sitting in darkness today if Thomas Edison hadn't invented the lightbulb, but what a simple device it is. Anybody could do it. Except he did. Thomas Edison, by the way, had a third grade education, the greatest inventor of our time.

It's a little like music. There are only eight notes in the musical scale. Anybody wants to put those things together in any way they can from the beginning of time to right now, but every day new music is written, new songs are written. And I have some of the sheet music here. Louis Armstrong, What A Wonderful World, just eight notes, page after page of eight notes. Or George Gershwin's Rhapsody In Blue, page after page, eight notes. Different music, different song. The Beatles, Let It Be, same thing, page after page. Different music, different songs, same eight notes. It's how you put it together that makes the new song. It's how you take the components and put them together, and that's what Ron did.

Now, if it was all old and well-known, why didn't Maier introduce it? Why didn't JECS, Kawasaki or Polaris introduce it? Why didn't any of the competitors introduce it? Why if it was all old and well-known?

Certainly the same people that now say it's old and well-known would have had the same incentive to create the same ideas. The fact is everybody had the notes, but Ron had the song. He put it together, and he made it work, and he proved it was a concept that was worthwhile.

(Transcript, April 24, 1997, pp. 1756-1757).

EMPOWER THE JURY

The grand finale -- empower the jury, challenge them to do what's right:

Mr. Gill said you sit as the conscience of the community. We agree, you do. You have the power. This is one of the beauties of this system. Eight people or ten people or twelve people come from a community without any knowledge or anything about this case and they have the power to send the message back. Is it okay to misappropriate? Is it okay to lie? Is it okay to mislead? Is it okay to take some information and ship it off to Japan? That's the question. You have the power to answer those questions.

Now, it's been said, and I think about this this afternoon, that the cruelest lies in life are [t]old [in] silence. It's not what you say. It's sometimes what you don't say that is the worst lies. And where is that silence from that one Exhibit 12 from Mr. Hedlund? We have two options, we can buy it or blank.

Now, when they got caught they paraded these

defenses in front of you. Robert Goddard, an interesting man, he invented a rocket in 1928, his dream came true in 1969 long after he had passed, but he said it's difficult to say what's impossible [for the] dream of yesterday is the hope of today and the reality of tomorrow.

Well, Ron Chasteen had a dream. 1978 through 1987 he tried to perfect that dream, and his hope was he could share it with Polaris. They would become partners, and they would exploit it together. That was his hope. And the reality was he got not a cent, not a penny, nothing. They shattered that dream. And you have the right to tell them when you go back and deliberate in this case that that's not right, our community doesn't accept that as conduct and behavior that we will tolerate. Thank you again.

(Transcript, April 24, 1997, pp. 1811-1812).

The final recovery changed Ron Chasteen's life for the better, I hope. He quit his day job, created a camp for homeless children and started his own construction business. We set up an annuity for him and his family as a gift of our appreciation for his role in the trial. Without him, we had nothing. With him, we slew Goliath once again. It was a great moment. A story appeared on the front page of The Denver Post the day after the verdict in which a quote by my law partner, John Janka, appeared (we even had shirts made imprinted with it): *"In America, you can't steal people's ideas and not pay."*

EXPOSING THE CHEATERS

Dastgheib v. Genentech,
Civil Action No. 2:04cv1283 (E.D. Pa., Nov. 2006)

Sometimes it doesn't pay to swing for the fences. This was one such case. At trial, we turned down a huge settlement offer. The final result, unfortunately: a defense verdict. We got zero.

Alex Dastgheib was a genius. Born in Iran and educated in England. He immigrated to the United States after graduation from the University of Paris Medical School. His post-doctorate studies included a stay at Johns Hopkins in ophthalmology and at Duke for more specialty training in ophthalmology. While at Duke, he found proof for his theory that a protein called VEGF was the causal link to macular degeneration, the leading cause of blindness in the civilized world. More than 250,000 Americans a year get the wet form of macular degeneration and lose their vision. And Alex set out to prove that it was an over-abundance of VEGF in the retina that caused the disease.

Alex obtained access to some rare slides at Johns Hopkins, wrote a paper on his findings and got the attention of Dr. Robert Cuthbertson, a researcher at Genentech who needed proof to get a project approved for an anti-VEGF drug called Lucentis. We had evidence that Genentech acted on Alex's slides to get the evidence it needed and the approval for the anti-VEGF project. The crucial date was February 28, 1996 when key meetings took place at Genentech to decide whether or not to go forward with the anti-VEGF project based upon tests on our client's samples. But what can you do when the other side cheats in discovery? Expose it and hope for the best:

Q.   So, Dr. Cuthbertson, trust and honesty is important to you, right? You just said that?

A.   Absolutely.

Q.   So, you have in front of you this book which you call your daily book, is that right, Exhibit Number 37? Do you recall testifying about that? It's Defendant's Exhibit 37. I think it was identified as your daily book. Do you have it there?

A.   Yes.

Q.   Do you have the original?

A.   Not here. This is a copy.

Q.   When did you last see the original?

A.   I really don't recall. I provided it to the Genentech lawyers some time ago.

Q.   You gave it to the Genentech lawyers? How long ago did you do that?

A.   It would have been some years ago. I'm sorry. I don't --

Q.   And just to -- for the record, it was spiral bound, correct? See these spirals on the side?

A.   Yes.

Q.   So, it wasn't like you could pull a page out without tearing it out of there, right? Right? Did you tear any pages out?

A.   No. Not --

Q.   So when you gave --

A.   -- not that I recall, not that I recall.

Q.   -- when you gave it to the lawyers, all the pages for every day were there, right?

A.   I couldn't say that, sir. I just said I didn't tear any pages out. I didn't go through it.

(Transcript, November 2, 2006, pp. 1384-1385). So he didn't take any pages out. Then who did?

Q.   Let me show you the entry for February 11th, again, with the spiral binding on the side, and this is your handwriting, right?

A.   Yes.

Q.   What does it say?

A.   It says, "Decision on eye slides today."

Q.   Decision on eye slides today. That's a reference to the eye slides that Dr. Dastgheib sent to you, correct?

A.   I -- I'm not sure about that specifically but it -- it could have been. I'm not sure. It doesn't say that.

Q.   But it says -- by the way, that's February 9 -- it's a little difficult to read. I'm trying to -- do you see it? It says "Friday, February 9"?

A.   Yes.

Q. And you don't recall that that's referenced to the eye slides that were sent to you by Dr. Dastgheib in December?

A. It doesn't say. I don't recall. It could be but I don't recall.

Q. Now, when these documents were produced, Genentech put a consecutive number at the bottom -- Genentech 28555, the next page is 556, and so forth. Now, those identifications weren't on the book when you gave it to them, right --

A. No --

Q. -- the lawyers?

A. No.

Q. And this covers three days at a time, right? Isn't that the format for it, for three days?

A. Except for the weekend, I think.

Q. Right. And if it's on a weekend, then you get a fourth and fifth day, right?

A. I think that's correct, yes.

Q. Okay. I want to take you to February -- and again, it's a little difficult to see so I'm going to try to zoom in on it. Sunday, February 25. Do you see that?

A. Yes.

Q. That's on the page 28559. Now, if I go to the next page, that's 28560, I see that you jumped ahead to February 29th. Do you see that?

A. Yes.

Q. You're going from February 25 to February 29th and therefore, one of the pages is missing, right?

A.   I guess. I mean --

Q.   Well, you didn't keep your book spiral bound so that you jumped from one date, February 25 to February 29, did you?

A.   I -- I'm not sure what you're asking me, sir.

Q.   And February 28th would be missing from the book, right? Right? At least in the copy you have?

A.   Yes. From what's in front of me, yes. That's -- I don't --

(Transcript, November 2, 2006, pp. 1384-1387).

The most important entry was deliberately taken out of the book -- February 28:

Q.   Now, am I correct, that was a pretty important day, wasn't it, February 28th?

A.   In what sense?

Q.   Well, let me show you Exhibit 36. I'll put them back out for a minute. These are minutes of a meeting and referring to an agenda -- tentative agenda for a meeting to be held on February 28th. Do you see that? A tentative agenda, February 28th, right?

A.   Yes. I see -- I see that, yes.

Q.   That's the day that your notebook page is missing, right?

A.   I agree, from what I've got in front of me, yeah.

Q.   And somebody was stamping these things consecutively, so the page was torn out of the book, right?

A.   I can't say that, sir. Not --

Q.   On this day, February 28th, it says "Tentative agenda, status of studies in progress, immunohistochemistry of human AMD eye sections, A. Ryan, A. Cuthbertson." On February 28th, 1996, the day that's missing from this book, you were presenting the status of the studies on the immunohistochemistry of human AMD eye sections, correct, sir?

A.   Well, that's a tentative agenda, or that was the proposed agenda.

Q.   Have you seen the minutes of that meeting?

A.   No. I -- in fact, I don't know that the meeting took place. It was a tentative agenda. They changed all the time.

Q.   Are you aware of any minutes, any notes, any documents, anything, that says what happened on February 28th, 1996?

A.   No, I'm not, and I'm not aware that the meeting actually took place, sir.

Q.   You don't remember?

A.   I don't remember it taking place.

Q.   And you have not seen and there has not been produced in this litigation, any document, any minute, any note, any record of any kind as to what happened on February 28th, 1996, correct, sir?

A.   As far as I know.

(Transcript, November 2, 2006, pp. 1387-1388).

Why the fuss about a missing notebook page? Well, the page that was missing was the single most important date in the case: February

28, 1996. Our client had given Genentech tissue samples to show that a protein VEGF was the causal link to macular degeneration -- the leading cause of blindness in the world. We argued that Genentech used the slides to prove the causal link. And February 28, 1996 was the day the internal test results were going to be discussed. But the notebook page was missing. This is how we used the missing page in closing; it was part of Genentech's cover-up:

> [T]here are a lot of things they didn't say. And there's an old saying that the cruelest lies are told in silence. Think about it. Where's the silence here? Where's the silence.
>
> Where are the lab notebooks for that time period? They didn't keep them. We had somebody testify, "We found lab notebooks" in all other kinds of time periods, but not a single lab notebook for Dr. Cuthbertson, Noel Ryan, Noel Dybdal, Carrie Kyle Byrne, Dr. Ferrara, nothing.
>
> Where are the slides? They disappeared. Where are the photographs that Anne Ryan said you ought to take? Surely, if you're doing a peer review article or if you're just trying to collect data, you would take a photograph. The slides fade in time. You'd take a photograph of the results, just like Dr. Dastgheib did.
>
> They did it. You don't see them. The February 28 meeting between Ryan, Dybdal and Cuthbertson. Not a note, not a minute, not a discussion. Pathology reports don't exist.
>
> So, what do you have here? Remember the diary? Remember the diary? 1996 diary, and they put a copy in front of Dr. Cuthbertson. "This is your diary.
>
> "Yes.
>
> "You remember this meeting?
>
> "Yes, I do. I went to Boston."
>
> This is the guy who was in Philadelphia last Tuesday

meeting with Genentech's lawyers when we were playing his video. After Genentech was ordered to produce that original diary and it came in overnight, what did you see? You saw there were two pages missing out of 104. Two pages missing.

Not one, two. Said there was a copying error. And those two pages contain reference to three meetings, February 7, February 27, February 28. It's almost illegible. You can't really read it. But you know what? You can read enough to know there was an all-day meeting on February 27th, and a one-hour meeting between -- at least scheduled, between Dr. Cuthbertson, Anne Ryan, Noel Dybdal on the 28th.

Ask yourself why in 104 pages of a document, a diary that they put before the witness, only two are missing. And they said -- and by the way, is that a coincidence, an error? You have to decide that. Why in the world if you're copying something do you not copy, by mistake, by error, the two pages that reference all the meetings that are taking place during this time period?

And I'm going to show you why this story doesn't stick together. You'll recall that they said, "Well, the original --" initially Dr. Cuthbertson said, "The original was sent to the lawyers to copy. I haven't seen it in years." And then the next day he said, "You know what? I found it in Australia." And they made a copy of what I sent them, which was a copy.

I'm going to show you the original, that is, the copy of the original. 'Cause we don't have the original. This is a copy of the original, and then the copy of the copy, what they had the first day. Now, I don't know if you're going to be able to see this, but I'm going to see if I can show this in a way -- look at the copy -- or look at the original for a minute. And you see this down here? 8:15. And you see this up here? Big thick line. Now, if you're going to copy that, if you're going to copy that, let's see what you get.

Are you going to get this? 8:30, 8:45? You can add that to a copy machine? And look at this. There's a narrow line up top, not a thick line. You go from thick to narrow? And you go from can't see 8:15 or 8:30 and 8:45 to 8:45. No way was that a copy of the copy.

Now, what does that tell you? That somebody was making a copy of the quote, unquote "copy of the original" when these pages disappeared. I don't know who it was. And does it really matter? They came to this federal courtroom, put a document in front of a witness on critical dates, and it didn't have the critical information.

You know, this reminds me of a poem that I think Sir Walter Scott used. I told it to my kids at times. "Oh, what a tangled web we weave when first we practice to deceive."

There's a web here. It's tangled. And why is it? Why did Dr. Cuthbertson forget that he had the original in Australia? Why was the 1995 diary here but not the 1996? Why are only the critical pages missing? Why isn't there a note or a memo or a minute of February 7 or February 27 or February 28 meetings? And why can't anyone remember anything about it?

(Transcript, November 7, 2006, pp. 1885-1888).

The result of the Genentech case was not favorable. We turned down a huge settlement offer and got nothing. Bad karma? Maybe. A client from Iran? Maybe. A single juror who led the crusade against us? Maybe. A client who lost credibility by not having a single note or document to support his position? Maybe. But that's the beauty of the system: you don't have explanations as to why you win or lose; you simply take the hit and move on.

TAKING A DEFENSE TO ABSURDITY -- PRACTICING THE PRIOR ART WILL KILL THE PATIENT

Sakharam D. Mahurkar v. C.R. Bard, Inc.,
Civil Action No. 92 C 4803 (N.D. Ill., Aug. 1994)

This case was about hemodialysis catheters -- the medical devices that connect people with failed kidneys to a dialysis machine that cleanses their blood of impurities and keeps them alive. Unfortunately, the average life-expectancy of a dialysis patient is ten years. Without dialysis, it is a matter of days before the toxins become fatal. I actually saw patients getting dialysis treatments at a Veterans Administration Hospital in Chicago (which was not a nice experience).

Dr. Mahurkar was an Indian immigrant who worked at Cook County Hospital in Chicago. He specialized in nephrology (the treatment of kidney disease) and recognized the huge problems in removing and returning blood to the body. This was necessary to prevent the lethal build-up of toxins that normal kidneys remove, but failed kidneys don't. The key to Dr. Mahurkar's catheter design was a double-D cross-section that allowed blood to be removed and returned efficiently without damaging the cells or creating blood clots.

Bard had copied Dr. Mahurkar's catheter design. But they also had prior art -- French Granger Patent No. 2297640 that disclosed a double-D cross-section -- and a prominent expert from the University of Chicago, Dr. Woodle, who would testify about it. Woodle testified the French patent showed Dr. Mahurkar's design. Hemodialysis catheters are inserted into veins, however, not into the smaller arteries that can be blocked. Both, of course, are blood vessels. This is how I undid Dr. Woodle and the prior art all at once:

Q.   You mentioned the manner in which you place the catheters and what veins you use. I believe you said that you can pick any number of veins.

A.   Yes.

Q.   But your preference is -- overwhelmingly your preference is to insert the catheter into the jugular vein; isn't that right?

A.   Either the external jugular or internal jugular veins.

Q.   All right. And when it's inserted through the external or internal jugular vein -- and excuse me because I don't know very much about medicine --

A.   Okay.

Q.   -- the catheter actually rests inside the vena cava?

A.   Actually -- can I just show you?

Q.   Sure.

A.   What happens -- let's just say we bring it from the left side, left eternal jugular, it will come through there, go through the innominate vein, through the vena cave, and we actually have our tips sitting in the upper portion of the atrium.

Q.   So the catheter feeds itself way through the vena cava?

A.   Yes, sort of makes it an S-like curve.

Q.   Is that true if you insert it through the other jugular as well?

A.   The internal jugular, yes. They both have to negotiate the amount of vein here, which forces it to make a bit of an S turn.

(Transcript, August 23, 1994, pp. 1749-1750). Now I set the hook -- 1/4 to 1/2 of your blood passes through the vena cava vein:

Q.   And [the] vena cava is a major vein in the body, correct?

A.   Yes.

Q.   It supplies about one-fourth of the blood to the heart?

A.   Actually probably more like a half of the cardiac output goes through the superior vena cava.

(Transcript, August 23, 1994, p. 1750). Yet, this prior art taught blocking the blood vessel (an artery) for four and five hours. No one would want to block a vein for any period of time, much less for four to five hours:

Q.   It's not a vein you would want to block for any period of time?

A.   Um, if you block the superior vena cava, I think that -- if you're talking about either the superior vena cava or the inferior vena cava, the superior vena cava, if you block it completely, a hundred percent, you get what's called an acute superior vena cava syndrome and there's acute venous hypertension in the upper extremities.

The collateral circulation -- there is some collateral circulation that goes around the heart that can come up back through. ***But in general it's a fairly significant physiologic insult.***

(Transcript, August 23, 1994, pp. 1750-1751; emphasis added). "A fairly significant physiologic insult." Are you kidding me? What gibberish. The cross-examination continued:

Q.   It's not a procedure you would recommend?

A.   However, the inferior vena cava down below the heart is a little different. Once you get down in the inferior vena cava, for example, the renal veins, one can occlude the vena cava -- let's put it this way. We do a liver transplant, we occlude the vena cava for an hour completely and don't bypass the blood and those patients do very well.

Q.   Would you recommend blocking the upper part of the vena cava where these catheters --

A.   This right here?

Q.   -- would be placed for a period of four hours?

A.   A complete occlusion?

Q.   Yes.

A.   A hundred percent occlusion for four hours ***would be difficult to tolerate physiologically.***

(Transcript, August 23, 1994, p. 1751; emphasis added). Fairly significant physiologic insult? Difficult to physiologically tolerate? It would likely kill the patient, as our client, Dr. Mahurkar, testified. Look at what the prior art French patent taught. The Kevorkian catheter was born -- use it to kill people, not save lives:

Q.   ... This is the so-called Granger disclosure. Is this a hemodialysis catheter that's shown here or not?

A.   They call it as a oxygenation catheter in the patent.

Q.   And it would be used to do what?

A.   It should not be used -- it should not be used to do anything.

Q.   Well, let's assume that you wanted to oxygenate somebody's blood because of kidney failure --

A.   Lung failure.

Q.   I'm sorry, lung failure, you want to oxygenate blood. Does the description of this patent describe a procedure for doing that?

A.   Yes.

Q.   Now, if such a design were used for hemodialysis, I think you testified that you typically remove -- what did you say, how many cc's?

A.   250.

Q.   -- 250 cc's per minute of blood.

A.   Correct.

Q.   And then you would send 250 cc's of blood, right?

A.   Right.

Q.   In order to do hemodialysis?

A.   Right.

Q. Now, how much blood flows through the vena cava --

A. 2,500 --

Q. -- vein?

A. 2,500 cc's.

⚬ ⚬ ⚬ ⚬ ⚬

Q. 2500 cc's. What is the balloon that's in the middle of the [prior art] catheter? What does that do?

A. It is a balloon which will collect the blood, expounding blood, the whole vena cava, as it is doing now.

Q. If 250 cc's are moved out and 250 cc's are moved in, what happens to the 2200 cc's of blood that's supposed to be flowing through the vena cava if somebody were to use a design like this?

A. If that much -- if that blood, which is normally supposed to go to heart for pumping, if it is stopped dead, 2,500 cc's -- 2,200 cc's of blood will not go to the heart and *the patient will be dead*.

Q. *If you were to use a device like this for hemodialysis of a patient and put a device like this in the vena cava, what would happen to that patient in your professional opinion*?

A. *Patient will be dead on the spot*.

(Transcript, August 11, 1994, pp. 591-592; emphasis added). Our expert, Dr. Ash, reached the same conclusion:

Q. Let me show you one more catheter that was illustrated. This is the so-called Granger catheter. Do you recognize this?

A.   Yes, I do.

Q.   Again, what do you understand the purpose to be of this balloon in the middle of the vein?

A.   That balloon is there to purposely block the vein, to stop the blood from going around the balloon so that a very large tube can suck all the blood out of the body.

Q.   Is this a hemodialysis catheter?

A.   No. This catheter would be totally unsuitable for hemodialysis.

Q.   If one were to take the amount of blood flow in and out of the catheter that is customary for hemodialysis, 200 to 300 milliliters per minute, what happens to the rest of the blood that's supposed to go through the heart?

A.   It would just stop.

Q.   ***What would be the consequence of that?***

A.   ***The consequence is I agree with Dr. Mahurkar. The patient would die.***

Q.   Would you use a catheter like this for hemodialysis?

A.   No I would not.

(Transcript, August 12, 1994, pp. 757-758; emphasis added). Okay. So there you have it. Prior art that teaches blocking the blood vessel for four to five hours. There were two problems, however: (1) the Mahurkar patent was not limited to hemodialysis only and (2) the Granger

(French) design was virtually indistinguishable from the Mahurkar design. Nonetheless, this is how I used the testimony in closing:

> The Cropp catheter, the Ash gastrointestinal treatment system, concepts back in 1938, the Granger French patent that Dr. Ash said and Dr. Mahurkar said isn't something that they would recommend you put in the vena cava because it will block it, that's what was out there. But nobody was putting it together. Nobody was writing the song.
>
> Every invention is made up of old parts. The light bulb in the projector that Edison invented had old parts, but he put it together in a new combination. And the plastic that was used for the overheads, all those elements were old too, but somebody put them together in unique combination. And it's easy to say, oh, it's old as the hills, I could have done it. But it's a lot more difficult to do it. And Dr. Mahurkar did it.
>
> And the evidence here is not clear and convincing that this invention would have been obvious at the time the invention was made that the nine different components, like the eight different musical notes, could be put together like he did. Invention comes in funny ways. Alexander Fleming discovered penicillin back in 1928, and it was an accident, because he was growing some mold and noticed that the mold spores were killing the infections. And he won the Nobel prize 20 years later. …
>
> And in a sense, that's what invention is. It's creating something new from some old components and putting them together in a unique way.

(Transcript, August 26, 1994, pp. 2103-2104). The case was won; the prior art was a failure. Dr. Mahurkar was paid in excess of $5 million. And, by the time we were done, maybe $100 million in royalties.

TAKING ON THE INVINCIBLE EXPERT

Westinghouse v. Southwestern Engineering,
Civil Action No. 82 Civ. 681 (D. Del., Oct. 1986)

HOW DO YOU UNDERMINE DR. DOOM?

In this case, we represented the defendant, Southwestern Engineering (a Los Angeles company), accused of infringing two Westinghouse patents on heat exchangers used in nuclear power plants. They were called moisture separator reheaters (MSRs) (what, in chemical engineering, we called steam-steam shell and tube heat-exchangers). For our client, this case was life or death. Its entire business was in MSRs. A loss meant going out of business. And Southwestern's President, Bob Weisberg, reminded me of that fact daily.

Westinghouse was represented by Tom Arnold of Arnold, White & Durkee (now Howrey & Simon). The key witness for Westinghouse was its expert, Dr. Warren Roshenow, Professor Emeritus of Mechanical Engineering at MIT. A giant in his field with a voice and presence to match his pedigree.

Our client said Roshenow was never on the losing side of a case. He was Dr. Doom, Darth Vader and Dr. Death all in one package. If he testified against you, you lost. Period. We had no deposition testimony to work with and no idea (or at least not much) about what he would say on direct. Our client kept asking me over and over again how we were going to deal with Roshenow. And, over and over again, I said I simply did not know. Finally, I couldn't take it anymore. And when Bob Weisberg asked for the twentieth time, I thought back to the chant Bundini Brown created for Muhammad Ali: "float like a butterfly, sting like a bee." That was what I was going to do.

His voice was amazing. I closed my eyes, just to listen. Powerful. Deep. Pure. Overwhelming. His direct went on for hours. He described technical details that I could not begin to understand. Then it occurred to me. None of this was even in the two patents and so began the "No. No. No." cross-examination.

CROSS-EXAMINATION -- NO! NO! NO!

Q. You are familiar with the two patents, the Ritland and Coit patents?

A. Yes.

Q. And you understand the claims of those patents?

A. I think I do.

〰 〰 〰 〰 〰

Q. Now, in -- referring to the patents, and you are familiar with them, do the patents define the temperature ... of the tube side fluid?

A. No.

Q. Do they define the temperature of the shell side fluid?

A.   No.

Q.   Do they define the pressure of the tube side fluid?

A.   No.

Q.   Do they define the pressure of the shell side fluid?

A.   No.

Q.   Do they define the Delta-T?

A.   No.

Q.   Do they define the length of the tube?

A.   No.

Q.   Do they define the tube diameter?

A.   No.

(Transcript, June 27, 1986, pp. 1147, 1149-1150). But Roshenow spent hours on all this in direct. You mean, it's not even in the two patents?:

Q.   In the patent. The L over D ratio therefore isn't defined?

A.   That is right.

Q.   The timing of any cycles for subcooling, or the duration of any cycles for subcooling isn't defined in the patent, is it?

A.   Right.

Q.   The presence or absence of noncondensables isn't defined in the patent?

A.   Right.

Q.   Both patents, correct?

A.   Right.

Q.   The tube materials aren't defined in the patents, are they?

A.   That is right.

Q.   The co[r]rosion characteristics of any tube materials aren't defined; isn't that right?

A.   That is right.

Q.   The patents don't talk about vapor sheer control, do they?

A.   No.

Q.   They don't talk about gravity control, do they?

A.   No.

Q.   They don't talk about flow regimes, do they?

A.   No.

Q.   They don't talk about the annular flow or stratified flow; isn't that right?

A.   Right.

Q.   There are no equations in the patents; isn't that correct?

A.   That is right.

Q.   There is nothing about steam velocities in the patents?

A.   That is right.

Q.   And the patents don't define what the flow rates are for the materials that might be passing through the tubes or across the shell; isn't that right?

A.   Right.

Q.   Are the words "cyclic subcooling" used in any place in either of the patents?

A.   No.

Q.   In fact, in the Ritland patent, the word "subcooling" only appears once; isn't that right?

A.   I will take your word for it.

(Transcript, June 27, 1986, pp. 1151-1152). So all of this technical "mumbo-jumbo" he testified about was not even relevant enough to be discussed in the two patents. The professor was unraveling.

DID THE PRIOR ART DO THE SAME THING?

It would be devastating to the Westinghouse patents if air-cooled condensers had the same problem and solved it in the same way as the patents did for MSRs:

Q.   It is your testimony and belief that air cooled condensers at least had a different problem, and that there was a different solution to whatever problem they had, thus making air cooled condenser technology not applicable to MSR's, is that right?

A.   Let me embellish that just a little bit.

Q.   Well, if you could answer it first, then you could embellish. Is that right or wrong?

A.   Halfway.

◆ ◆ ◆ ◆ ◆

A.   Yes. The bulk of the air condensers that are in operation are at sub atmospheric pressure. Most of the writings and the discussions in the technical journals [are] on those condensers. In those cases, the writings that we find and the general knowledge that I believe others have are that the problems do not have to do with this cyclic subcooling, but they are due to the noncondensable gasses freezing, corrosion, that kind of thing. And that is what is mentioned in the literature, and prior to the 1980's, about all we heard about -- in 1982.

Now, above atmospheric pressures, I da[r]e say not many people would have thought that they would have cyclic subcooling either without the kind of explanation I just went through, and I couldn't have given you this kind of explanation without having the experience from the MSR. So, we never -- I never heard of, or no one I know of, has heard of cyclic subcooling in above atmospheric condensers or failures resulting from them. ***And I -- if you know such things, I would love to have that in my file.*** Just have not heard of failures in those cases.

(Transcript, June 27, 1986, pp. 1170-1172; emphasis added). The hook was set: if he had heard about air-cooled condensers addressing the same problem, he would keep a copy in his file.

A COPY FOR HIS FILE

He would love a copy in his file. And, he was about to get one:

Q.   You have never heard of any such thing?

A.   Prior to 1972.

Q.   All right. You have never heard of any such thing and you would like to have a copy for your files?

A.   That is what I would like to have, yes.

Q.   Do you know Dr. Rabas?

A.   Who?

Q.   Dr. Rabas?

A.   Rabas?

Q.   Yes.

A.   Sure I do.

Q.   He's sitting in the courtroom?

A.   Sure.

Q.   Has he done extensive work on MS[R]'s?

A.   Sure.

Q.   More work that you have on that subject?

A.   On MSR's?

Q.   Yes.

A.   Yes.

Q.   Have you consulted with him generally in the course of your consultation work for Westinghouse?

A.   Yes. Briefly.

Q.   Have you consulted with him with respect to the subject matter of this case?

A.   Yes.

Q.   Do you know whether Dr. Rabas has done any studies on the subject of flow instabilities in MSR tubes?

A.   Yes. He made temperature measurements, which he'll tell you about.

Q. Are you also aware of the fact that he's done studies on flow instabilities in the air-cooled condensers?

A. I didn't know that.

Q. Do you think he's a designer of ordinary skill in the art?

A. He's superior skilled.

Q. Do you know that he worked on both air-cooled condensers and MSR's?

A. I knew -- yes.

Q. Do you know that he made a comparison between the flow patterns in both MSR's and air-cooled condensers?

A. Yes.

Q. Do you know that he identified that the water hammer and cyclic subcooling existed in MSR's?

A. In MSR's?

Q. Yes.

A. Yes.

(Transcript, June 27, 1986, pp. 1172-1174).

THE WESTINGHOUSE DOCUMENT

Here it comes (in a Westinghouse document no less):

Q. Let me show you a document that we have marked as Defendant's Exhibit 285. It's an article written by Dr. Rabas entitled "Two Types of Flow Instabilities Occurring Inside Horizontal Tubes with Complete Condensation."

I would like to ask you a few questions about that.

A. *Shoot*.

Q. Okay. You see that the article begins with the statement that the data is presented which demonstrates the two different types of condensing instabilities can exist in the horizontal U-tube heat exchangers used in moisture separator reheaters. Do you see that?

A. Yes.

Q. You agree with that; is that correct?

A. Yes, I think so.

Q. And those two types of instabilities are the water hammer and then this other cyclic subcooling which you talked about; correct?

A. Yes.

Q. Two types of cyclic subcooling?

A. Right.

MR. ARNOLD: I am not acquainted with this document being on any 282 list or exhibit list. Have I missed it somewhere that's listed and I should know about?

MR. NIRO: It's not on any 282 list and the pretrial order says for cross-examination we are not limited to things that are on the pretrial order list in terms of cross-examination.

MR. ARNOLD: I will accept that.

MR. HARDING: May we have a copy, Mr. Niro, so we can follow the questions?

MR. NIRO: Sure. I thought this came from your files but I don't know if it did.

BY MR. NIRO:

Q. Dr. Rabas goes on to say, on the second page, that the purpose of this paper is to present a data base which illustrates the types of instabilities that can exist in moisture separator reheaters.

And then he says two separate and distinct types of abilities can exist, a condensate chucking type at low inlet vapor flow rates and cyclic type at high inlet vapor flow rates.

And then on the third page, he actually shows a photograph, or a sketch. I think you can see it.

A. Yes.

Q. It's identical to your Plaintiff's Exhibit 16.12; isn't that right?

In fact, it shows the hot steam going in the same direction and the cold condensate going in the other direction and the flooded tube.

Do you see that?

A. Yes.

Q. It almost looks like one was prepared from the other; right?

A. It was. Dead copy.

Q. Then, after he discussed the situation of these two types of cyclic subcooling, he says, at page 120 -- and I will read it to you -- he says:

"The writers were unable to find any temperature" -- I'm sorry -- "any temperate or pressure variation measurements for air-cooled condensers. Lock Shonn, 1920, did mention that holes and annular cracks may appear during unstable hydraulic conditions and that leaks in some tubes in the region of the welds occasionally occur in service."

And then he says, or they say:

> "*It is apparent that one or both types of instabilities encountered in moisture separator reheaters may then also cause failures in air-cooled condensers.*"

Do you see that?

A.   Yes.

Q.   Do you agree with that?

A.   I don't know. I didn't know about it.

Q.   Pardon?

A.   I didn't know about that.

Q.   *That is one that perhaps you can add to your file, then.*

A.   *That is good.*

(Transcript, June 27, 1986, pp. 1174-1177; emphasis added). Did he really say "Shoot" when I showed him the document? And did I really say, "You can add [this] to your file"? What fun. Dr. Doom was crushed. And he was *livid*.

After the judge left the courtroom, Roshenow literally ran off the witness stand to confront me: he stood directly behind me as I was gathering my papers and, in his now-shattered (but still booming) voice, screamed, "What kind of lawyer are you?" I slowly turned and politely said, "You just saw what kind of lawyer I am."

My client's company was saved. The case was over. And the plaintiff actually paid our client $17 million to settle our counterclaim. Months later, we had a big party in LA on Rodeo Drive. It is better to win than to lose. Dr. Doom was done in by his own arrogance.

RUNNING THE TABLE

<u>Black & Decker (U.S.) Inc., et al. v. The Coleman Company, et al.,</u> Civil Action Nos. 96-656-A, 96-216-A and 96-1512-A (E.D. Va., Aug. 1996)

The SnakeLight® flexible flashlight was the most successful product launch ever from Black & Decker. Retailers couldn't keep them in their stores. And it was a flashlight that sold for $25 when most flashlights sold for $5. The key to the product was a flexible core that allowed "hands-free" use. You could twist it, turn it, wrap it around your head or a pipe.

Dion DiMucci of Dion and the Belmonts (only crazy 60s nuts, like me, remember Dion and the Belmonts) recorded a remake of his famous song "The Wanderer" to promote the SnakeLight®: "It's the SnakeLight from Black & Decker. It goes around, around, around, around...."

Of course, success invites copying -- and was this product ever copied. The Chinese manufacturers couldn't make them fast enough. As soon as we shut one down, another appeared. Coleman had a Chinese-made copy called the Coil Light. One day in August 1996, my son, Raymond, and I ran the table in a federal courtroom. (For those of you who have not made their money during college playing billiards or pool, this is pool talk for getting every ball in the correct pocket before your opponent gets to shoot.) Every defense witness was taken down; one after another. It happens once in a lifetime. Here are some of the highlights (remember, this is cross-examination of the defense witnesses):

WITNESS ONE -- MAKING SURE THE JURY KNEW THIS IMITATION WAS MADE IN CHINA

Q.   Mr. Hawkins, you are employed by the Coleman Company; is that correct?

A.   Yes, I am.

Q.   You have been there for slightly less than two years, correct?

A.   Yes.

Q.   And you joined them when, in about November of 1994?

A.   Yes.

Q.   And you are currently the group product manager for hardware and general purpose lighting; is that correct?

A.   Yes, it is.

Q.   That's a correct description of your title?

A.   Yes.

Q.   And your responsibilities include overall management responsibilities for the product that's at issue in this case, the Coil Light, correct?

A.   Yes, specifically marketing the product.

Q. You have marketing responsibility, but other responsibilities for the product as well; is that correct?

A. Yes.

Q. And Coleman began developing this Coil Light product, the flexible flashlight product, around April of 1995, correct?

A. We began concept drawings in the very early -- like January of '95.

Q. Am I correct that you began development of the product, not concept drawing, but development of the product around April of 1995? Is that correct?

A. Yes, as recognized by Coleman management. That is what we define as official development.

Q. And by December of that year, you had a product that was available, ready for the market; is that correct?

A. That's correct.

Q. That was what we have referred to as the first Coleman design, correct?

A. That's correct.

Q. *Okay. And Coleman and its supplier in China, Dorson, were able to take all the steps to design, develop and introduce that product in eight months, between April and December of 1995, correct?*

A. *Yes.*

Q. *The name of the company that assisted in development is Dorson; is that right?*

A. *Yes.*

Q. *Where are they located?*

A. *They are located in China.*

(Transcript, August 20, 1996 AM, pp. 52-54; emphasis added).

WITNESS TWO -- THEY TOOK THE SNAKELIGHT® APART TO COPY IT

Q. Do you know that he looked at that issue specifically by taking a Black [&] Decker SnakeLight apart before --

A. No, I don't. You would have to ask him. I wasn't present when he took it apart.

Q. You don't believe he looked at it, but you saw one in his office taken apart?

A. I saw one in his office taken apart. I don't know what he looked at and, you know, what his thought pattern was when he did that.

Q. Am I correct that you saw a SnakeLight flexible flashlight disassembled in Mr. Bamber's office?

A. Yes, after we had already tooled our own products.

Q. That is when you saw it?

A. Yes.

THE COURT: I take it you don't know when he took it apart?

THE WITNESS: No.

THE COURT: Next question.

BY MR. NIRO:

Q. Now, am I correct, you know that this company did -- that is, Coleman, did a competitive analysis --

A. Can I add to that?

THE COURT: Add to --

THE WITNESS: I am trying to clarify, I am thinking through what you just asked me; just for clarification --

THE COURT: All right. Go ahead.

THE WITNESS: -- please. Thank you.

When I saw the SnakeLight taken apart, what I am referring to is when I saw it taken apart in his office when I walked by. We were already tooled for our product. That was very late in our own design.

THE COURT: I will ask you again. You don't know when he took it apart, do you?

THE WITNESS: No. My assumption is then, specifically, no.

THE COURT: You don't know?

THE WITNESS: Right.

THE COURT: Next question.

(Transcript, August 20, 1996 AM, pp. 65-67).

BY MR. NIRO:

Q. My question to you is: Did anyone take apart a Black [&] Decker SnakeLight flexible flashlight to determine how the resilient sleeve was held in place to both the working end and the base housing?

A. Did anyone?

Q. Yes.

A. David took one apart. Again, I don't know what he did and why.

MR. NIRO: Your Honor, may I read to the witness from page 67 of his deposition, taken on February 8th?

THE COURT: If it is different from the answer given, yes. You must read the whole question and answer.

BY MR. NIRO:

Q. Question: -- page 68, beginning on line 6 of your deposition taken on February 8th, 1996.

> "Question: Let's talk about some of the similarities for a minute. Did anyone take apart a Black [&] Decker SnakeLight flexible flashlight to determine how the resilient sleeve was held in place to both the working end and the base housing?
>
> Answer: I believe David Bamber did."

Did you give that answer to that question at that time?

A. I am saying the same thing, listening to what you just said.

THE COURT: Answer the question. Did you give that testimony on that day?

THE WITNESS: Yes, I did.

THE COURT: All right, next question.

(Transcript, August 20, 1996 AM, pp. 65-67).

WITNESS THREE -- COLEMAN ONLY SPENT $125,000 DEVELOPING ITS COPY; BLACK & DECKER SPENT $6 MILLION

Q. The document that you prepared, Coil Light profit assumptions, I wanted to ask you a few questions about that, if I could.

On the first page of this, it identifies outside consultant, I believe, outside design, and has one dollar. Does that mean a thousand?

A. I have rounded to thousands of dollars.

Q. The total outside cost for the design of this product is $1,000; is that right?

A. Yes. Most of the design was done internally.

Q. Okay. And I see the next line says "internal design," but it says "marketing." Does that mean that the marketing expenses for the total work done on this product was $125,000?

A. We have a group that we refer to internally as the marketing department. Their main function, however, is not limited to simply marketing. In fact, probably their main function is to design products.

Q. All right. But they have a marketing function as well?

A. I believe they do.

Q. So the total expense for outside design and internal design in marketing, to get this product that's accused of infringement into the marketplace, is $126,000?

A. Yes. The $1,000, however, was a one-time expense that will not repeat. The $125,000 is an annual number associated with that.

Q. That is what it cost Coleman for research and development and design and introduction and marketing, $126,000?

A. Again, that is not directly -- that is an annual number that is associated with the group of people who will routinely support any additional design or marketing of Job Pro Coil Light.

(Transcript, August 21, 1996 AM, pp. 13-14).

WITNESS FOUR -- HE TESTIFIED THAT THE BLACK & DECKER PATENT WAS INVALID BECAUSE THE DIMENSIONS SET FORTH IN THE CLAIMS WERE NOT SUPPORTED, BUT HE DOESN'T UNDERSTAND PATENTS

Q. Mr. Bamber, let's begin, if we can, where you ended, and that's with the '803 patent. You said that you couldn't find support in the patent specifications for the varying ranges that are set forth with the dimensions, set forth in the claims; is that right?

A. Yes, sir.

Q. You understand, of course, that a patent examiner skilled in the technology examined this application and disagreed with your opinion; isn't that right?

A. I don't know, sir.

Q. You don't know that protests were filed contending that there was no support for those ranges, and the Patent Office disagreed?

A. I am saying I don't see the dimensions or drawings.

THE COURT: That isn't the question he is asking.

THE WITNESS: I'm sorry.

THE COURT: He asked whether you knew about certain Patent Office proceedings.

THE WITNESS: I heard about that yesterday.

BY MR. NIRO:

Q.   You didn't know that beforehand?

A.   No, sir, not until Mr. Dossas talked about it yesterday.

Q.   And nobody told you your opinion was different from the Patent Office's opinion?

A.   You are telling me now, sir.

⟊ ⟊ ⟊ ⟊ ⟊

Q.   Would you agree that you can't under[stand] patents?

A.   I would agree, I would tell you I am not an expert on patents.

Q.   Now, my question to you is: Are you a person who, "I design flashlights; I can't understand patents?"

Would you agree with that?

A.   It depends on what level of understanding. I am not an expert.

Q.   Let me read to you from page[s] 264 and 265 of your deposition, beginning at line 23.

"Question: How about someone who designs flashlights; what kind of qualifications would that person need?

Answer: A person who -- I design flashlights. I cannot understand patents."

Did you give those answers to those questions at your deposition?

A.   It happens, like an insurance policy, yes, sometimes.

Q.   Your answer is you can't understand them then, and you can't understand them now?

A.   No.

Q.   It is not correct?

A.   I understand these patents.

Q.   Did you give that testimony at that time, sir?

A.   No, I didn't.

Q.   You are saying that there is a mistake in this testimony?

A.   I am saying my experience has changed, yes.

Q.   It has changed from the date of this deposition?

A.   Yes.

Q.   So, from July 18th, 1996 to August 21st of 1996, you have changed from somebody that cannot understand patents to somebody who can understand patents; is that right, sir?

A.   I can understand these two patents, yes.

(Transcript, August 21, 1996 AM, pp. 76-77, 80-81). Amazing: he learned it all in a month.

WITNESS FIVE -- THE COIL LIGHT HAS EXACTLY WHAT THE SNAKELIGHT® HAS

Q. Doesn't the SnakeLight design have precisely the same shaped receiving bore for that part?

THE COURT: What was your question, Mr. Niro?

BY MR. NIRO:

Q Doesn't the SnakeLight design have exactly the same type of receiving bore for the sleeve?

A. I would have to take your word for it. I haven't looked at it that closely.

Q. You didn't see that when you took it apart?

A. No, sir. If I did, I don't remember.

Q. Are you certain, sir, that in the first and second design that you don't have what's called a bore?

A. Not a longitudinally extending bore; I have a small clamp diameter. You take a hose, a garden hose, and you put a clamp on it.

Q. In relation to the housing, don't you have a longitudinally extending bore?

A. No, sir.

Q. Let me read to you from page 222, 222 of your deposition, taken on July 18th, I believe, of this year, beginning at line 7.

"Question: *But it has a bore, correct?*

Answer: *It has, yes.*

Question: *And in relation to the housing, it extends longitudinally, correct? You accepted it was, although a short distance, correct?*

Answer: **Yes.**"

[emphasis added.] Did you give those answers to those questions at that time?

A.   Yes, I did.

(Transcript, August 21, 1996 AM, pp. 94-95). Impeached.

WITNESS SIX -- THE GLOVE DOES FIT -- MS. LASATER'S DECLARATION WAS WRONG

Ms. Lasater swore in her declaration that the shorter version of the Coil Light was sold in the big radio "Golf Mania" promotion. But the measurements we did in Court proved her declaration was false:

Q.   Good afternoon, Ms. Lasater. The declaration that you filed with the Court under oath is dated August 7, 1996, correct? You recall filing that?

A.   I don't have that in front of me.

Q.   Okay. Let me show you the declaration. Is that your signature on the last page of the document?

A.   Yes.

Q.   It is dated August 7, 1996?

A.   Yes.

Q.   And in this sworn statement to the Court, you say "Coleman did not provide any advertising or promotional material to the Golf Mania promotion," correct?

A.   Correct.

Q.   That turned out to be incorrect; is that right?

A.   No.

Q.   Did you send to Mr. Burden at the radio station a facsimile dated June 20, 1996?

A.   Yes.

Q.   You sent that to him?

A.   Yes.

Q.   And you said to "Please use the starred information to write your copy," correct?

A.   Correct.

Q.   And the copy he was writing was for the Golf Mania promotion, correct?

A.   Correct.

Q.   And what you sent him was information on the, among other things, the Model 5320-718, 2D Coil Light, correct?

A.   Correct.

Q.   And it's your testimony here today that that was for the third version design, correct?

A.   Yes.

Q.   Not the first version design?

A.   No.

Q.   This document came from the files of Mr. Burden, correct?

A.   Correct.

Q.   You didn't have a copy in your files that was produced for us?

A.   No.

Q.   In this document, it's a facsimile that was sent to Mr. Burden. To the right of the unit, where it says "unit dimensions," do you see that?

A.   Uh-huh.

Q.   I will circle it "Units dimensions: length, width and diameter," and to the right of that is what appears to be a photograph of the Coil Light, correct?

A.   Correct.

Q.   Can you determine from that whether it was the first, second or third version design?

A.   Not from that picture.

Q.   And you don't have the original document that you sent to them?

A.   No.

R. NIRO: Now, with the -- your Honor, if I might get the assistance of the [M]arshal?

THE COURT: Yes.

R. NIRO: Exhibit -- there is a collection of them there, a green stickered exhibit, it has a green sticker, on the Golf Mania promotion.

THE COURT: All right, hand that to the witness.

MR. NIRO: Exhibit 789B, would you take a look at that for a moment.

(Plaintiff's Exhibit No. 789B premarked for identification.)

THE WITNESS: (Complied)

BY MR. NIRO:

Q.   Is that sticker, the green sticker on that, something indicative of the fact that that was sold by Target as a part of this promotion?

A.   I had not seen this green sticker until I was in court yesterday.

Q.   Does that now indicate to you that that, in fact, was part of the Coleman product that was sold as a part of that promotion?

A.   Coleman is not listed on the sticker, but it is on the product.

Q.   Okay. Does that indicate to you that it was that version, that is the first version design -- if you could hold it up -- the first version design that was sold as part of the Golf Mania promotion, at least, correct?

A.   Could you restate that.

Q.   I'm sorry. Is that the first version design that you have in your hands?

A.   Yes.

Q.   And the green sticker indicates it was part of the Golf Mania promotion, correct?

A.   Yes.

Q.   And there is also the shorter version in a package, if you can -- would you look at that for a moment and give us the Exhibit Number?

A.   Defendant's Exhibit 2.

(Defendants' Exhibit No. 2 premarked for identification.)

BY MR. NIRO:

Q.   Okay. That's the third version design?

A. Yes, I believe so.

Q. And that's shorter -- can you hold them up together?

A. (Complied)

Q. That is shorter than the first version design?

A. Yes.

Q. Now, if you would hand the second version to the [M]arshal, I would just like to ask you to do something. If I could have it for a moment.

The dimensions on the packaging of this unit indicate a length of something like 14-1/2 inches. Do you recall that?

A. No, I don't.

Q. The length that's identified in your promotional material that you sent to Mr. Burden is 17.75 inches; is that right?

A. That's what's on the paper.

Q. That would indicate to you that was the longer version unit, the first, not the third version unit; isn't that right?

A. This paper indicates it's referring to the first version.

Q. So, what was sent on June 20, 1996, for use by Mr. Burden in the promotion was a sell sheet for the first version design, correct?

A. That is correct. But the dimensions of the product would not be information that would be put in a radio commercial, so that was not an important component on the sale sheet.

Q. The photograph shows the first version design?

A.   I can't tell what the photograph shows.

Q.   *On the basis of the length of the package, would you agree it was the first version design that was the subject matter of this document [not the third version, as she said in her declaration]?*

A.   *I would agree.*

(Transcript, August 21, 1996 PM, pp. 19-25; emphasis added).

This was important because the longer, first version (the one she swore was not part of the promotion) was an admitted infringement of the Black & Decker patent. Remember the OJ Simpson trial, where the prosecutor asked OJ to put the glove on? He lost control the moment he did that. Not once in my cross-examination of Ms. Lasater did I let her do the measurements. I did that. We proved her declaration was false and that the infringing design had been sold at the promotion.

WITNESS SEVEN -- THE DAMAGES EXPERT WHO TESTIFIED AN EIGHT-CENT ROYALTY PER FLASHLIGHT WAS REASONABLE

Bill Lee was a former law partner of mine who had been hired to testify about a reasonable royalty: his opinion was an 8¢ per-unit royalty was reasonable. But, my son, Raymond, noticed his report referred to an earlier case we had against GSL, where he also said an 8¢ royalty was reasonable. However, a jury in the same Virginia courthouse earlier found a reasonable royalty to be $13.60 per flashlight. Quite a difference:

Q.   Mr. Lee, you are a patent attorney, correct?

A.   Patent and licensing law firm.

Q. Like Mr. Harmon and Mr. Chestnut and his colleagues here, you are with a law firm in Chicago; is that correct?

A. I am of counsel in a law firm, yes.

Q. You are being paid for your time to be here and to prepare and to go through the processes and preparation for your testimony, correct?

A. Yes.

Q. And you have done that, correct?

A. Yes, I have.

Q. And you've been working on this case for a number of months, correct?

A. A few months, yes.

Q. And you have spent in excess of 100 hours working on this, haven't you?

A. I wouldn't think it would be that much, but it could be 50 hours; I am not sure, 50 to 100 hours.

Q. Fifty to a hundred hours. You are paid $300 an hour, so you've been paid $20,000?

A. I don't think I have been paid that much yet, but this month might bring it to that level.

Q. Well, you, on page 12 of your report, refer to the Black [&] Decker v. GSL case, in which the jury awarded royalty damages in the amount of $13.60; is that right?

A.   That is correct. But that has to do with another patent which is not here involved, because the Court has held it not to be infringed by Coleman.

Q.   But you deal in your report with the situation in which a jury in this courthouse awarded Black [&] Decker royalty damages of $13.60 for each infringing flashlight that infringed a patent on the internal [structure] of the SnakeLight; is that right?

A.   I don't know, other than what I have been told, that there was what I consider a royalty far out of line under the ordinary and proper licensing negotiation technology.

Q.   You disagreed with Mr. Arnold's opinion in that matter, is that correct, relating to the '206 [patent]?

A.   You are talking about his testimony today?

Q.   No, in terms of his analysis of reasonable royalties in connection with their patent that is referred to in your report; you disagreed with his conclusion, correct?

A.   Well, his conclusion had no basis --

THE COURT: Can you answer yes or no?

THE WITNESS: I disagree with it, yes.

BY MR. NIRO:

Q.   Your conclusion was that a reasonable royalty in connection with that patent would be 8 cents, just like you have testified to here today, correct?

A.   Yes.

Q.   Mr. Arnold said $13 dollars, correct?

A.   Pardon?

Q.   *Mr. Arnold's opinion was $13 dollars per unit?*

A.   *And I disagreed with that.*

Q.   *You disagreed, you said 8 cents, and he said $13, and the jury said $13.60?*

A.   *That is what I have been informed. I don't know. I know nothing about the GSL, the factors involved in that case.*

Q.   *And in connection with the '392 patent, you say it should be 8 cents, correct?*

A.   *Yes.*

Q.   *And Mr. Arnold says $13.60, correct?*

A.   *He does, and I disagree with that.*

Q.   *And you say 8 cents on the '803 patent and he says $13.60; you disagree with him?*

A.   *And I disagree.*

Q.   *And it would be up to the jury to decide, of course, who they want to accept, if anyone, on this subject, correct?*

A.   *I think that's correct.*

(Transcript, August 21, 1996 PM, pp. 65-66, 70-72; emphasis added). The evidence showed Black & Decker made as much as $14 for each SnakeLight® flashlight. The jury awarded $13.60 (not the 8¢ Mr. Lee thought was reasonable). The table had been run. The case was over, in large part, because of our cross-examination of 7 defense witnesses. Thank you, Raymond, and the rest of the trial team, for giving me the ammunition and inspiration to win on cross-examination.

BAITING THE HOOK

Sufrin v. Hosier,
Civil Action No. 94 C 608 (N.D. Ill., Dec. 1996)

It is not possible to destroy every adverse witness on cross-examination (much as you might want to), but there are times when you can still use cross-examination to set the stage for a later, sometimes fatal, blow to the credibility of that witness based upon the testimony of another witness. I call it "baiting the hook." Sort of a delayed impeachment. Tom Scavone and I still laugh about the delayed impeachment we did in a case about plastic clamps for Ray Wenk's company, Matrix IV. I was cross-examining a witness named Dennis Plesha, the President of Bowthorpe Inc., the opposing party. Bowthorpe had a patent on the plastic clamps; Matrix had a trade secret suit against Bowthorpe. I asked Plesha whether he had ever been accused of misappropriating trade secrets. He said, "No." But, I had misplaced my copy of his deposition transcript where he previously said, "Yes." So I moved on, rather than fumble and bumble. That night, I was beside myself. How could I be so dumb? I had this guy and let him off the hook. Tom was taking another witness the next day and we developed a plan to do the impossible. The cross-examination went something like this (unfortunately, I cannot find the transcript).

Q. Did you hear Mr. Plesha testify yesterday?

A. Yes.

Q. Did you hear him say he had never been accused of taking the trade secrets of his employer?

A. Yes.

Q. Let me read to you Mr. Plesha's deposition testimony:

Question: Were you ever accused of taking a prior employer's trade secrets?

Answer: Yes.

Q. When was Mr. Plesha telling the truth, yesterday or in his prior deposition?

A. I don't know.

We couldn't believe there was no objection.

A "less extreme" example occurred in the trial of <u>Sufrin</u> v. <u>Hosier</u>, a case concerning one of the most unusual law partner disputes in the annals of patent law. Much of the dispute depended upon what Barry Sufrin was told in a critical meeting with the firm's accountant, Paul Duggan. Barry denied he had a meeting.

In 1976, Jerry Hosier and I left Hume, Clement, Hume & Lee (the law firm where we both started as associates in 1967 and 1969, respectively; it is now known as Brinks Hofer) and, because of our experience, became partners in three years. For a time, I feared we would be without any work, but that was not the case: two of the biggest and best clients of the firm came with us. We were off and running. We pioneered contingent-fee representation on a large scale in patent cases.

In 2011, <u>Intellectual Asset Management Magazine</u> said this about me in an article about the top 50 people in intellectual property:

> Disregarding for a moment the controversy surrounding patent trolls (a term apparently coined for him), it would be tough for anyone to deny that patent plaintiffs litigator Ray Niro has made a significant impact in the IP world. He has done this by giving many big businesses something to fear. Before Niro arrived on the scene, all too often large corporations had been able to infringe patents without the fear of any comeback, as the small companies and individuals whose rights they infringed lacked the financial clout to do anything about it. Niro was one of the first lawyers to offer alternative fee arrangements to such entities, even taking stakes in companies in lieu of direct payment. It has made him a very rich man and won him any number of enemies. While Niro may not be to everyone's taste, he blazed what has become a well-trodden trail and in so doing helped to change the way that patents are viewed and used -- no small achievement.

Jerry and I were hugely successful, but life was stressful. Eventually, Jerry left to start his own firm, taking with him one of our associates, Barry Sufrin. Barry was an employee of Hosier & Niro. Jerry offered him a job with his new firm. That led to the formation of Hosier & Sufrin.

Jerry, of course, went on to achieve enormous success and wealth for a prolific (some would say infamous) inventor named Jerome Lemelson. He achieved settlements totaling over $1.5 billion, netting more than $500 million in contingent fees in the process. Not surprisingly, this stunning accomplishment captured the attention of the legal community. In 1994, <u>American Lawyer</u> put a photograph of Jerry on its cover with a fitting backdrop of Aspen Mountain. They called Jerry the richest, most successful patent litigator ever. And he was. In 2001, Forbes magazine listed him as the country's top-earning attorney.

As is often the case, when large sums of money are involved, people come out of the woodwork demanding a share for themselves. (An example is the post-trial litigation to divide the spoils in the RIM case where $600 million was recovered.) This case was no different. Sufrin had a falling out with Hosier in December 1989 and left the firm. But, Sufrin claimed that, because some of the Lemelson contingent-fee matters were pending at the firm while he was still a partner, he was entitled to $70 million of the contingent fee.

The problem for Hosier was that Sufrin's claim had a ring of plausibility. They were 50/50 shareholders in a law firm named "Hosier & Sufrin." And when the two of them started the firm, they created a one-page agreement addressing how they would be compensated. That document (not much more detailed than a "back of the napkin" deal) was hardly a model of clarity. Sufrin was to receive 3/4ths of his "billings" and 1/3rd of the "residual profit"; Hosier was to receive all of his "billings" and 1/4th of Sufrin's "billings," plus 2/3rds of the "residual profit." Just as the proverbial shoemaker's children go barefoot, these two sophisticated lawyers failed to define "billings" and "residual profit"; they also failed to explain how the formula applied to contingent-fee cases.

There was another problem for Hosier: he did not exactly treat Sufrin in a warm and fuzzy manner before -- or after -- his departure. Later, when Sufrin raised accounting issues relating to the wind-up of the firm, Hosier threatened to shut off Sufrin's promised $1 million share of proceeds from another contingent-fee recovery for a client named Telesonics. According to Sufrin, he separately agreed to take only $1 million of $43 million in fees in the Telesonics matter because he believed that Telesonics was already a Hosier client matter before the formation of Hosier & Sufrin. When Sufrin continued to press Hosier on accounting issues, Hosier instructed Telesonics not to pay the remaining sum of the promised $1 million due Sufrin ($419,000), a move that could be described as "playing hardball" or, as Judge Posner called it during the Seventh Circuit oral argument, "extortion."

Sufrin sued Hosier in Chicago, claiming a right to $70 million from the fees generated up to that date from the Lemelson recoveries. He also added a claim for the Telesonics share ($419,000), plus punitive damages. Jerry asked me to represent him (because, as he put it, "I trust you"), and I reluctantly agreed because this was really not my kind of case. Despite our prior differences, Jerry remained a respected friend and he needed help. I could not turn him down.

A jury trial was scheduled to start one week before Christmas 1996 -- not the best time to be defending a lawyer who made hundreds of millions of dollars in a few years. In the weeks before trial, we toyed with paying Sufrin the $419,000 Telesonics money because Hosier's defense to that claim was, in a word, weak. But we elected not to do that in the belief that the jury -- particularly a Christmas jury -- would want to award Sufrin something. Though some viewed that decision as crazy at the time, I saw it as a safety valve to allow the jury to vent any displeasure in a claim that was a very small part of the dispute.

Going into the trial, it was my goal to portray Sufrin as an opportunist who did no work, but still wanted enormous rewards, principally by showing that his interpretation of the agreement was at odds with his dealings with Hosier before, and just after, the breakup. Unfortunately, I got off to a rocky start, as both Hosier and I, apparently, had annoyed the trial judge. Maybe we both made too much money. In any case, my opening statement was abruptly terminated the second the judge clocked me at 20 minutes and then, during my cross-examination of Sufrin, the judge repeatedly sustained objections to my questions. A few examples give the flavor of what was happening:

> Q.   So every one of the 42 clients that went with you no longer became an asset and you left, right?
>
> A.   In the way that you are arguing it, yes, I would say that's correct.
>
> Q.   But it's your position that the three clients that were left with Mr. Hosier were assets of the firm, is that right?
>
> MR. REZNER: Objection, your Honor. Asked and answered.
>
> THE COURT: Sustained.

(Transcript of Proceedings, December 18, 1996, p. 128).

> Q.   But after you left, you believe Jerry Hosier's contingent fee billings were an asset of the firm, correct?
>
> MR. REZNER: Objection, your Honor. Asked and answered.
>
> THE COURT: Sustained.

(Transcript of Proceedings, December 18, 1996, p. 129).

> Q.   So the answer is you don't believe that you have any obligation to pay any money of any kind for any work

that you did after you left the firm to Jerry Hosier, correct?

MR. REZNER: Objection, your Honor. Asked and answered.

THE COURT: Sustained.

⚜ ⚜ ⚜ ⚜ ⚜

Q.   And it was only the one-page document, the one page agreement that governed your relationship with Jerry Hosier, is that correct?

MR. REZNER: Objection, your Honor. Asked and answered.

THE COURT: Sustained.

BY MR. NIRO: Q. Am I correct that it's that agreement that defines how you would divide the profits from the law firm when you practiced there together?

MR. REZNER: Objection, your Honor. Asked and answered.

THE COURT: Sustained.

(Transcript of Proceedings, December 18, 1996, pp 130-131).

I simply could not get any traction with this trial judge. So I turned to the fact that Sufrin's prior lawyers had prepared a draft complaint that did not square with his claim now. The judge also shut this down:

Q.   Well, Mr. Flaherty prepared a complaint on your behalf, didn't he?

MR. REZNER: Objection, your Honor. Relevancy.

THE COURT: Sustained.

BY MR. NIRO: Q. Am I correct that Mr. Flaherty prepared a complaint on your behalf in which he did not name Jerry Hosier as a defendant?

MR. REZNER: Objection, your Honor.

THE COURT: Now, I sustained the objection as irrelevant and you went ahead and asked the question again, as you've done several times, Mr. Niro. *I am warning you*.

I ask the jury to disregard the question.

(Transcript, December 18, 1996, p. 143; emphasis added). *Things were getting tense*.

I decided to go where I could not get cut off: Sufrin's annual settlement of amounts due under the agreement, typically done in a meeting with the firm's accountant, Paul Duggan. I love Paul. A big, likeable Irishman from the South Side of Chicago. This was an area I wanted the jury to remember when Duggan took the stand later -- first, we had to set the hook:

Q. Mr. Sufrin, I'm going to ask you a question about how this contract is handled each year.

Am I correct at the end of each year there would be a settlement under this contract between you and Mr. Hosier?

A. I don't know if the word "settlement" is correct, but after the end of each year the calculations would be run and checks would be cut as appropriate under the agreement.

Q. And Mr. Duggan was involved in that process?

A.   Yes, he was.

Q.   And under the contract as it existed, if there had been a wind-up, then that would have ended Mr. Hosier's obligations, is that right?

A.   It would have ended both of our obligations.

Q.   So if you had met with Mr. Duggan and followed the normal procedure in 1990, then that would be the end of it, correct?

A.   I didn't meet with Mr. Hosier, that is Ed Hosier, would give him the numbers and he'd run the numbers from what Ed Hosier gave him.

Q.   You never met with Mr. Duggan at the end of each year?

A.   The end of each year? No, I might have met with him at the end of one year, but it was more or less a procedure that he was doing.

〰 〰 〰 〰 〰

Q.   Mr. Sufrin, you testified about your meetings with Paul Duggan and the fact that you had at one point in time him [sic] I think you said drop a bunch of documents on you in a jumbled fashion, do you recall that?

A.   Yes, he dropped off a bunch of documents.

Q.   *Is it your testimony that you never personally met with Paul Duggan in your offices at Laff in 1990?*

A.   *I received the documents from him at my offices at Laff. I don't believe that I had any kind of meeting with him.*

Q.   *That is your testimony and belief, right?*

A. *To the best of my recollection, yes.*

Q. And it is your testimony that it was Mr. Duggan and not you that suggested that all you wanted was the hourly value of your time in the Mattel cases, assuming there were any recoveries?

A. That is indeed my testimony.

(Transcript of Proceedings, December 18, 1996, pp. 143-144, 156; emphasis added).

This was not high drama, nor was it any sort of immediate, knock-out punch. But, the jury was just starting to grapple with the claim and the personalities. Sufrin seemed to be a sympathetic witness, and his wife and children were sitting in the front row. Yet, this seemingly innocuous line of questioning would later prove vital for several reasons. First, Sufrin had denigrated the importance of his meetings with the firm accountant, Paul Duggan, and even suggested there was no meeting whatsoever after the breakup. Second, this heightened the importance of Duggan's later testimony. Third, if the jury believed Duggan, Sufrin's credibility would take a serious blow.

But, there were several more stops on the way to Duggan's testimony, and my struggles continued. Sufrin's counsel called to the stand a purported licensing expert, Stanton Hadley, who opined that 80% of the royalties achieved by Hosier for the Lemelson patents were attributable to a contingent-fee engagement for the so-called "CIA patents" signed before Sufrin left the firm. This was an important issue because the CIA patents were a small subset of Lemelson's patent portfolio, the entirety of which Lemelson retained Hosier to enforce after Sufrin departed.

On cross-examination, I established that efforts to license the CIA patents alone had been unsuccessful:

Q. Well, when Mr. Lemelson and Mr. Hosier tried to license those patents alone in 1989, in 1990, in 1991 and in 1998 -- I'm sorry '88, '89, '90 and '91, no license was signed by any licensee, isn't that correct?

A. That's correct.

Q. And no royalty income was derived, isn't that correct?

A. That's correct.

Q. Under these engagement letters called the CIA engagement, isn't that correct?

A. That's correct.

Q. They got zero royalty income, correct?

A. Yes.

Q. And it was only after the 12/3/91 entire patent portfolio license engagement that there was success in licensing the Lemelson technology, isn't that correct, sir?

A. I would say that success might have ensued had further time been allowed with the negotiations that went on for the CIA patents alone. So the fact that the other patents were thrown in and then a license was signed, in my view, was not decisive.

Q. Am I correct, sir, that it was not until -- it was only after the 12/3/91 engagement that any of the monies that are claimed in this case for the licensing of the entire portfolio patents, that any for those royalties were achieved, isn't that correct?

A. That is correct.

(Transcript of Proceedings, December 19, 1996, pp. 232-233). But then I encountered more trouble:

> Q. And you, of course, know that before Mr. Hosier represented Mr. Lemelson, he had very little success either in court or in the licensing of his patents, isn't that right?
>
> A. That's my understanding.
>
> Q. In fact, Mr. Laff, Barry Sufrin's partner, said he was a loser, isn't that correct?
>
> MR. REZNER: Objection, your Honor.
>
> THE COURT: I'll see you at sidebar.

(Sidebar conference had out of the hearing of the jury)

> THE COURT: A number of the questions that you have been asking this witness you have asked with no foundation whatsoever. *I am admonishing you not to continue*.
>
> MR. NIRO: Okay, your Honor.

(Proceedings resumed within the hearing of the jury)

> THE COURT: The last question is stricken as improper.
>
> BY MR. NIRO: Q. In your preparation for your testimony in this case, did you review deposition testimony of any witness?
>
> A. Yes, I did.
>
> Q. Did you review the deposition testimony of Mr. Laff?
>
> A. I did not.

THE COURT: *I told you not to go forward with that*.

(Transcript of Proceedings, December 19, 1996, pp. 235-236; emphasis added). This was the cross-examination of an expert. What is so bad about asking him what he did in preparation? Did he talk to Laff? Did he read his deposition? Incredible. I moved on.

While I was able to take some shots at Hadley's methodology, I was also stymied in my attempt to introduce the key fact that the CIA patents were ultimately held to be unenforceable:

Q.   Now, the CIA patents that you referenced as being the 19 patents that are part of the engagement that took place before Mr. Sufrin left the firm, those CIA patents have now been held unenforceable by a United States District Court, is that correct?

MR. REZNER: Objection, your Honor. Lack of foundation.

THE COURT: Sustained.

Move on.

(Transcript of Proceedings, December 19, 1996, pp. 252-253; emphasis added). This was an expert. He surely knew this critical fact; if he didn't, that was significant also:

Q.   Did you consider whether the validity or enforceability of those patents had been challenged by any of the parties that you mentioned, Chrysler or Ford or Motorola?

A.   I considered the fact that they had been challenged by most of the licensees through their files, all the way back to the earliest context, and certainly it was challenged in lawsuits.

Q. You relied upon, and I think you had before you, pleadings that you looked at from the Ford case, correct?

A. Yes, I do.

Q. And you're aware, are you, that Ford challenged the enforceability of the CIA patents, correct?

A. Yes.

Q. And what was the result of that challenge?

MR. REZNER: Objection, your Honor. Relevancy.

THE COURT: Sustained.

(Transcript of Proceedings, December 19, 1996, pp. 253-254). Not only was this relevant, it showed the CIA patents had no value -- they were unenforceable. The judge was making things difficult. Sometimes that happens. My advice: *let it blow by you like the wind*.

Next up was Sufrin's damage expert, who opined that Sufrin was entitled to damages in the amount of $72 million. At the close of Sufrin's case, I asked for a sidebar and attempted to present our motion for judgment as a matter of law, and the following exchange occurred:

MR. NIRO: We would like to present our motion at the end of the plaintiff's case.

THE COURT: All right. *I will consider it presented and denied*.

MR. NIRO: We have a written motion.

THE COURT: Well, there is not time for me to review it, much less opposing counsel to review it and to argue it.

MR. NIRO: Well, I would like to file it.

THE COURT: **Well, no, you may not** because we have not been given notice. We have not had a chance to review it. Nor has counsel had an opportunity to respond to it. You may submit it at the end of the case and give it to counsel so he has a chance to review it and argue it.

MR. NIRO: Your Honor, we do not waive any of our rights with respect to the JMOL at the conclusion of the case.

THE COURT: Well, I --

MR. NIRO: There is a danger, and this is our concern, that we would be put in a position of waiving if we do not move formally and have some record of that.

THE COURT: Well, you have moved orally. I have considered your oral motion and I have paid close attention to the evidence. I think the plaintiff has made a prima facie case as to all his claims.

(Transcript of Proceedings, December 19, 1996, p. 302; emphasis added). I won't say here what I was thinking.

After I recounted the bases for the motion, the judge made clear what she thought about it (and perhaps me):

THE COURT: I find that the defendant's motion is predicated on mischaracterization of the record, upon misconstruction of the law in that it views the evidence and credibility issues in the light most favorable to the defendant, which of course is improper. Instead of viewing the evidence and the inferences reasonably drawn from the evidence in the light most favorable to the plaintiff, which is the proper standard at this junction. The motion is denied.

(Transcript of Proceedings, December 19, 1996, pp. 304-305). Hopefully, I was on better paper with the jury at that point.

Jerry Hosier then took the stand. From the jury's reaction, Hosier's testimony was a mixed bag; it was difficult to put a positive spin on some of the things that had happened in the course of the firm's break-up. On the other hand, the jury seemed to get the fact that Sufrin's acceptance of $1 million of the Telesonics recovery did not square with his claim for a share of the Lemelson recoveries. As I saw it, that claim would stand or fall on our next witness, Paul Duggan.

The battleground was an alleged May 21, 1990 meeting between Duggan and Sufrin. Sufrin claimed that there was no meeting with Duggan; Duggan simply dropped off a "jumble of papers" containing proposals which Duggan initiated. And Sufrin had to do that dance because there was a suggestion in that jumble of papers that Sufrin wanted to be paid on an hourly basis for the limited time he had spent on contingent-fee cases. The May 21, 1990 meeting was looming so large that I served Duggan with a trial subpoena the night before he testified, calling for him to bring his time records to court. I knew that there would be an evidentiary brouhaha about the issue but, hopefully, the jury would get the message that there were contemporaneous records of the meeting. A written record of an actual meeting would undermine Sufrin's claim that none took place.

The jury immediately took to Duggan. He is a big, likeable Irishman from the south side of Chicago, and I highlighted that background up front: Brother Rice High School; Loyola University; starting his own CPA firm three years after graduation. The jury also heard that Duggan considered himself to be a friend of both Hosier and Sufrin. I then walked him through each year-end calculation that he performed for the firm, undercutting the notion that Sufrin was entitled to a portion of Hosier's contingent-fee billings. I was trying to build as much drama as one can with an accountant's testimony to the climax of the May 21, 1990 meeting, and we finally got there:

Q. Now, Barry Sufrin has testified in this case that it was you that suggested to him that you should value his time in the Mattel case and do this calculation in the way that you've indicated. Is that correct or incorrect?

A. That's incorrect, and I just know that from my note that I have in my file.

Q. Explain that to us.

A. I met with Barry Sufrin on the 21st of May 1990. I went to his office at Laff, Whitesel. In fact, I pulled my time sheets out yesterday to verify that I went there on that day.

MR. REZNER: Objection, your Honor.

THE COURT: Sustained.

MR. REZNER: I move that answer be stricken.

THE COURT: It's stricken.

BY MR. NIRO: Q. Let's begin with the page 001278 from Exhibit 17. It says question "BWS 5/21 '90." Are those your notes?

A.   Yes.

Q.   What do they reference in terms of the circumstances of your preparing those notes?

A.   This was a request made by Barry at the end of the meeting to resolve the issue so the year-end could be put to rest.

Q.   All right.

A.   And I took the notes, made a phone call to [J]erry Hosier and he said "pass," meaning he said I'll pass on it until Dr. Gol[d]berg pays [h]is bill.

Q.   Yesterday Barry Sufrin testified that he didn't meet with you in 1990, that you only dropped off jumbled papers. Is that correct or incorrect?

A.   That's incorrect.

Q.   Approximately how long did you meet with Barry Sufrin on May 21, 1990?

A.   Three hours.

Q.   How do you know that?

A.   I reviewed my time sheets.

MR. REZNER: Objection, your Honor.

THE COURT: Unless you produce these.

MR. REZNER: Can I ask this be stricken?

THE COURT: Yes, it is stricken.

(Transcript of Proceedings, December 19, 1996, pp. 442-444). This again reminds me of the movie "The Verdict." The nurse kept her own copy of the admittance record and it said the patient had eaten 1 hour before admittance. The physician charged with giving a general anesthetic shortly after the patient had eaten forced her to change 1 to 9. The written record and the testimony from the nurse won the case for Paul Newman (see p. 146.).

> BY MR. NIRO: Q. Mr. Duggan, were you requested in the subpoena that was served on you to appear here today to bring with you time records?

A.   Yes.

Q.   Did you bring them along?

A.   Yes.

Q.   Do you have them here?

A.   Yes.

> THE COURT: Have you furnished them to counsel?

> MR. NIRO: We have them now, your Honor, that is the extent to which we have them. I don't have them.

> THE COURT: All right. Well, we'll take that into account when we schedule cross-examination of this witness.

> BY MR. NIRO: Q. Do you have them physically with you?

A.   Yes, I do.

> MR. NIRO: Your Honor, may I offer them at this time? Not into evidence but --

> THE COURT: No, you are not going to be offering them but you will be making them available to counsel at the close of this session.

MR. NIRO: Okay.

BY MR. NIRO: Q. Based on those records, can you tell us why it is that you know that you spent three hours?

A.   It's indicated on my time sheet for that day as to what I did, where I did it and who I did it with.

Q.   Who does it indicate that you met with?

A.   Barry Sufrin, from 10:00 o'clock in the morning until 1:00 p.m.

Q.   Where did you meet with him?

A.   Laff, Whitesel.

Q.   Were the papers that you presented to him jumbled?

A.   Not that I recall.

Q.   Do these notes indicate in any way what was said during the course of that meeting?

A.   Yes.

Q.   Now, the area I want to focus you on is called "gross up John S.L.'s time on" maybe you better read this.

A.   "on Lemel" L-e-m-e-l.

Q.   "Lemel"?

A.   "Lemel at Stan" for standard rates "…and add to associate billing."

Q.   Who was it, if anyone, that told you to do that?

A.   Barry. It was Barry's request at that meeting, that I was understating associate profit. Or in fact, my first calculation showed that there was a loss on this residual profits. And he said there won't be a loss if you add that back.

Q.   Did you redo that calculation?

A.   Yes, I did.

❖ ❖ ❖ ❖ ❖

Q.   Let me ask you this, at any time that you've known Barry Sufrin and worked for Hosier & Sufrin, that firm, did he ever suggest to you in words or substance that he was entitled to any portion of contingent fees that were earned and billed by [J]erry Hosier?

A.   No.

Q.   Did he ever suggest to you, in words or in substance, that he was entitled to any contingent fee billings for work that he didn't do?

A.   No.

Q.   Did Barry say anything to you when he left the firm as to what kind of work he wanted to do?

A.   My recollection is Barry said he was going to do hourly work and [J]erry was going to do contingent fee work. He took the hourly clients.

(Transcript of Proceedings, December 19, 1996, pp. 442-446, 448). We were done for the evening, but the jury had not actually seen the May 21 time sheet. So that night, I had that document blown up into a large poster board. *I would take a chance*.

The next morning, on re-direct, I immediately turned to the May 21 meeting, this time, with a large, blown-up exhibit of the time sheet in hand:

BY MR. NIRO: Q. Mr. Duggan, since we're on the issue of friendship here, you consider Barry Sufrin to be a friend.

A. Yes. I haven't seen Barry since May 21st, 1990 until yesterday, but I always considered Barry my friend.

Q. You testified on cross-examination that what Barry Sufrin asked for on Mattel was the hourly rate value of his time. When did he say that to you?

A. Looking at my notes the first time I received that information from Barry would have been April 6th of 1990, in terms of the physical numbers. So that would be the first time I can say with assurance that he raised the issue.

Q. Was that discussed at the May 21, 1990 meeting?

A. Absolutely.

Q. And yesterday you produced for us and for Mr. Rezner your actual time entry records is that correct?

MR. REZNER: Objection, your Honor. Scope.

THE COURT: I haven't heard the complete question. Would you finish the question. Don't answer until I hear the question.

BY MR. NIRO: Q. I would like to put before you your time records.

THE COURT: Well, those were not the subject of cross-examination.

MR. NIRO: I think that he asked about the time and date and circumstances of when Barry asked for on the Mattel matter the hourly value. I want to establish that date through his notes, if I may.

THE COURT: I'll have to hear the question. All right. Go ahead.

MR. NIRO: Thank you.

BY MR. NIRO: [Placing board of the May 21 timesheet on a tripod before the jury] Q. Let me just show you if I may, Mr. Duggan, the time entry page -- You have those notes in front of you?

MR. REZNER: I object, your Honor, to the use of these documents in the way that I don't think I can handle outside sidebar.

THE COURT: Are those in evidence?

MR. NIRO: We don't propose to put them in evidence, your Honor.

THE COURT: Well, then, don't put it in front of the jury if it is not in evidence.

MR. NIRO: I would ask, your Honor, then, that this document, the notes which were subpoenaed and produced by Mr. Duggan yesterday for both parties, be introduced in evidence.

THE COURT: No, they are not part of the pretrial order. They were not properly marked. No.

⚕ ⚕ ⚕ ⚕ ⚕

Q. Was it at the meeting of May 21, 19- -- was it at that meeting of May 21, 1990 that Mr. Sufrin again said to you that what he wanted on Mattel was the hourly rate value for the time he had spent?

A. Yes.

MR. NIRO: I've nothing further. Thank you.

(Transcript of Proceedings, December 20, 1996, pp. 485-486, 488). Though the May 21st timesheet was never introduced into evidence, the jury had a good look at the three-hour entry: "Meeting with Barry Sufrin."

There was additional testimony in the trial, but Duggan's testimony about the meeting -- coupled with Sufrin's evasiveness about it -- doomed the $70 million claim.

I returned to the issue in closing, because I wanted to be certain that the jury remembered the conflict in testimony:

> Remember Barry Sufrin's testimony about May 21, 1990? I asked him "Do you deny meeting with Paul Duggan in 1990?" And he said yes, he dropped off a bunch of papers and they were jumbled, we had a meeting with him. Paul Duggan came in and he said "I met with him. Do you know why I met with him, and I know why I met with him, because I got a time record that shows I met with him." Why would Barry Sufrin lie about a meeting in May of 1990 with Paul Duggan where Paul Duggan has records that show what he did? And Barry Sufrin says well, that's not true. Why would he lie about that? Because at that meeting Barry Sufrin said I'm not entitled to one-third of Mattel or any of the other cases, just give me the hourly value of my time, that's what he said.
>
> Let's talk about the meeting itself. Duggan has notes, "5/21/90, BWS" Barry Sufrin. He has questions. Are these questions that [J]erry Hosier would ask? Barry Sufrin said, by the way, it was Paul Duggan that told me I should take the hourly value of my time and not my one-third, and I told him pass. But Paul Duggan said that's not true, Barry Sufrin said I'll take the hourly value of my time.

✦ ✦ ✦ ✦ ✦

Now, it's been said -- and I think I'm about out of time -- it's been said that the cruelest lies are told in silence. And think of silence here. Barry Sufrin says I'm entitled to one-third. But did he say that to Bruce Sperling? ... Did he say it to Paul Duggan, the accountant? Did he say it to [J]erry Hosier? And if Barry Sufrin hadn't remained silent, he admitted [J]erry Hosier could have said that's it, let's go our separate ways right now in 1987 or 1989. But he didn't do that. He could have said let's modify the agreement now, what's done is done.

(Transcript of Proceedings, December 23, 1996, pp. 720-721, 728).

I also had to get my grandchildren into the closing. Sufrin's case was based upon "make believe" scenarios and I hit hard on that, referring to basketball games when kids get to "make believe" they are NBA stars:

... You know, I'm blessed with eight grandchildren. Six of them are six years old and under. And two of the boys I take over to the Union League Club on Saturdays occasionally. And they like to play basketball up on the 21st floor with the reduced-size baskets. And the six year old wants to be Michael Jordan, so does the four year old, but the six year old, being more persuasive says, I'll be Michael Jordan, you be Scottie Pippin. And I watch them pretend to be Michael Jordan and Scottie Pippin. And that's what children do; they pretend. They engage in make believe. And it's a wonderful world to make believe especially at this time of year. But Barry's Sufrin's case, when you think about it, when it comes down to its essentials, has a make-believe part to it. Remember the Example A that Mr. Rezner showed you and said this is the way the contract should be interpreted? What case was he talking about? What case? What case for which they now ask forty-six million dollars did Barry Sufrin do half the work in? Because that is the assumption in the make-believe case. He did the same amount of work that Jerry Hosier did, five hundred hours and they collected a half a million dollars and they go through the calculation. That case never happened. And in the real world, Jerry Hosier spent eleven thousand hours, thirty thousand hours plus of time of other lawyers, a commitment of five million dollars to other lawyers and experts, a total commitment of ten million dollars in expenses. That's the real world.

(Transcript of Proceedings, December 23, 1996, pp. 715-716). I wanted to cast Hosier as a superstar who earned his money through hard work (he was the Michael Jordan of patent litigation):

Michael Jordan didn't get to be Michael Jordan by dealing with hypotheticals. He had to perform and he performs every night to earn the fifty or seventy million dollars he makes. And so did Jerry Hosier. He performed for Mr. Lemelson. And he performed well for him, as Mr. Lemelson himself said and as Mr. Hadley said, he is the best licensing lawyer I have ever seen, the most successful and the best at what he does. But he didn't get there by accident. He had to work hard. He had to dedicate his life to doing that. He negotiated 63 licenses and got 537 million dollars for his client. ... Make believe in a child's world is okay because nobody gets hurt, but it has no place in a federal courtroom. And there is no basis for an award of 46 million dollars in this case.

(Transcript of Proceedings, December 23, 1996, pp. 716-717). I ended with the testimony of Paul Duggan and our theme -- Hosier did the work, not Sufrin:

I would just like to end by saying this, Barry Sufrin

wrote these words. He created this contract. He knew what they meant and he never modified them. They modified them in this courtroom, just as is shown here in red. Year end and year out he agreed to what Paul Duggan did. He sat with Paul Duggan and told him what to do. There isn't a letter, a memo, a note that says Paul, you're doing the wrong thing here. In 1993 it all changed. And in the end, this case really comes down to what is right or wrong. The world of make believe is a wonderful place for children, but it doesn't have a place here. And you don't take people's property away from them and you don't take what they've earned away from them on the basis of some phony cases somebody creates here.

What is right here is that Jerry Hosier did the work, he was never told, ever, that Barry Sufrin said he was entitled to a third of the contingent fees. And he is not entitled to 47 million or 4 million or 400,000 or a dollar because he didn't do the work. He is not entitled to something for nothing. Thank you very much, ladies and gentlemen.

(Transcript, December 23, 1996, pp. 729-730).

The jury deliberated for four hours on December 23 and returned its verdict: for Hosier on Sufrin's claim for $70 million, and for Sufrin for the $419,000 Telesonics money plus $419,000 in punitive damages. Though it was technically a split decision, in reality, it was a big win for Jerry Hosier. And the key to it all was setting the hook with Barry Sufrin, getting him to say he did not meet with Paul Duggan for three hours when Duggan's time records (which Sufrin did not know existed) had showed that he did.

Jerry was happy, and we flew to Aspen that evening on his Gulfstream 3 (he now has a Gulfstream 550).

THE SPACE MAN COMES
BACK TO EARTH

Black & Decker Inc., et al. v. **Robert Bosch Tool Corp.,**
Civil Action No. 04 C 7955 (N.D. Ill., Sept. 2006)

Joe Domes was a carpenter in upstate New York. He was a simple man. But he invented something unique -- a radio charger that construction workers could use for news or entertainment that alternatively could be powered by, or could charge, power tool batteries. It sounds simple, but no one had the idea before Joe.

Black & Decker/DeWalt purchased Joe Domes' patent for $3 million, making him a wealthy man. Bosch, a DeWalt rival, infringed the patent.

A DeWalt executive, Christine Potter, explained the product's success:

Q. It mentions up at the top part, as well, "This Charger Rocks." That was the theme of this advertising?

A. Yes, and it still is the theme of the product.

Q. Why did you say, "This Charger Rocks"?

A. We thought it was a great way to communicate the new innovative feature, that now you could charge your batteries while listening to your radio, and thought it was a great way to capture the essence of the product.

Q. Now, DeWalt introduced this in the spring of '99, you say?

A. Yes.

Q. And was it a hit?

A. Yes, it was.

Q. What happened in terms of sales, let's say, in the first six months?

A. Well, in the first six months we sold about $17 million worth of the product.

Q. How about the first year?

A. About $24 million.

Q. And what have the sales been to date, let's say, just in the last six years?

A. Well, from the introduction up until the present, we've sold over $140 million of this product.

Q. Over $140 million worth of sales of this product alone?

A. Yes, of the radio charger.

Q. Does the product, as you understand it -- the radio charger -- help you sell power tools, as well?

A. Yes, it does.

Q. Why is that?

A. Well, because, again, customers value that idea of a cordless system and it saves time and money if you can interchange your batteries amongst a variety of different products.

So, the radio charger fits wonderfully into that system because of that interchangeability. And you can also use the radio charger to help sell other products.

From time to time, we've run promotions. For example, the combination kit on the table, it would sell typically for $500; and, for periods of time, we've done promotions where, if you bought that kit, you could mail a coupon to DeWalt and subsequently get a free radio charger.

And we see tremendous sales increase as people value that system.

Q.   All right. So, the radio charger may help sell power tools and vice versa?

A.   Yes. We hear, quite frequently, that people buy into a system and they like to standardize their equipment. If you have multiple different types of batteries, you've always got to worry about, "Do I have the right one charged;" where, if you standardize on the battery, you always know you have the right one charged and you're ready to go.

(Transcript, September 13, 2006, pp. 200-202).

To say Joe Domes was a character is an understatement. He went through the eleventh grade, quit school, joined the Navy and learned construction. His grandfather worked for Thomas Edison, so he had some family history with invention. He described his excitement with his late-night conception of his idea and waking up his wife to tell her about it:

Q.   ... Now, let's go to the heart of this whole thing. I want to ask you to tell the jury, in your own words, how you came up with the ideas that resulted in these two patents. Just explain it to them like it happened.

A.   Well, it was in December, 1996. I was remodeling our kitchen; and, after I cleaned up and finished what I had to do, the only thing on the table was a beat up old radio that I had and a Makita drill -- cordless drill.

And I kept getting up adjusting the volume; and, you know, it was -- it had no antenna and all that stuff. And then I sat back down and I looked at it and I said, "I can put these two together to make them rugged for a jobsite."

So, I basically just put two and two together and, you know, got a gut feeling in me and put them together.

Q.   What year was that?

A.   That was '96 -- December, '96.

Q.   1996. It was December?

A.   Yes, it was.

Q.   Was it around Christmas time?

A.   It was just before Christmas. We were trying to get everything finished.

Q.   How late at night was it?

A.   It was, like, 3:00 o'clock in the morning.

Q.   Why were you working so late?

A.   To try to get it ready for my wife to start decorating the next day.

Q. And you were working on your kitchen?

A. Yes, I was.

Q. What was the problem, as you saw it, that had to be solved by this whole thing?

A. Well, the problem was, you know, on my jobsites, the radio, you know, falls off the shelf or ladder or something; it breaks; you got duct tape you got to roll around it.

The first thing that breaks is the antenna. So, you would have to stick a piece of wire in it or something. The cord would break out or something like that.

And, you know, I just figured, "Make it like an ABS plastic," something hard, rigid, that will hold up to my jobs because my guys were -- some of my guys were -- pretty bad with the radios.

Q. What about the idea of having an AC plug to power the radio and charging batteries at the same time? How did you come up with that?

A. Well, because we always had a charger that was always separate and you had to have different chargers for different batteries at the time. So, I put the radio and the battery charger inside the radio.

Q. Were you excited about this idea?

A. I was very excited, yeah.

Q. What did you do?

A. Well, I went upstairs and I woke my wife up and I told her that I had a great idea and she said, "Tell me in the morning. Go to bed."

(Transcript, September 14, 2006, pp. 375-377).

Joe also described his search for a patent attorney. He saw the advertisements on television but, as he put it, he wanted to find a lawyer who actually had an office in a building:

Q.　Now, Mr. Domes, you had the idea. You drew it up. You had some drawings. What did you do next, in terms of going forward with this whole thing?

A.　I asked a friend of mine if he knew a lawyer that -- a patent lawyer, because I didn't want to do anything on TV -- you know, the lawyers on TV. So, he gave me a number and I called my lawyer. ...

Q.　You had seen some lawyers on TV?

A.　Yeah.

Q.　Patent lawyers?

A.　You know, you don't want to -- Daley said, "Don't go near them."

Q.　It's news to me.

A.　So, I didn't.

(Laughter.)

BY MR. R. NIRO:

Q.　*But you didn't go to the guys you saw on TV?*

A.　*No, I went to a lawyer that had a building.*

(Transcript, September 14, 2006, pp. 385-386; emphasis added).

My favorite part of this case, however, was the cross-examination of Bosch's expert, Professor Paul Horowitz from Harvard University. I began with his keen interest in tracking extra-terrestrial beings from outer space:

Q.   In your report, you identify some of the [] various articles that you've written on, "SET Pioneers," "Interview in the SETI Factor," "High Resolution SETI Experience." "SETI" means search for [extra] terrestrial intelligence, right?

A.   Do [you] want to try that, again?

Q.   Why don't you tell me what it means?

A.   "The Search For Extraterrestrial Intelligence."

Q.   Sorry about that. Extraterrestrial. That's "ET" -- they made the movie on ET?

A.   Yeah, ET is the middle here (indicating).

Q.   I see.

A.   "ET" is my middle name.

Q.   And you built an 84-foot tower at Harvard University looking for radio contact with extraterrestrial beings in outer space, right?

A.   No. Actually, the radio telescope was already there.

Q.   You're operating it?

A.   Not anymore.

Q.   You had graduate students working on this project?

A.   Yes, I did.

Q.   And you have written articles on the subject, right?

A.   Yes, I have.

Q.   Numerous articles?

A.   Well, several.

GO FOR IT!

Q. "Radio Search For Extraterrestrial" -- I'm sorry, I can't pronounce that word -- "ET Intelligence," right?

A. Yes.

Q. And "The Great ET Debate, Meyer and Horowitz Discuss the Search For Intelligent Life Elsewhere," right?

A. Yes, indeed.

Q. Am I correct, Professor, that one of the articles talked about a radio search -- a radio search -- for ET intelligence, right?

A. Yes. This was at a conference, yes.

Q. You actually wrote this (indicating), correct?

A. Yes. It may have been transcribed from a talk. I'm not sure.

Q. Okay. And one of the things you did is -- for getting all the equations -- you have a theory on galactic communication via microwaves; is that right?

A. Yes. This (indicating) shows the amazing fact that you could communicate to any of the million nearest stars for a dollar per word.

Q. All right. And "Inter-Stellar Telegrams Are Cheap"?

A. Yes. That's was actually drawn by my mentor, Purcell.

Q. In this article, I think they show -- or you show -- the actual 84-foot tower that you built or somebody built, right?

A. Where are you going with this? Yes, that is -- I did not build the tower. That dish was there, as I said.

Q.   Okay. I'm just going to finish it real fast. Am I correct that one of your colleagues at Harvard sharply criticized your work, saying it was a waste of the University's money and a waste of the resources of the graduate students there?

A.   Yes.

Q.   That was Professor Meyer?

A.   Yes.

Q.   He said, "The search for intelligent life on other worlds is a waste of time and money," right?

A.   I think he said it was a deplorable waste of the taxpayers' money; but, perhaps, I should tell you about the petition, or at least --

THE COURT: Dr. Horowitz, just answer the question that is posed, please.

THE WITNESS: Okay.

BY MR. R. NIRO:

Q.   He said, "The chance of success is virtually nil"?

A.   He said that, yes.

Q.   All right. And you have even described what you think these ET beings are going to look like, right?

A.   I don't remember, but I'm happy to entertain whatever you've got there.

Q.   *"I guess we're narrowing our search to civilizations that are not only smart, but also are able to construct the technological paraphernalia to communicate; but, they don't have to have two hands that match; and, if they go around on wheels, that's okay," right?*

A.   ***Yeah. Sounds like me.***

(Transcript, September 21, 2006, pp. 1672-1676). Crazy. They go around on wheels and don't have two hands that match.

Professor Horowitz couldn't let it go. On redirect, he addressed me -- he was going to make me a believer:

BY MR. TREMBATH:

Q.   All right. Let's start with probably the most interesting topic, SETI -- "Search For Extraterrestrial Intelligence." Could you tell the jury what that's all about? Are you looking for ET?

A.   It's close to lunch. Let me keep it brief. There's every reason to believe that what happened on the ordinary planet, circling probably an ordinary star in a galaxy of a hundred -- 400 billion stars, 400 billion in a universe of a hundred billion such galaxies happened elsewhere.

There is life elsewhere in the universe. There's every reason to believe that evolutionary processes happen there, too. And, therefore, there's every reason to believe that there's advanced civilizations out there, some much more advanced than we. We are ordinary.

Technology now permits communication between civilizations over these distances. This is understood. It's a fact. It's not a supposition. It's not conjecture. We can do it with radio waves, if there's someone to communicate with. And, likewise, with lasers.

SETI is the scientific search for signals of such sorts; and, it's been endorsed by -- every decade by -- the astronomical communities that review; it's been high on their priority list; it's been endorsed by a number of signatories to a petition in 1982, including seven Nobel Prize winners; and, including those who don't think it's going to succeed, like my friend Ben Zuckerman and many other places.

This is good science and you can make fun of it. Have a good time. But it's one of the greatest questions that can be asked.

And when the answer comes, you'll change your tune, Mr. Niro.

(Laughter.)

MR. R. NIRO: *I didn't realize I asked a question.*

(Transcript, September 21, 2006, pp. 1708-1710; emphasis added). I had completely unnerved the guy. And the jury was getting it.

Professor Horowitz did an experiment to prove there was no infringement. But I showed it did not work (thanks to my son, Dean) -- it actually destroyed the radio:

Q. Professor, you did some surgery on this radio (indicating), right?

A. Yes, I'm now another kind of doctor, I guess.

Q. All right. Indeed. Do you want to show the jury how you can operate the radio now on battery power?

A. I cannot operate the radio anymore.

Q. You can't operate it?

A. It's been -- it's had --

Q. It's been killed?

A. One critical component has been removed from the radio.

Q. I see. And if I try to run it on AC power, it won't operate?

A. No, because I took out something that was part of the radio.

Q. I see. So, by taking out the switch, you prevent this radio (indicating) from operating the way it was intended to operate, correct?

A. Let me answer carefully.

Q. Is that "Yes" or "No"? I don't want a speech.

A. I am not going to give you "Yes" or "No."

Q. Okay. I am going to ask you one more time. If you can't answer it "Yes" or "No," you tell me why you can't answer it "Yes" or "No." By taking out that switch (indicating), you have disabled this radio to operate the way it was intended to operate; "Yes" or "No"?

A. I will give you a "Yes."

Q. Pardon?

A. I will give you a "yes" on that.

Q. Okay. And by removing the voltage regulator, you prevent this radio from operating the way it was intended to operate, correct?

A. Do you want a "Yes" or "No," again?

Q. Yes.

A. [I]f I take it out of the radio, yes, it will not operate.

Q. *Okay. So, to put it in surgical terms, if you were a physician, you killed the patient, right?*

A.   *Well, the surgery was successful, but the patient died.*

(Transcript, <u>Black & Decker</u> v. <u>Bosch</u>, Civil Action No. 04 C 7955 (N.D. Ill.), September 21, 2006, pp. 1665-1666; emphasis added). Things got tense because I wanted yes or no answers and Professor Horowitz simply could not do that:

> MR. R. NIRO: Your Honor, I am going to ask him to answer, so we can finish sometime this week.
>
> BY MR. R. NIRO:
>
> Q.   "Yes" or "No"?
>
> A.   No.
>
> THE COURT: Wait a minute, counsel. Dr. Horowitz, please listen to the question and answer the question. Mr. Niro, wait until you ask your next question until the witness answers.
>
> MR. R. NIRO: Okay.
>
> BY MR. R. NIRO:
>
> Q.   Am I correct, sir, that when you plug in the AC outlet, the AC power was converted to DC power and enabled charging of the battery; "Yes" or "No"?
>
> A.   That's not a good question. I can't answer it.
>
> Q.   Okay. And when you plugged the AC power in, the battery was, effectively, disconnected from the radio, right?
>
> A.   Yes, by JK1.
>
> Q.   And by taking the switch out, you destroyed the radio?

A.   Well, it no longer functions.

Q.   And by taking the voltage regulator out, you destroyed the radio, correct?

A.   It no longer functions, yes.

(Transcript, September 21, 2006, pp. 1668-1669). The spaceman was brought back to Earth.

In closing, I gave Joe Domes' original patent back to him and challenged the jury to take it away. They did not. The jury's verdict: patent valid and willfully infringed:

> Now, Joe Domes was not building an 84-foot antenna to determine whether alien beings are communicating radio waves to the world as we know it. He was working as a carpenter in New York. He was living the American dream. He was creating an invention and getting a reward for himself for the invention that he created.
>
> And, you know, just like somebody invents something and they have the ability to manufacture and they build a plant and they have a product, he didn't have that opportunity. He had $5,000 that he couldn't even pay to get a patent.
>
> And what did he do? He sold it to somebody. Now, that guy that bought it has no incentive ever to do anything like this, again, if their arch competitor can take the same product, take it to China and copy it.
>
> You know, the one thing that bothered me, quite frankly, about one of the questions that was asked of Mr. Cheung is the question that was brought up here a moment ago:
>
> "How did you feel, Mr. Cheung?
>
> "I was insulted. I feel terrible that they would say that I copied." I have another question. "How did you

feel, Joe Domes? How are you going to feel if it's okay to take your invention and give it away?"

And, you know, some of the greatest inventions we have aren't invented by Corporate America. They're invented by individuals. And there aren't going to be any more individuals inventing anything if there's no reward at the end of the rainbow. If big Corporate America can run them over, it's over, and we're entering the dark ages of innovation in this country.

He's a regular guy. He got two patents. He got a reward for those patents. And I've been thinking about it each day when I take these patents (indicating) in and I put them right here (indicating), which is what I like to do. These are originals (indicating). This one's (indicating) an original, this one's (indicating) a copy. It's one of an a kind. It's one of a kind. They give it to you and that's it. It's got a nice little ribbon on the side (indicating).

And I was thinking about my dad who got a third grade education. He came here when he was 18 years old from Italy, an immigrant. My mom was an immigrant. And they lived the American dream. They gave me the opportunity to do what I do.

But there is no incentive -- zero -- to invent if you can run over people's patents.

And my dad, on the side of his certificate -- I don't know if they still do that -- when he became a citizen, had a little ribbon just like this (indicating). Just like this (indicating).

And before you take this patent away from Mr. Domes -- and I'm going to give it to him because I've just borrowed it.

It's yours, Joe. (Document tendered.)

BY MR. R. NIRO:

Before you take these patents away, be sure. That's what they're asking you to do.

(Transcript, September 21, 2006, pp. 1810-1812; emphasis added). Joe Domes got his patent back. And the jury didn't take it away.

My son, Dean, saw the spaceman leaving. He asked him nicely if he was taking a plane or a spaceship.

THE COWBOY LEARNS NOT TO DANCE IN THE END ZONE

IMS Technology, Inc. v. Haas Automation, Inc., et al.,
Civil Action No. 97-1043-A (E.D. Va., Aug. 2000)

The coach of the Green Bay Packers, Vince Lombardi, called over an excited running back who had just spiked the football and then danced in the end zone. He angrily said: "Next time you're in the end zone, son, act like you've been there before. And that you're going to be there again." Good advice.

Gene Haas had a cowboy mentality and (like the running back) liked to dance in the end zone -- rich, arrogant, the sole owner of the biggest U.S. manufacturer of machine tools. His personal income exceeded $325 million per year. Despite the fact that virtually every major machine tool manufacturer in the world had taken a license under our client's patent, Haas decided to fight. He was going to show us. And he did. Just before trial, the district judge (see the TFD case at page 143) changed her mind about claim construction and found our client's patent not infringed. Haas told everyone who would listen: "I told you guys not to settle. I won. I showed them." He was dancing in the end zone

A year later, the Federal Circuit reversed the district judge. No more dancing, Mr. Haas. Before we knew it, we had a trial. This was an important invention: having a conversation with a machine about the product you wanted to make. And the industry recognized its importance by accepting patent licenses.

I hit hard in the opening about Haas being a hold-out. What did he know that the likes of Fanuc, Nissan, Yamazaki, Okuma, Cincinnati Milicron, Hitachi, Brother, Allen-Bradley and 70 other companies who accepted licenses did not:

> IMS decided to share it. And you will hear a stipulation that in the course of the past six years, five years, 38 separate companies, the biggest companies in the machine tool industry, paid $36 million to IMS for rights under this patent. These are companies that control about 95 percent of the market and have billions of years in sales -- billions of dollars a year in sales; Mitsubishi, Okuma, Hitachi, U.S. companies, Japanese companies, French companies, Swiss companies, Italian companies, Israeli companies, around the world all recognizing this patent.
>
> The reason we are here today is there is one holdout; it is Mr. Haas and his company. They are one of the biggest manufacturers of machine tools in the United States. They don't have a single patent that they have ever gotten on anything they have done. Mr. Haas has one personally. The company doesn't have any. They are owned or controlled by Mr. Haas. And in the past four years have had sales of nearly a billion dollars of products we accused of infringement.
>
> Mr. Haas was offered a license in March of 1999 and again in May of -- I am sorry, March of '97 and again in May of 1997 in letters that were sent to him urging him to take a license under the same terms and conditions that everyone else was offered. Those letters were never answered, not a response, not a "I'm not

interested," nothing. In July of '97, three years ago, this lawsuit was filed.

(Transcript, July 31, 2000, pp. 111-112).

In a stipulation, we identified the companies who accepted licenses and the amount they paid:

> MR. NIRO: Yes, Your Honor. We have totaled the numbers in the stipulation. We can put that in the record now, if the Court would permit it.

◦ ◦ ◦ ◦ ◦

> MR. NIRO: All right, I'll read it one more time. Maybe I can get my math right. [$]26,559,898.

◦ ◦ ◦ ◦ ◦

> THE COURT: That's the total -- as I understand it, that's the total amount of the license numbers paid to the plaintiff that can be publicly revealed?

> MR. NIRO: Right. That does not include -- that's correct, Your Honor. That does not include four settlements in which the licensees requested that the amounts they paid be maintained in confidence and not disclosed or -- and it does not include the commercial value of the license with Siemens, which involved some commercial considerations. So those five license agreements and their value were not included in the [$]26,559,898.

(Transcript, August 1, 2000, p. 285).

Now, for Gene Haas. I called him as an adverse witness and began by showing how much money he made (not highly relevant, but who cares?):

Q. Would you state your full name, please?

A. My name is Gene Francis Haas.

Q. And you're the president of Haas Automation, is that correct, the defendant in this case?

A. Yes, I am.

Q. You own a controlling interest in Haas Automation, correct?

A. Yes, I do.

Q. It's a Subchapter S corporation, correct?

A. Yes, that's correct.

Q. That means that the profits of the company flow through to you personally, correct?

A. Yes, that's correct.

Q. And you are the only shareholder of Haas Automation, correct?

A. Yes.

Q. Now in order to authenticate one of the documents that I'd like to show you, I'd like to review with you the revenues, 1997 revenues of the company. As I understand it, those revenues were around $325 million; is that correct?

(Transcript, August 1, 2000, p. 287). The Court permitted the testimony because it related to commercial success -- a factor relevant to the issue of obviousness.

The invention had to do with a conversational language that allowed a machine tool operator to effectively talk to the machine. For example:

[Machine] Q.	What do you want to make?	
[Operator] A.	A cylinder.	
[Machine] Q.	What diameter?	
[Operator] A.	Four inches.	
[Machine] Q.	What length?	
[Operator] A.	Twelve inches.	

It was quick and easy. Haas's version was called Conversational Quick Code. I got Haas to admit it was innovative, simple, flexible and valuable:

Q. Okay. Now QuickCode, as you understand it, is innovative; isn't that correct?

A. Well, it's a way of teaching G code to people who don't understand what, what G code is, because G code is a somewhat encrypting language. I mean, I think a lot of people think that G code is something that's very hard to understand, but if I may for the jury, it's really very simple. It's like if you went down to the candy machine to get a candy bar and you wanted a Snickers --

Q. Well, is it innovative or not? That's my question to you.

A. I think it's innovative, yes.

Q. Right. And "innovative" means something that's unique and new; isn't that correct?

A.   Well, we're always trying to improve our product. I think that's, that's what we're in business for.

Q.   And QuickCode combines the simplicity and flexibility of G code programming with English descriptive sentences to enable even a beginning programmer to construct most two-dimensional parts; isn't that right?

A.   That's what it says, yes.

Q.   And I think you've said that one of the benefits of this QuickCode is its simplicity, correct?

A.   Yes, I think that's a true statement.

Q.   And Conversational QuickCode allows the machine to prompt the operator for information that's necessary to create a program, correct?

A.   Conversational QuickCode does put questions on the screen, yes.

Q.   All right. So there are questions on the screen, and then the operator interacts with the machine by responding to those questions, correct?

A.   Well, he inputs data, yes.

Q.   Well, for example, one of the questions might be, "What is the feed rate?" And the operator would respond by putting in the feed rate, correct?

A.   That's in Conversational QuickCode.

Q.   Okay. Now that's what your manuals say, correct?

A.   Yes.

(Transcript, August 1, 2000, pp. 295-296). Haas also admitted there were savings associated with Quick Codes:

Q. Now there are savings associated with QuickCode in terms of using that type of a system; isn't that right?

A. I, I wouldn't -- I don't think I could say that, because I think QuickCode really teaches an operator how to use G code programming. G code programming actually would be quicker to use rather than QuickCode, because the problem is is that when you're running something like QuickCode and even if it's Conversational QuickCode, it's asking you questions, and it's much like, you know, calling up the phone company and they say, "Push button 1," or, "Push button 2." Sometimes it's better just to dial the number than it is to have to go through a question-and-answer format.

Q. So you deny that there are savings in time associated with the use of QuickCode?

A. QuickCode teaches you how to use G code, but once you learn how to use G code, G code would be quicker than using the QuickCode.

Q. Okay. Let me read to you from page 142 of your deposition taken in this case, at line 13:

> "Question: So there's some savings in time associated with the use of QuickCode?
>
> Answer: If you use QuickCode."

Q. Did you give that answer to that question at that time?

A. Yes, because if you use QuickCode, you're going to learn how to use G code programming faster, which will bring you up to speed faster, which makes the machine more productive faster.

Q. So there are savings in time associated with use of QuickCode, correct?

A.   Well, the faster you learn something, I think the more productive you can become.

(Transcript, August 1, 2000, pp. 296-297). He admitted his company had only gotten one patent in eighteen years. Hardly an innovative company. Then, I confronted him with his personal attack on the inventor, Jerry Roch -- someone he claimed was from a cornfield in Indiana:

Q.   Is it fair to say that you have little or no respect for the creativity and inventions of Jerry Roch?

A.   No, I think Jerry Roch seems to be a fine person.

Q.   Well --

A.   I respect him tremendously.

Q.   Don't you think that it's absurd that someone from a cornfield in Indiana could invent interactive control for a machine tool?

A.   Well, those are words I used in a deposition after you grueled me for two or three days, so I think I was probably a little bit upset, but at the same time, Mr. Roch invented a product in 1976 that already existed, with all due respect. Those are the facts.

Q.   You consider it absurd, in your words, that someone from a cornfield -- and I assume you're referring to Jerry Roch -- in the middle of Indiana could invent interactive control; isn't that correct?

A.   Mr. Niro, you're using words that I used in the heat of the moment, and I think that they certainly weren't in -- directed at Mr. Roch personally.

(Transcript, August 1, 2000, pp. 302-303).

Amazingly, Haas had designed Conversational Quick Code for his machines, but there was not a single document showing what research he did to develop his design (the implication -- he copied):

Q. Am I correct that you have no documents that relate to the design of Conversational QuickCode, correct?

A. No. It was, it was one of those think sessions where you put it together in a few hours and, you know, just come up with the idea. It wasn't, it wasn't really all that complicated.

Q. So the answer is you don't have any documents?

A. No. I don't have any documents, no.

Q. Not a single document that evidences what research and development work you did to come up with this feature, correct?

A. Well, I do most of my thinking in my head, and then when I've solidified the answer, then usually I'll sit down with the engineers and discuss with them what I want.

(Transcript, August 1, 2000, p. 310). He also received no legal advice on whether or not his Conversational Quick Code infringed:

Q. Am I correct, sir, that you have no document anywhere that references any legal advice that you ever got on the question whether QuickCode infringes or whether the Roch patent is valid?

A. There's certainly a lot of expert witness reports about whether we infringe or not and the validity of the patent. You have all of those, sir.

Q. Let me read to you from page 1230 of your deposition.

"Question -- this is line 23 -- "Do you know of any document anywhere that references any legal advice that you've received?"

Answer: No, I don't."

Did you give that answer to that question at that time?

A.   Well, I may have given that answer, but I certainly had attorneys working for me, and it's the job of the attorneys to, to basically respond to those type of invalidity and infringement issues, sir.

(Transcript, August 1, 2000, p. 312).

The key to the validity portion of the case was proving that Haas was simply second-guessing the patent examiner. He knew of no prior art more pertinent than what the examiner had already considered. This is how it went:

Q.   Okay. I want to turn finally to some of the statements that have been made about the prior art, that is, stuff that existed before. Do you recall that at the time that your deposition was taken, that you were designated by the corporation to testify as its witness on all of the defenses that existed in this case?

A.   Yes. I was selected as the witness for the corporation.

Q.   Okay. And at that point in time, you believed that three patents that had been considered by the patent examiner during procurement of the Roch patent disclosed each and every element of each and every claim of the patent, right?

A.   Mr. Niro, if you read my entire deposition into the record, you will find out that I thought all the prior art was pertinent.

Q. Well, my question to you is did you believe that there were three patents considered by the patent examiner, specifically, the Anderson patent, the Henegar patent, and the Evans patent, that disclosed all the elements of each claim of the patent?

A. Mr. Niro, I --

THE COURT: Mr. Haas, you have to answer the question. Then you can explain or your counsel can ask you on cross examination to amplify, but an answer -- I let you go a long time, but if an answer is either yes or no, that is the appropriate answer. He simply asked you as to these three patents, not anything else, all right? Mr. Niro, ask the question again.

MR. NIRO: Yes.

THE WITNESS: I'm sorry.

BY MR. NIRO:

Q. Did you believe, sir, that the three patents, Anderson, Henegar, and Evans, that were considered by the patent examiner during the procurement of the Roch patent, disclosed all the elements of each claim of the patent?

A. I don't exactly remember what I said, and I'm sure you can probably read it back to me so I can have a better understanding of what I said.

Q. You don't recall? All right, let me read to you from page 201 of your deposition: "One of the areas in which -- or categories in which you've been designated to testify is the factual and legal basis for each affirmative defense asserted by Haas. That's Item A on the deposition notice. Are you prepared to answer questions on that subject?"

"Answer: Yes, I am."

You did say that, correct?

A.   Yes, I did.

✦ ✦ ✦ ✦ ✦

Q.   Do you see that? I'll read it to you. It says, "What about patents and printed publications? Are there any patents or printed publications that in your view describe each and every element of each of the claims of the patent?" referring to the Roch patent.

   "Answer: I believe the Anderson patent describes each and every element of the claim."

Did you say that?

A.   I don't see that. What page is that now? 208?

Q.   Page 208, line 23.

A.   Oh, yes, I found that.

Q.   You did give that answer to that question at that time?

A.   Yes, I did.

Q   And do you see that on the face of the patent reexamination, there is identified as a reference cited -- okay, let me see if I can zero in on this. Do you see where it says Anderson, 3,783,253?

A.   Yes, I do.

Q   So that, that item of prior art was considered by the patent examiner, correct?

A.   Yes, it was.

Q. And then I went on to ask you, "Any others?" And you said, "The Henegar patent."

    "Question: That discloses each and every element of each of the claims?"

And you said, "I believe so."

And I said, "Is that the Henegar patent 3,746,845, the one that was considered by the patent examiner?"

And your answer was, "Yes."

Did you give those answers to those questions at that time?

A. Yes, I did.

Q. And Henegar is right here as well, disclosed right on the face of the patent as something the examiner considered, right?

A. Yes, but, Mr. Niro, I'm not a legal expert.

Q. I'm not asking you to be. At page 209, I asked you, "Any others that disclose each and every element of the claim?"

And you said, "I believe that the Evans patent discloses each and every element of the claim.

    "Question: Evans is shown where?

    Answer: That was in the first -- the initial patent application.

    Question: And that's Evans 4,010,356 that's cited in the patent?

    Answer: Yes."

Did you give those answers to those questions at that time?

A.   Yes, I did.

Q.   Okay. And Anderson -- I'm sorry, Evans on the face of the original patent is shown right here; isn't that correct?

A.   Yes.

Q.   4,010,356?

A.   Yes, it is.

Q.   Okay. So it was your belief as of the date that your deposition was taken in this case that three items of prior art that were considered by the patent examiner disclosed each and every element of each and every claim of the patent in suit, correct?

A.   Yes, at that time.

(Transcript, August 1, 2000, pp. 320-325). He admitted patent examiners do a good job:

Q.   And you believed the patent examiner didn't do a very good job, right?

A.   No, I believe the patentee mischaracterized some of those patents.

Q.   You realize that patent examiners are trained in the technology, right, the relevant technology?

A.   Yeah, I think they do a good job.

Q.   All right. They're trained in the patent law as well as the technology?

A.   Yes.

Q.   Right?

A.   Yes.

Q.   In fact, one was in our jury pool yesterday, said she taught -- she was taught about patents and so forth, right?

A.   Yes.

(Transcript, August 1, 2000, p. 325). Well, if that is so, and the best prior art was considered by the patent examiner, how can the patent be invalid?:

Q.   Now all the prior art that you relied upon in this case, every single item of prior art that you're bringing to the attention of the jury at some point is cumulative of what the patent examiners considered; isn't that right? It's no better, it's no more pertinent?

A.   I don't believe so.

Q.   Well, am I correct that you as of the date of your deposition were unaware of any item of prior art that was more pertinent than Anderson, which the examiner considered?

A.   There was quite a bit of prior art. I always considered all of it pertinent.

Q.   Would you turn to page 216 of your deposition -- I'm sorry, 214 of your deposition? Did you say in response to my question,

> "Question: And that would be true of Anderson, for example? It is as pertinent as any of the other items of prior art that you've familiarized yourself with, correct?
>
> Answer: Yes."

Did you give that answer to that question at that time?

A.   Yes, that appears to be what I said.

Q.   And I went on to ask you, "And you have produced for us many, many items of prior art that you believe are relevant to the claims of the patent, correct?

   "Answer: Yes."

You did give that answer, correct?

A.   Yes.

Q.   And do you recall that as of the date of your deposition, you had boxes filled with items of alleged prior art?

A.   Yes.

Q.   Including the 15 items of prior art that you're relying upon in this case, isn't that right?

A.   Yes.

Q.   And you concluded there was nothing in those boxes more pertinent than Anderson, Evans, and Henegar, as well as the Eaton patent, all of which were considered by the examiner; isn't that right?

A.   Well, that's what my statements say, but I guess I don't fully understand the implications of the word "pertinent" as it applies to patent law.

Q.   You don't understand what "pertinent" means?

A.   Well, I understand that it has importance, but when you have all these different documents and you start talking about is it cumulative, it becomes -- it's not easily understood, and I have, I have had a little difficulty with that myself.

Q.   Well, at page 220 of your deposition, you were asked these questions, and I think you gave these answers:

"Question: Of those that you went through, which is the most pertinent?

Answer: They all carry equal weight.

Question: None is more pertinent than the other?

Answer: Not at this time."

Did you understand what "pertinent" meant when you gave those answers to those questions?

A. Well, I, I think what I'm -- I understand. I think what I'm trying to say is that at that time, I was thinking that the prior art, to me, they all had some importance, and I can't specify that I thought one was more important than the other, but at least to me, "pertinence" means that this is important, but I'm not trying to maybe say this one's more important than the other one.

Q. Would you turn to page 222 of your deposition, line 20? You were asked the question, "All right. Now for those patents that you've reviewed and have familiarity with, which do you believe most in depth and thoroughly describe what's contained in the claims of the IMS patent?"

Your answer was, "I'd pick Anderson and Evans."

"Question: Okay. Evans being U.S. Patent 4,010,356; is that right?

Answer: I believe so.

Question: And Anderson being the other patent, 3,783,253?

Answer: Say that number again now?

> Question: It's right on the cover page of the patent. 3,783,253, that's Anderson, right?
>
> Answer: Yes."

Did you give those answers to those questions at that time?

A.   Yes, I did.

Q.   And that answer was given after you had assembled all of the prior art that you're relying on in this case; isn't that right?

A.   This is really only six months after the -- I was sued, and I tried to do my best. You know, maybe I didn't get it exactly right, because I'm not exactly sure about pertinence and importance of prior art as it pertains to this patent, but these are, these are things I've said.

MR. NIRO: We have no further questions. Thank you.

(Transcript, August 1, 2000, pp. 325-329).

End of the game. The best prior art was before the patent examiner. He considered it and he allowed the IMS patent after a reexamination. So what was Haas doing (other than second-guessing the Patent Office)? I hit hard on that in closing but, first, I talked about the burden of proof and how it makes the jury's job easier:

> Well, how do you go about this task? Fortunately, Judge Brinkema will tell you that there is something called burdens of proof that assist in that process. It is a little like thinking about a screen that allows the sand to go through and the rocks to stay behind.
>
> It is a way to filter and sift through this stack of

evidence. You know, when you come through the front of the courthouse, in addition to seeing the rabbit and the turtle or the hare and the turtle, you see that there is the blind lady of justice, blind-folded, holding the scale in the balance. And if it tilts one way, then you decide the issue for one side. And if it tilts the other, you decide the issue for the other side. And that's the preponderance of evidence standard, the burden of proof. That's the screen for decisions on infringement, which is going to come later.

In this phase of the case, that burden of proof is by clear and convincing evidence. That's the defendants' burden and that screen now filters very tightly. Indeed, instead of a slight tipping of the scales, it has got to be pretty heavy tipping of the scales for somebody to satisfy that burden of proof.

(Transcript, August 3, 2000, p. 971). Then, I emphasized that patents are property:

And when you think about that, it summarizes the deficiencies in what the defendants are trying to sell here. They are asking you to take somebody's property away from them, because a patent is property, just like your house or your car or your lot or your watch or your ring. It is personal property.

And they are saying: Take it away from Jerry Roch, nullify it, do something the Patent Office didn't do, and say that two patent examiners were wrong, examiners that spent over eight years examining the first application and one year reexamining it.

This isn't a case about a slight shifting. This is a case in which the defendants have a substantial, clear burden. And as Judge Brinkema will explain to you, you have to have a firm conviction, an abiding conviction to take somebody's property away.

(Transcript, IMS v. Haas, Civil Action No. 97-1043-A (E.D. Va.), August 3, 2000, pp. 971-972). Haas was using hindsight. If I could use hindsight, I could have been a Beatle too:

> Remember, I told you about the patent which has been sitting over in the right-hand corner of our table. That's the original with the certificate and the seal and the ribbon, one of a kind. You can make copies of it, but Jerry Roch has one of them. And only you can take it away from him. But in order to do that, as the Court will explain, you have to be sure.
>
> Now, what have they given you as a basis to do this? They say, you know, this invention is old, and it is easy and it is obvious and anyone could do this, but, you know, what they don't tell you is that it takes 20/20 hindsight to do it. Think about their analysis. We went through it yesterday with Mr. Herndon.
>
> They take a look at the invention, they break it into all its pieces. They go out and find bits and pieces of it out there in this collection, this hodgepodge of prior art, and then in hindsight they put it all back together again. You know, I like to think of it a little like this (indicating), and I mentioned it a couple times in the course of the case. I have got sheet music for four different songs here, What a Wonderful World, Louis Armstrong. If you look inside here, there are the notes, all eight of them put in some combination to create a beautiful song. Or Paul McCartney and John Lennon, Let It Be, exact same eight notes that were used to create a totally different song, or George Gershwin's Rhapsody in Blue, piano solo, same eight notes that were used to create the other two songs and Beethoven, same eight notes. It is not going out and saying, you know, these notes are old, anybody could create this music, it is showing the combination.
>
> If somebody said to me today write What a Wonderful World, and they handed me in hindsight

this sheet music, I could do it. I could have written any of these songs and so could you. But I know I couldn't do it at the time these songs were written. Why? Because I didn't know how to put them together. That's what happened here. It is so apparent. Nobody knew how to do it, nobody taught you how to do it, nobody said how to do it, nobody described how to do it, nobody built a machine to do it, until Jerry Roch did it. And now in hindsight they want to come back and say: Well, I could have done it. I could have been one of The Beatles or Louis Armstrong.

That's not the way you judge invention.

(Transcript, August 3, 2000, pp. 972-974). The elements were old and well-known, but nothing showed the combination:

I mean, what's the light bulb but a bulb, a filament that glows, a fuse, and some gas inside the bulb, four little things, all old, all available. But only Thomas Edison created it. He did it first.

And if that were the patent that was involved in this case, these defendants would be telling you that because all the components were old, you ought to invalidate that patent and live in darkness.

Remember Mr. Herndon's cheat sheet, what I called the cheat sheet? And I didn't mean to insult him. It wasn't my intention to do that. But what it was is a little summary so he could remember all these combinations because he couldn't keep it in his mind. And I don't blame him. I don't think anybody could.

He had all the pieces, but he didn't have anything that showed the combination. When I went through it with him, he admitted, he had to have blank spaces for every piece of prior art, all 15 that they are relying on. If they had a single piece of prior art that showed it all, they would have put that chart out in front of you and said: Here it is, it shows everything. And if it is so easy and obvious and simple, why did he need a summary chart that he read from throughout his testimony to tell you why this patent is invalid?

(Transcript, August 3, 2000, pp. 974-975). I returned to our theme -- they were second-guessing the patent examiner:

> What's their analysis when it comes right down to it? I mean, think about what they are really saying. They are saying that the Patent Office examiners weren't good enough to figure out whether this invention was patentable, whether it was new, whether it was nonobvious. And the fact of the matter is, as was established repeatedly, they were smart enough, they are trained in the patent law, they are trained in the technology, and they considered the very best prior art. Now, how do we know that?
>
> Remember Gene Haas when he testified the first time, when I took him through the prior art? And we went through it in kind of a difficult fashion because he didn't want to say what he had said in his deposition. Well, what he said ultimately is: You know, I have spent all this money, I have done all this effort, I have collected all this prior art and do you know what I think is best, most pertinent? Evans, before the examiner; Anderson, before the examiner; Eaton, before the examiner; Herndon, before the examiner. Now, what's he saying? And what did he say? What he said is: I don't have anything better than what they considered. So what are we left with? Second-guess the patent examiners.

(Transcript, August 3, 2000, pp. 975-976). I hit hard on the promises made in their opening that were not kept:

> And remember the promises that Mr. Pianko made in his opening? He said the patent process is one-sided because the competitors don't get to go in and tell the

examiners about the prior art. And you learned that was not true. There was nothing that would have prevented Mr. Haas and his company from going before the Patent Office and starting a reexamination just as Hurco did and putting all this collection, this hodgepodge of prior art before the patent examiners. And you know why it didn't happen? It is obvious why it didn't happen. Because they knew it wasn't going to fly. The examiners weren't going to reexamine based upon the same thing that they had already seen.

And he said Hurco made false statements to the patent examiner. Did you hear any evidence about that? Did you see any evidence about that? Where else was the silence? And this is the one that I really want you to think about. These defendants had millions of dollars to spend in defense as apparently they do. You think they could afford to get one lawyer on the face of this earth to write a single opinion in writing that this patent is not infringed or this patent is invalid. Jerry Roch didn't invent anything. And here's why? They spent $45,000 to have an expert study the prior art and reach no conclusion, but they didn't spend a penny to get an attorney to come up with an opinion that they could put in front of you and say: By the way, we acted on the advice of this attorney and he told us it is invalid. Why not?

Because nobody would do it. Nobody would put their name on a piece of paper like that. That's because it is not true. And that silence is deafening.

◌ ◌ ◌ ◌ ◌

And that tells you a lot about their case when you think about the fact that they scoured the earth for this prior art and they couldn't find anything better than what the examiners had. That's not clear and convincing evidence.

(Transcript, August 3, 2000, pp. 980-981, 982).

And I reminded the jury that Gene Haas had made fun of the inventor, Jerry Roch, someone from a cornfield in Indiana. But wasn't Thomas Edison born on a farm also?:

> And then you have, of course, Mr. Haas, who masterminded this facade. And he pretty much admitted, if he likes something, he copied it. And he said he couldn't conceive of a person in a cornfield in Indiana inventing interactive control. Remember that? He said, oh, it was after you badgered me for two days, come on. What did he invent? What did he create?
>
> You know where the greatest inventor of our time came from? He was born in Milan, Ohio on a farm. They have cornfields there too. And his first invention was when he was 15. And in time he had over a thousand patents. And he brought us the light bulb, the phonograph, movie camera. He had a third grade education, greatest inventor of our time, Thomas Alva Edison, and he grew up on a cornfield.
>
> That's the level of respect that Mr. Haas and his company have for the patent system, for Jerry Roch, and for the invention that's involved here.

(Transcript, August 3, 2000, p. 983). And, of course, I mentioned my favorite inventor, Robert Goddard. He invented the rocket and said a great thing about dreams, hope and reality:

> There is another great inventor named ... Robert Goddard, ... there is a space center named after him. And in 1914 he invented the rocket. He got a patent on it. And you saw all these patent numbers 4 million and so forth. This is 1,102,653, if you would put that up for a minute, Bob.
>
> And he said something I think is really amazing. He said: I can't tell what's impossible because yesterday's

hope is today's dream, and tomorrow's reality. Hope, dream, reality.

And his dream came true in 1969, years after the 1914 patent when we put a man on the moon. And I remember well because I was right here in Washington going to school, Washington suburbs. And Jerry Roch had a dream too. His dream started in 1974 when he got this idea. And it became a reality in the mid-1980s when everybody in the industry started using his invention. And, you know, like a lot of good inventors, you know, far too many, I would say, he has great creativity, but he wasn't good at business. It takes money to innovate. It doesn't take as much to copy, because you can pick and choose what you want to copy, but when you are innovating, you have got to take those chances that sometimes not every one works. Well, he wrote -- his business failed, but he wrote a hit record.

And it wasn't until 1995 when his patent was reexamined that he finally had a chance and the company that he founded had a chance to offer this to the infringers that were copying that patent. And Hurco didn't choose to keep the technology to itself. It chose to share it, to be paid compensation for the use of the invention, even though they had the right to exclude.

And one by one every major manufacturer and every major company that makes machine tools or controls accepted licenses. Siemens AG, Hitachi, Mitsubishi, Bridgeport, Cincinnati Milacron, one after another. You heard the stipulation. Companies from the United States, from Germany, from the United Kingdom, from France, from Italy, from Japan. They all accepted licenses.

Are they all wrong? They had the resources. They had the fire power. They had the legal talent. They had the ability to come here and say: This patent is no good, it is invalid. But they copied the invention and they paid. And who are those licensees? Fanuc,

$8.8 million for a license, biggest machine tool control manufacturer in the world. Cincinnati Milacron, they made the Acramatic, what they say is prior art, paid $1.75 million. Now, if they believed the patent was invalid, would they do that? Mitsubishi, a confidential number, but Mr. Bollinger, who was the supervisor of Mr. Poo was their expert. If he knew the patent was invalid, why would he have his client pay what they paid for a license?

And you have Okuma, at $1.8 million, and Toyota and Mitsubishi, all of whom opposed the patent in Japan, and they accepted licenses. And there are 38 of them. And the number is well in excess of $26 million.

(Transcript, August 3, 2000, pp. 985-986). I stressed to the jury, "Don't take the patent away unless you are sure":

By copying Jerry Roch's invention, these companies that accepted licenses, unlike the defendants here, were saying you have a good invention, you have a good product, you wrote a hit record. It is wrong, and it would be wrong to invalidate this patent on this record in this case, on the hodgepodge of prior art that was presented to you by the defendants in the way that it was.

This patent is one of a kind and there simply is no basis by clear and convincing evidence to take it away.

(Transcript, August 3, 2000, p. 987).

The jury found the IMS patent valid. After the second phase of the trial on infringement and another round of testimony from Haas, Mr. Haas had enough. He called our client and said he wanted to talk. At his hotel, we found him sitting in a chair twirling a roll of duct-tape as though it was a rubber band. This guy was breaking down. Although he would not look at me directly, he did mumble that he had seen enough and only wanted to go home. When I told him he would have to pay more than any other infringer, he whined some, but relented after I explained to the cowboy that I wanted him to remember the moment. **"Remember this moment, Mr. Haas."** In fact, I recall saying something like: "You are going to pay the most because you laughed at us and I want you to remember this." Haas had laughed at me in a deposition. I told him then, "Let's see who is laughing when this is over." He signed the settlement that night and went home. Mr. Haas paid our client more than $8 million within ten days.

The cowboy was not finished, however. A few years later, some federal agents visited us. They were investigating Haas for tax fraud. He was billing his company using phony invoices and keeping the cash. According to The New York Times:

> "The tax fraud schemes in this case stem from defendant Haas's dislike of the federal judicial system and anger towards a federal judge (Judge Leonie M. Brinkema) who presided over a patent infringement suit" that Mr. Haas lost in August 2000, according to the court papers. The indictment said that the primary purpose of the "tax fraud schemes was to recoup the patent infringement settlement payment by defrauding" the government.

Johnston, David, "*Executive Accused of Tax Fraud and Witness Intimidation,*" The New York Times, 20 June 2006 (quoting from the Indictment). Mr. Haas served a couple of years in jail. *No dancing in the end zone there. So much for the cowboy.*

MEASUREMENTS COUNT

<u>Black & Decker Inc., et al. v. Porter Cable Corp.</u>,
Civil Action No. 98-436A (E.D. Vir., Feb. 1999)

Preparing a winning case is sometimes like putting together a puzzle. Every piece counts. It is not just about finding the pieces, but also how to put them together so it makes sense to a judge and jury. When complete, the puzzle becomes a stunning picture, but not until the pieces come together.

In a trial, you may know all the elements of your case and where they belong in order to paint the picture you want the jury to see. But what if one of the essential pieces is missing? In the case of <u>Black & Decker</u> v. <u>Porter Cable</u>, we needed the testimony of a key expert witness about a measurement he had made to conclusively prove infringement. I owe my son Dean for the idea on how to cross-examine Porter Cable's expert. But first, our case.

Greg Moores was a Black & Decker mechanical engineer who found a way to improve a product known as a plate jointer. A plate jointer is a power tool that is used by woodworkers, carpenters and tradesmen to make openings in two opposing pieces of wood so they can be securely joined together. In my opening, I briefly explained the differences between the old plate jointer model (Model 555) and Moores' invention (Model 682).

> This is a Porter-Cable device called the Model 555. This is what existed before Mr. Moores' invention.
> You will see it has a crude-looking fence here. It can only cut at one angle. And then you have to get an Allen wrench to take it off and flip it around the other way to make a different cut. It is time consuming.
> It doesn't have that flexibility, the angular, the quick angular and vertical adjustability.
> With this invention, you don't have to take the tool, take it apart, put another piece on. And that became, that invention became an enormous, enormous success.

(Transcript, February 8, 1999, p. 67).

Porter Cable, seeing the success of the DeWalt product, copied the invention and introduced an identical product in 1998 (Model 557), six years after the debut of Moores' invention. Porter Cable asserted there was one thing, only one element, which differentiated their product from Moores' -- the location of the pivot point relative to the opening on the face of the product.

The claims in Moores' patent required that the pivot point on the plate jointer be located rearward of the opening on the face. If the pivot point is located in front of the opening, then the equipment tilts and the product no longer works properly. The rearward location of this pivot point was essential to get accuracy when cutting wood at a particular angle. Porter Cable claimed that its product, the Model 557, had a pivot point that was coplanar to the opening of the face and, for that reason alone, they did not infringe upon Black & Decker's product.

Q. Did you, in this opinion, conclude that the pivotal axis of the Porter-Cable plate jointer fence is coplanar with the front face of the plate jointer that contacts the work piece, and through which the blade protrudes?

A. I believe so, yes.

Q. And what you were saying there is if the pivot axis is coplanar with the front face, then you conclude there is no literal infringement, right?

A. I believe I concluded that, yes.

Q. In fact, that's right in the beginning of this, right on the first page, underlined there in this exhibit, where it says:

"Brief conclusion: The pivotal axis of the Porter-Cable plate jointer fence is coplanar with the front face of the plate jointer, that is, where the blade emerges from the front face that contacts the work piece and through which the blade protrudes."

That was your basis for concluding that there was no literal infringement, correct?

A. That was the vision of the design-around and the basis for this letter, yes.

(Transcript, February 17, 1999, pp. 181-182).

Q. And am I correct that Mr. Smith told you that the only basis that he knew of for designing around the '204 patent was location of the pivotal axis?

A.   I don't recall the exact conversation, but it's my understanding that we were -- did not infringe if we were coplanar with the front face.

⬌ ⬌ ⬌ ⬌ ⬌

Q.   Turn to page 258 if you would -- I'm sorry, 260, beginning at line 21?

A.   Yes.

Q.   (Reading) "Question: Sir, as you sit here, the only thing you can recall that Mr. Smith told you about designing around the '204 patent is the location of the pivotal axis; is that correct?

Answer: Yes, I believe so."

Did you give that answer to that question at that time?

A.   Yes.

(Transcript, February 9, 1999, pp. 225-226).

So there it was: If the pivot point was co-planar, there was no infringement. If it was rearward of the opening, there was infringement. Unfortunately, the location of the pivot point in relation to the opening of the face was something that the naked eye could not perceive. And, while we had run several tests that showed the pivot point on the Porter Cable product was, in fact, located rearward of the opening on the face (and not co-planar as Porter Cable claimed), their tests showed just the opposite. Or so we thought. It was our word against theirs until the cross-examination of their expert.

On direct, Porter Cable's expert, John Smith, testified he didn't change the height of the fence during his test because the pivot axis was co-planar. If it were rearward, he would have had to change the height of the fence. The case was now about a single measurement:

Q.   Why don't you take the first board and show us how you made the cut.

A.   The first board was a cut at 135 degrees, which I determine[d] the height setting and locked that in position, and I moved the fence down to 135 degrees and positioned the red indicator mark on the pencil line that I had made, and made the cut.

I then moved over and made a second cut, doing the same thing, and that is all I did to this piece of wood.

And then I went and took the fence to 90 degrees, but I didn't change the height. And then once again --

Q.   Let me ask you, why didn't you change the height?

A.   Because of the location of the pivot axis, you don't need to do that. ...

(Transcript, February 18, 1999, pp. 230-231).

There it was: no infringement because they didn't change the height. Case over, right? Well, not so fast. Here is the cross-examination with the witness standing directly before the jury too:

Q.   Mr. Smith -- by the way, if you want, you can just stay there for a moment.

When you did this test that you just demonstrated, did you use any of the units that are on the floor here?

ATTORNEY R. NIRO: Maybe you can come over and pick them up, with the Court's permission.

BY ATTORNEY R. NIRO:

Q. Did you use Plaintiff's Exhibit 126?

A. I couldn't tell you. What do you mean?

Q. Could you hold it up?

A. (Complied)

Q. Plaintiff's Exhibit 126, that has been an exhibit marked in this case, did you use that?

A. No, I don't believe so.

Q. And 127 is another one down there. Did you use that?

A. No, I don't believe so.

Q. And 128, would you hold it up, if you would?

A. (Complied)

Q. It is one of your units, right?

A. Yes.

Q. Did you use that?

A. No, I did not.

Q. And Exhibit 415, that is also there. Did you use that?

A. Not that I am aware of.

Q. And the unit that you used, you don't have here to show us today; is that right?

A. That's correct.

Q. And you testified that what you did in making this test, to make it flush, is you didn't move the position vertically; isn't that right?

A. That's correct.

(Defendant's Exhibit No. 582 premarked for identification.)

BY ATTORNEY R. NIRO:

Q. Now, you recognize this exhibit here, one of your company's exhibits, called Exhibit 582 [see diagram]. Does that show the wood that you used and the device that you used?

ATTORNEY ROBERTSON: Objection, your Honor, foundation.

BY ATTORNEY R. NIRO:

Q. It details a comparison of devices, DeWalt's 682, Porter-Cable's 557, and it shows this pivotal axis flush or forward.

I will have to see if I can focus it better.

It says it shows the different points, you've done the measurement, and it shows one flush fit and one not.

(Transcript, February 18, 1999, pp. 232-234).

Comparison of Devices

DeWalt's '682
Pivotal Axis Rearward

Porter Cable's '557
Pivotal Axis Flush or Forward

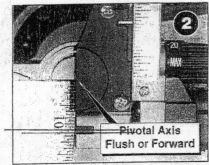

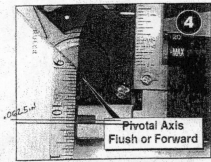

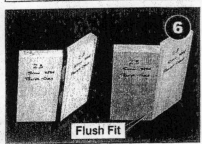

DX 582

I had him. He *did* have to change the height:

Q.   Do you recognize those wood pieces?

THE COURT: Are you persisting in the objection or not?

ATTORNEY ROBERTSON: I withdraw the objection.

THE WITNESS: It's hard to see the wording, but it looks like this side over here are these pieces.

ATTORNEY R. NIRO: All right.

BY ATTORNEY R. NIRO:

Q.   In fact, you have some writing on there, don't you? Is that the same writing?

A.   I can't really see it real, real well.

Q.   It says --

A.   "2B."

Q.   -- "show side Porter-Cable, 2B"?

A.   Uhm-hmm.

Q.   Is that it?

A.   Looks to be.

Q.   Yes.

Now, when you -- did your measurement -- you actually had a scale that you put right beside, say about 10-1/8, 7-1/8, something like that, do you see that?

A.   I see that.

Q.   When you made the other measurement, you are about 10-1/4, right? Do you see that?

A.   I see it. I didn't do this.

Q.   I see.

A.   This demonstrative.

Q. Ten and an eighth isn't ten and a quarter. It moved an eighth of an inch vertical; isn't that right?

A. I don't believe that is true. I would like to see the top one, if I could.

Q. Just a shade underneath; isn't that right, sir?

A. Could I see the bottom one, please?

ATTORNEY R. NIRO: I will let you look at the whole thing, if you want.

BY ATTORNEY R. NIRO:

Q. You moved it vertically, wouldn't you say, about an eighth of an inch?

A. That's not an eighth of an inch. It would be a 16th of an inch. It did move.

(Transcript, February 18, 1999, pp. 235-236). He admitted he had lied. He **did** have to change the height of the fence to make the two pieces fit:

Q. And if it did move a 16th of an inch, it wouldn't ma[t]e up to that one, would it?

A. No, it wouldn't. It would be out a little bit.

Q. Now, if it's off that distance, you did move it vertically, right, a 16th of an inch, right?

A. It should be.

Q. What the jury is looking at is one where you moved it vertically, not one where you did it exactly the same vertical height, right?

A. No, I didn't move the vertical height.

Q. These photographs are wrong; is that what you are saying?

A. No.

(Transcript, February 18, 1999, pp. 236-237). Moving the height vertically 1/16th or 1/18th of an inch is not "I didn't change the height." I had nailed him. Using his own pictures, the evidence he had to prove his case had done just the opposite. He flat-out lied to the jury and, in exposing this misrepresentation, I had destroyed the expert's credibility and gained the trust of the jury.

This theme of deception was repeated, with Porter Cable's patent lawyer who "changed" the definition of the word "opening" so they could fudge his opinion:

Q. I want to take you to the sequence of events in terms of your dealings with your patent attorneys, to see if we can develop a chronology here and put these measurements in the chronology. I would like to start with the August 28, 1997, opinion.

Now, prior to receiving that opinion from Merchant and Gould, your lawyer, Mr. Sumner, you had been told that there might be a problem with the '204 patent based on the initial design that you were working on, correct?

A. Yes.

Q. And that occurred sometime in the '95, '96 time frame?

A. It occurred earlier. I am not sure when it was.

Q. Okay. By August 28, 1997, you actually had a written opinion, that is, the first Sumner opinion; is that right?

A. Yes.

⸪ ⸪ ⸪ ⸪ ⸪

Q. In that first opinion, Mr. Sumner said, in essence, that the Porter-Cable 557 plate jointer is coplanar with the front face that contacts the work piece, correct? It says that down here at the bottom, right?

A. Yes.

ATTORNEY R. NIRO: So, that's August in the chronology. I will place that up here, in the chronology, August 28, 1997, Mr. Sumner, the Porter-Cable 557 plate joiner is coplanar with the front face that contacts the work piece.

ATTORNEY R. NIRO:

Q. Now, the next thing that happens in the sequence of events that brings us here today is that Black [&] Decker filed a complaint against Porter-Cable for infringement of the '204 patent, right?

(Transcript, February 10, 1999, pp. 23-25).

Now, John Smith made some measurements that showed there was infringement:

Q. Do you remember when you were served with the complaint?

A. I don't recall the date.

Q. Would it be after March 30?

A.   I don't know.

Q.   You do know that it was June 24, 1998, that John Smith made the measurements on the location of the pivotal axis that are shown on the chart 404 that is up there, right?

A.   Yes.

Q.   So the sequence of events, we have an opinion that says it's coplanar, we don't infringe. And then there is a complaint filed, and then there are some measurements, right?

A.   Yeah. There was a complaint filed, and we measured, because in real life we have engineering tolerances that make the axis drift in either direction.

(Transcript, February 10, 1999, pp. 26-27).

Q.   June 14th, 1998 -- and we will scratch out the date it was filed. June 14, 1998, there was service of the complaint. And then ten days later Mr. Smith does the measurements, right?

A.   Yes.

(Transcript, February 10, 1999, p. 29). Now, for the second opinion and the new definition of "an opening":

Q.   Okay. Then there was a second opinion written, this time by Mr. Sumner, and that's Exhibit 303. And that was written on July 15, 1998, right? That is Exhibit 303. Do you have it up there?

A.   I don't have it.

(Transcript, February 10, 1999, p. 29).

Q. Now, when you received the second opinion, you realized that there had been a shift in what you understood an opening meant; isn't that right?

A. In the first opinion, we asked for a decision on "coplanar with the axis in the front face," with no thought that engineering tolerances would be a problem. The second opinion reflected engineering tolerances of real life components.

Q. Now, am I correct, sir, that when you received the second opinion, you had a different understanding of what opening meant? Is that right?

A. The understanding I had of "opening" would have -- would reflect what John Sumner, what John Sumner's opinion of what the opening is.

Q. And it changed, didn't it?

A. Well, I don't know.

Q. Didn't Mr. Sumner change from the opening being the front face to the opening having some thickness, so that it could be moved back?

A. The second opinion does explain that the opening, in his opinion, has thickness.

Q. Okay.

A. Apparently, from the wording in the patent.

Q. And that definition came and that change came after the measurements, right, about a month after you did measurements?

A. Yes, the letter is dated after the measurements.

(Transcript, February 10, 1999, pp. 32-33). So what was going on? A first legal opinion with one definition; then some measurements and then a second opinion.

In my cross-examination of Mr. Sumner, I went after him on the inconsistencies:

Q. Now, when you went through your chronology of critical times and dates and events, you went through a whole series of letters, starting with your first opinion, and in fact it was an oral opinion on the initial design; then to the first written opinion that you gave in, let's see the date, August 28, 1997. That was your first written opinion, correct?

A. Yes, as I recall, that's correct.

(Transcript, February 17, 1999, p. 174). What was the basis for his opinion?

Q. And the only basis you gave in this opinion, as it relates to claim 1 of the patent, '204 patent for no infringement, is this conclusion that the pivotal axis of the Porter-Cable plate jointer fence is coplanar with the front face?

A. That's the analysis of literal noninfringement, yes.

Q. Okay. Seven months later a lawsuit was filed, right?

A. Yes.

Q. And three months later Porter-Cable did some measurements, correct?

A. Something on that time frame, yes.

Q. And those measurements were done by Porter-Cable to determine where the location of the pivot axis was; isn't that right?

A.   They were provided to me by Porter-Cable. I do not
     know how the measurements were done.

Q.   I am curious about that. Did they provide you with
     all the measurements, or did they just call you on the
     phone and give you one?

A.   I don't recall.

Q.   In your next opinion, you refer to measurements that
     were made. I think that's your opinion, your Defense
     376. Do you have that?

A.   Yes, sir.

Q.   And in that opinion you refer to measurements that
     were done on June 24, 1988, correct?

A.   That's correct.

Q.   That's about three months after the lawsuit was filed,
     right?

A.   To be honest with you, I don't recall. But we can
     assume that's true.

(Transcript, February 17, 1999, pp. 184-185).

Q.   And this is your second opinion, correct?

A.   Yes, sir.

Q.   It's confidential and privileged, correct?

A.   That's what it says.

Q.   And in it you give a summary of what your opinion
     is, correct?

A.   Yes.

Q.   And am I correct that you say that:

"We understand that on June 24, 1998, Porter-Cable took measurements of several of its recently manufactured Model 557 plate jointers"?

You said that right in your opinion; is that right?

A.   Yes.

Q.   Who told you that?

A.   Porter-Cable.

Q.   Who?

A.   I don't recall.

Q.   So, someone at Porter-Cable said, "We did some measurements as to where the pivotal axis is," right?

A.   That's correct.

Q.   But you don't know who it was?

A.   No, I don't recall.

Q.   And you don't have any recollection of them giving you a copy of the measurements; is that right?

A.   No, sir.

Q.   You did find out that, through these measurements, Porter-Cable found that recently produced Model 557 plate jointers had a fence pivotal axis that was about 0.015 inch behind the front surface of the tool, right?

A.   Yes, sir.

(Transcript, February 17, 1999, pp. 188-189).

Q.   So, you knew there were multiple measurements; is that right -- is that what you are saying -- of multiple tools?

A. That is what it says in my letter.

Q. Did you know how many measurements had been made?

A. No.

Q. Do you know by whom they had been made?

A. No.

Q. Do you ever think it might be worthwhile, as a patent attorney, to provide clearance for this product, to inquire of your client how many measurements it made, how they were made and what they showed?

A. No.

Q. It never occurred to you?

A. No, sir.

⊕ ⊕ ⊕ ⊕ ⊕

Q. And in this [second] opinion, you concluded that the opening had thickness; isn't that right?

A. Yes, it does.

Q. That was your opinion, correct?

A. Yes, as disclosed in the '204 patent, that has thickness.

Q. That's the opinion you had at that time?

A. That's what the drawing shows in the '204 patent.

Q. And that turned out, of course, to be incorrect, isn't that right, in terms of a definition?

A.	With all due respect to the Court, I believe that the opening has depth.

Q.	When you say "with all due respect to the Court," are you saying that your conclusion is inconsistent with what the Court said?

A.	My conclusion is that the opening is in the front wall of the tool, which, as illustrated in the '204 patent, is a wall with a thickness, and it's labeled as an opening 30, pointing to the thickness of the opening.

(Transcript, February 17, 1999, pp. 194-195, 196). He disagreed with the judge:

Q.	Sir, the term "opening" is defined as the open space in the plane formed by the front face of the base. Is that somewhere behind or in the front face?

A.	Where are you reading from?

Q.	I am reading from the Court's definition of what an opening means.

A.	There is also contained in that opinion that the opening has four sides to it.

Q.	Okay.

	Is this definition --

A.	Same opinion.

Q.	Is this definition, "the term 'opening' is defined as the open space in the plane formed by the front face of the base," is that something you don't understand?

A.	I also understand --

	ATTORNEY R. NIRO: Sir, answer [my] question. I know you may also understand a lot of things.

RAYMOND P. NIRO

THE WITNESS: Okay.

BY ATTORNEY R. NIRO:

Q. Am I correct, you understand the term "opening" as defined by the Court as being the open space in the plane formed by the front face of the base?

A. With all due respect, I disagree with the Court.

Q. Well, whether you agree or disagree with the Court, if that's the definition that we live by in this case, would you agree that that definition is this red line right at the front face?

A. Well, again, with due respect to the Court, if you can show me the Markman opinion, I can find other definitions of opening in there that are consistent with the patent.

Q. Did you write this second opinion after you learned about the measurements, so that you could have an opinion that somehow would say that you were coplanar, not behind?

A. I'm sorry, I think you are trying to mislead me again. Could you repeat the question?

Q. Did you write this opinion, this second opinion, where you gave the word "opening" thickness, did you write that so that you would have some basis to say that the measurement that you were aware of, which was behind, somehow would now become coplanar?

A. Substantially coplanar, yes, uhm-hmm.

(Transcript, February 17, 1999, pp. 201-203).

Enough said. To prevail, Porter Cable's attorney had to disagree with the trial judge's definition of what an opening was. (It is never a good idea to disagree with the trial judge.) Then a technical witness had to say he didn't fudge a test when he actually did. The jury found the DeWalt patent valid and infringed and awarded damages of $1,050,000 for past infringement. Not a lot of money, but a huge victory for Black & Decker against a direct competitor.

EVERYONE MAKES MISTAKES

Flint Ink Corporation v. Sharen E. Brower,
Civil Action No. 93-CV-73761-DT (E.D. Mich., March 1996)

Sharen Brower was a part-time artist and school teacher. She lived in Newell, Iowa, a town of 75 people. Her invention was a new soy-based ink, initially conceived for her art work but, later, determined to have huge commercial value as a non-petroleum-based ink that could be used in printing newspapers.

Flint Ink was the second-largest ink company in the United States, run by a curmudgeon named Flint (no less). Sharen visited Flint with her lawyer, Ed Sease, and was told she knew nothing about inks. Worse, after she left the meeting, Flint did two things: (1) it copied her formulation and (2) it filed a declaratory judgment suit against her in Detroit, claiming her patent was invalid and had been procured by her lawyers by committing a fraud on the Patent Office. The inequitable conduct phase of the case went to trial in May 1996. If we lost, the case was over. If we won, we got to the next phase of the trial. The Court found the technical misstatements made to the Patent Office by Mr. Sease material, but not intentional. There was no intent to deceive, thus, there was no fraud. Later, a jury awarded Sharen $48 million in damages.

The cross-examination of Flint's expert proved decisive in beating the inequitable conduct claim:

Q. Now, you've given some opinions about what's material and what's not under Rule 56.

Am I correct, sir, that you have testified in other cases in which you've urged courts to find a party guilty of inequitable conduct?

A. Are you correct in that? Yes, I have done that.

Q. And your testimony was found to be wrong; isn't that correct, sir?

A. The case that you refer to was 3M versus Johnson & Johnson, and the court did not accept my testimony in that case; that's correct.

Q. In fact, you said there was inequitable conduct, and the court found that there was not; isn't that correct?

A. I guess.

Q. Is that right sir, or not?

A. Well, I said there was inequitable conduct, but it was actually either a Magistrate or a Special Master. I believe it was a Special Master, so it wasn't really a court, as such.

Q. And then the court affirmed the findings of the Special Master?

A. I believe that's correct.

Q. And Judge Rich, Circuit Judge of the Federal Circuit, affirmed the court; isn't that right?

A. I don't even know if inequitable conduct was at issue before the CFC.

Q.   Well, I'll show you the case.

A.   Well, if -- if you say it was, I'll accept your word for it, but I don't recall.

Q.   Okay. And I heard you testify, I believe, that submitting materials to the Patent Office is a little like testifying under oath.

A.   Correct.

Q.   And, of course, you did so in the Johnson & Johnson case, right?

A.   I did?

Q.   Right.

A.   Yes, I believe so.

Q.   **_And in that case, your opinion was rejected, right_**?

A.   **_That's correct._**

(Transcript, May 3, 1996, pp. 172-174).

So the expert had been wrong before. That was a point in our favor. But, how about this case? Was the expert also improperly questioning the competence of the patent examiner?

Q.   Now, I wrote this down when you gave this testimony. I think I've got it right.

You were talking about the history of what happened in the Patent Office, and what the Examiner was saying as you interpreted it, and you said, referring to the Examiner, that you haven't shown by evidence what the improved results are.

Do you recall saying that?

A. I believe I said something to that effect in the -- in characterizing the final rejection in the first application, yes.

Q. And what caught my attention was the word evidence. That is the word you used, correct?

A. I believe so, yes.

Q. And that is what Patent Examiners consider; isn't that right?

A. Evidence?

Q. Evidence.

A. In appropriate cases, yes. It comes up where they feel that they have ... established a prima facie case of obviousness, based on the patents that they're relying on, or the prior art, and then the applicant attempts to rebut that prima facie case of obviousness, generally by showing some sort of unexpected results, and that is done frequently by submission of affidavits or declarations, as was the case here.

Q. And what the Examiners then are required to consider is the evidence, correct?

A. And the arguments. They will pay attention to all of it, if they do, yes.

Q. Well, let's talk about evidence.

    The Rule 132 Declaration, at pages 45 through 51 of the file history, is evidence; is that correct?

A. Yes.

Q. And the Rule 132 Declaration at pages 58 and 59 is evidence correct?

A. If that's -- I'll locate it. Is that the second declaration?

Q. Correct.

A. Yes, that's correct.

Q. And the three ANPA patents that were submitted to the Patent Examiner is evidence, correct?

A. Yes.

Q. As is the article, correct?

A. That's correct.

Q. And Patent Examiners, as you understand it, are required to consider the evidence, correct?

A. They are supposed to do that. Whether they do in detail in every case is a severe question. I don't believe that they do, because they -- they are very busy people, and do not have the time.

They're under a quota system. They frequently do not have the time to look at voluminous materials in detail, and again, this is the reason why the applicants have a duty of candor, so that the -- to help short-circuit this --

MR. NIRO: Your Honor, I move to strike that answer. It's, one, not responsive; two, absolutely contrary to -- I move to strike his answer.

MR. DINNIN: We object and oppose to strike. I think it's completely improper. He was answering the question and explaining the reasons for his answer, Your Honor.

THE COURT: Overruled. Go to your next question.

⸎ ⸎ ⸎ ⸎ ⸎

Q. You understand that it's not appropriate to question the skills or experience of a Patent Examiner; isn't that right?

A. Are you asking me to testify to some piece of law?

Q. I'm asking you a question, sir. Can you answer it?

A. Is that a legal question?

Q. That's my question to you. Can you answer it?

A. Okay. I have no such understanding.

Q. Take a look at that decision [of] the Federal Circuit, and tell me whether that changes your opinion.

THE COURT: Do you want to have it on the record, what you're showing him?

MR. NIRO: Yes. That's the Western Electric case that I discussed earlier with the court.

THE WITNESS: I don't think this changes my mind, at least the part that says it's in here. It says, "It is no more appropriate to question a Patent Examiner's technical expertise than it is to question the quality of a judge's law school education or judicial experience."

I'm not questioning the Patent Examiner's technical expertise, here.

(Transcript, <u>Flint</u> v. <u>Brower</u>, Civil Action No. 93-CV-73761-DT (E.D. Mich.), May 3, 1996, pp. 175-179).

Now came what proved to be a decisive moment. Flint's expert admitted he made mistakes too. But it wasn't fraud or inequitable conduct when he made a mistake because he didn't intend to do it (just like the Court found Mr. Sease did not intend to deceive the Patent Examiner):

Q. Now, in the 35 years that you've practiced patent law, preparing and prosecuting patent applications, have you ever made a mistake?

A. I'm sure I have.

Q. And when you made your mistakes in prosecution of [a] patent application, did you consider those to be a violation of Rule 56?

A. No, I didn't, because I think when I became aware of them, I corrected them on the record.

Q. And when you didn't become aware of them, you didn't correct them on the record, correct?

A. There may be a few out there that have never been -- that I'm still unaware of today; that's correct.

Q. *And you didn't feel you violated Rule 56, because you didn't intend to mislead, right?*

A. *That's correct.*

MR. NIRO: Thank you. Nothing further.

(Transcript, May 3, 1996, pp. 179-180; emphasis added). Well, Sharen Brower's lawyer did not intend to deceive either. The Court found no fraud and no inequitable conduct. The stage was now set to win $48 million for the artist/school teacher from the little town in Iowa.

WOULD AN EXPERT LIE
ABOUT HIS EDUCATION?

<u>USM Corporation</u> v. <u>Detroit Plastic Molding Company</u>,
Civil Action No. 6-72536 (E.D. Mich., Dec. 1980)

Like the <u>Brower</u> case, this case also took place in Detroit. It was a battle over injection-molded foam glove-box doors sold to General Motors. Our client had two patents on the injection-molding process. Plastic was heated by extrusion through a restriction setting off a chemical decomposition that created gas bubbles and, thus, a foam interior for the glove-box door.

Ernie Brooks (opposing counsel) was brought in about a year into the case as new counsel to battle me. He introduced himself like this: "I'm your new enemy." Well, an enemy he was. It was like hand-to-hand combat. But, his expert lied about his qualifications at trial. He testified on direct that he had graduated from Wayne State University with a Bachelor of Science degree in Mechanical Engineering. How did I know he was lying? I had the transcript from his deposition in another case where he testified he had not graduated. The testimony went like this:

Q.   Mr. Hendry, you graduated from Wayne State with a degree in mechanical engineering in 1942; is that right?

A.   Yes.

Q.   I'd like to ask you a few questions about the details of your educational background.

A.   Uh-huh.

Q.   Did you take any formalized courses in chemistry, in physical chemistry or organic chemistry?

A.   Very little. I'm not a chemical engineer.

Q.   In the course of your undergraduate studies did you take any course in heat transfer, fluid mechanical fluid flow?

A.   We had minor courses in those.

Q.   Did you take any courses in instrumentation?

A.   Just as we had it relating to stress and materials.

Q.   Did you take any specialized courses in plastic technology?

A.   No.

Q.   You're quite certain you graduated in 1942?

A.   Yes.

Q.   Did you previously give testimony, Mr. Hendry, in a civil action entitled "Union Carbide Corporation versus Borg Warner"?

A.   Yes.

Q.   Were you employed by Excello at that time?

A.   Yes.

Q.   Do you recall that your deposition was taken by Mr. Dugal --

A.   Dugal McDougall; that's right.

Q.   Who is he?

A.   He was an attorney, trial attorney, for Borg Warner.

Q.   I'd like to read -- you were on the same side of the case as Mr. McDougall then?

A.   Yes, I was.

Q.   I'd like to read you several questions and answers that you gave in a deposition taken on June 24, 1974 in that proceeding.

> Question: Would you give us, Mr. Hendry, a brief sketch of your formal education since graduating from high school?
>
> Answer: Well, I went to -- took some courses at Wayne State in Detroit. I did not graduate.
>
> Question: When did you take those courses at Wayne State?
>
> Answer: 1938, 1939
>
> Question: Any other formal courses?
>
> Answer: No.

Did you give those answers to those questions at that time in that case?

A.   Yes, I did.

Q.   That was the truth, was it not?

A.   Later on I took the rest of the courses to complete it and I can get you my graduate certificate.

Q.   Then you say later on you took courses, this deposition was taken in 1974?

A.   Yes.

Q.   Is it your testimony that you took courses after 1974?

A.   I took courses between that time and this time and got my graduate degree.

Q.   So, as of 1943 through that period of time until post 1974 you did not in fact have a degree in mechanical engineering?

A.   That's correct.

Q.   So your testimony that you gave earlier that you did receive your degree in mechanical engineering in 1942 was in error; is that correct?

A.   That's correct.

(Transcript, December 15, 1980, pp. 4345-4347).

That might have been good enough if it were true. Hendry claimed he had gone back to school after the war and completed his education in mechanical engineering. But, at a break, we checked and Wayne State had no record of him ever taking any courses in mechanical engineering -- **no degree**, **no courses**, **nothing**. I went back on the offensive:

Q.   … Mr. Hendry, I'd like to take you back just a moment to the receipt of your Bachelor of Science Degree in Mechanical Engineering from Wayne State. Was that a four-year course that you attended?

A.   No. It was done over a long period of time. If you would like me to, I can get the records. They're under Watson Hendry; it's an honorary degree, okay.

Q.   When did you receive this honorary degree?

A.   It's a -- it's not a degree exactly. It's a -- in recognition for things that you have done, okay? *I've already discredited the fact, how much longer are you going to go on with it?*

(Transcript, <u>USM</u> v. <u>DPM</u>, Civil Action No. 6-72536 (E.D. Mich.), December 15, 1980, p. 4374; emphasis added). He was coming apart:

Q.   When did you receive a Bachelor of Science Degree in Mechanical Engineering?

A.   It was an honorary degree, not a bachelor.

Q.   You don't have a Bachelor's Degree of Science in Mechanical Engineering?

A.   No, I do not.

Q.   When did you receive this honorary degree from Wayne State?

A.   It's not a degree, it's for recognition on things you have done in the plastics field. They gave three or four or 24 or 48, or whatever.

Q.   Can you tell me when you received this recognition?

A.   '76, '77.

Q.   So, you didn't take any course work subsequent to 1974; is that right?

A.   That's correct.

Q.   You did not take any course work from Wayne State University from 1939 to the present date; is that right?

A.   Yes, I did.

Q.   When did you take these initial courses that you --

A.   1939 and 1938. I worked at Burroughs Adding Machine Company and I went there after school and took some credits then.

Q.   Did you take any further course work?

A.   No.

Q.   At Wayne State thereafter?

A.   No.

Q.   So, just so that I understand this, you finished your last formal course work from Wayne State in what year?

A.   I think it was '39.

Q.   From that point to the present you've taken no further courses towards any degree at Wayne State or any other university, is that correct?

A.   That's correct.

(Transcript, December 15, 1980, pp. 4374-4376). Well, he was at least admitting he lied in his direct and initially on cross-examination.

After this testimony, we got an affidavit from the people at Wayne State. They had no record of Mr. Hendry ever attending any classes there. We went back before the Court and asked that Hendry be brought back to recant his perjured testimony and the Court ordered him to reappear.

What happened next was incredible. Ernie Brooks called Hendry to recant his prior testimony (it is not perjury if you recant before the proceedings end). Both Ernie (who knew about the lies) and the witness were represented by criminal counsel:

Q. Mr. Hendry, when I collected your direct testimony on Monday at page 4304 of the transcript, I asked you "Would you summarize for the Court, please, the extent of your formal education?" And you answered, "I went to Wayne State, got a Bachelor's Degree in Mechanical Engineering." Mr. Hendry, was that response true or false?

A. *That was false*.

Q. At Page 4303, I asked you "When did you receive your degree --" the top of the next page 4304, you answered, "In 1942." Mr. Hendry, was that testimony true or false?

A. *False*.

Q. Subsequently, Mr. Hendry, in USM's cross examination at page 4345, Mr. Niro asked you "Mr. Hendry, you graduated from Wayne State with a degree in mechanical engineering in 1942, is that right? And you answered, "Yes". Was that testimony true or false?

A. *False*.

Q. At Page 4345, Mr. Niro asked you "Did you take any formalized courses in chemistry, in physical chemistry or organic chemistry?" And you answered, "Very little. I'm not a chemical engineer." Mr. Hendry, did you ever take any courses ever in chemistry, in physical chemistry or organic chemistry?

A. *No*.

THE COURT: I'm sorry, what was your answer?

THE WITNESS: *No, I did not*.

Q. (By Mr. Brooks, continuing) Mr. Hendry, at 4345, Mr. Niro asked "In the course of your undergraduate studies, did you take any courses in heat transfer, fluid mechanical fluid flow? You answered, "We had minor courses in those." Did you ever take any such courses?

A.   *No*.

Q.   Was the testimony that you had minor courses true or false?

A.   *False*.

Q.   Mr. Niro asked you "Did you take any courses in instrumentation?" And you answered, "Just as we had it relating to stress and materials." Mr. Hendry, did you ever take any courses that involved instrumentation?

A.   *No*.

Q.   Was the testimony "Just as we had it relating to stress and materials" true or false?

A.   *False*.

Q.   Mr. Niro asked you at Page 4345, "Did you take any specialized courses in plastic technology?" And you answered, "No". His next question was "You're quite certain you graduated in 1942?" And you answered "Yes." Was that testimony true or false?

A.   *False*.

THE COURT: Excuse me, Mr. Brooks, you presented two questions and two answers to Mr. Hendry. Are the answers that --

MR. BROOKS: Let me redo it. I recognize the ambiguity now.

Q.   (By Mr. Brooks continuing) Let me take you through them one at a time. Mr. Hendry, at Page 4345, you were asked "Did you take any specialized courses in plastic technology?" And you answered, "No." To the extent that No implied that you had taken courses at all, was the implication true or false?

A.   I did not take any plastic courses.

Q.   At page 4345, you were asked, "You're quite certain you graduated in 1942?" And you answered, "Yes." Mr. Hendry, was that testimony true or false?

A.   *False*.

Q.   Mr. Hendry, at page 4346, Mr. Niro read to you from a deposition you gave on June 24, 1974 and he read the following questions and answers:

> "Q.   Would you give us, Mr. Hendry a brief sketch of your formal education since graduating from high school?"
>
> "A.   Well, I went to -- took some courses at Wayne State in Detroit. I did not graduate."
>
> "Q.   When did you take those courses at Wayne State?"
>
> "A.   1938, 1939."
>
> "Q.   Any other formal courses?"
>
> "A.   No."

Mr. Hendry, Mr. Niro then asked you "Did you give those answers to those questions at that time in that case?" And you said, "Yes, I did." Was that testimony true or false that you have given those answers in that earlier deposition?

A.   I did give those answers in earlier deposition.

Q.   Mr. Hendry, Mr. Niro then asked you, "That was the truth, was it not?" And you answered, "Later on

I took the rest of the courses to complete it and I can give you my graduate certificate." That's on Page 4347. Was that testimony true or false?

A.   *False*.

Q.   Page 4347, Mr. Niro asked you "When you say later on you took courses, this deposition was taken in 1974?" And you answered, "Yes" was that your understanding as to the timing of that deposition?

A.   The timing of the deposition? What time was it?

Q.   '74.

A.   I think so.

Q.   Mr. Niro then asked you "Is it your testimony that you took courses after 1974?" And you answered, "I took courses between that time and this time and got my graduate degree"[. Wa]s that response true or false, Mr. Hendry?

A.   *False*.

✻ ✻ ✻ ✻ ✻

Q.   (By Mr. Brooks, continuing) Mr. Hendry, did you ever at any time take any course at Wayne State?

A.   *No, I did not*.

Q.   Did you ever at any time receive any recognition from Wayne State?

A.   *No*.

Q.   Mr. Hendry, did you ever at any time receive any certificate from Wayne State?

A.   *No*.

Q. Mr. Hendry, did you ever at any time receive any degree in any form from Wayne State?

A. *No.*

MR. BROOKS: Your Honor, that concludes our continuing examination of Mr. Hendry.

(Transcript, December 18, 1980, pp. 4496-4500, 4502; emphasis added). I didn't have to ask a question.

End of case. Who would believe an expert who lied about his education? Judgment was entered for USM finding its patents valid and infringed. But, how sad and humiliating it must have been for this witness. He had lived this lie in his professional life for years. Yet, under the spotlight of cross-examination, the truth emerged. I felt sorry for him.

A TECHNICAL KNOCK-OUT ("TKO") IN THE FIFTH ROUND

National Business Systems, Inc. v. AM International, Inc.,
Civil Action Nos. 80 C 4915 and 81 C 6227 (N.D. Ill., April 1986)

They say your first million is the best million. Maybe. My first multi-million dollar contingent-fee case was AM International v. NBS. Our take was 35%. The payment was $3 million and our fee a little over $1 million. It does not sound like much now, but back then, Wow! We danced that night like there was no tomorrow.

The invention here was a dual-platen credit card imprinter that made better receipt imprints, which, in turn, meant better machine readability and less cost to sort the credit receipts. There were three patents on this invention. One claim of one of those three patents was held valid and infringed (under the doctrine of equivalents). Every other patent claim was either held invalid or not infringed.

Judge Nicholas J. Bua presided over the damages trial and he wanted a settlement badly. He asked me minutes before the trial began what our demand was. When I said $3 million, he said "That's ridiculous; we are going to trial." And so we did.

Defense counsel was Don Stout, who later became famous (and enormously rich) as a principal in NPT, the company that recovered

$630 million from RIM on its Blackberry phone. The cross-examination of NBS's President proved important. When it concluded, Judge Bua called a halt to the proceedings. He invited Don Stout and me into chambers. The question put to me was: "Is the $3 million still on the table?" When I checked with our client and replied that it was, he asked Mr. Stout to meet with him privately in a conference room next to his office. When they both emerged a few minutes later, Judge Bua announced: "The case is settled at $3 million. Let's go on the record." Don Stout looked like he had been hit by a truck. I felt sorry for him.

A week later, I called Don and asked what the Judge had said to him. (Remember, this was a bench trial.) The answer: "He told me he had heard enough evidence to make his decision and it was going to be a lot more than $3 million." Settling at $3 million was a bargain.

Here is the cross-examination of NBS's president, Clive Raymond. It showed a company that needed and used the invention to build market share and then spent $2 million to defend the right to sell something it later claimed was not important. ***Control on cross-examination is critical.*** I set the tone early -- answer "yes" or "no."

Q.   Mr. Raymond, in order to save some time, I'm going to ask you questions that I would like you to answer yes or no. If you can't answer my questions yes or no, why don't you let me know and I'll ask you another question. All right?

A.   All right.

(Transcript, April 23, 1986, p. 619).

Q.   And they [AM] were the dominant company in that market, and you replaced them, isn't that right?

A.   I don't know that we became the dominant market factor.

Q.   Weren't they the dominant company until you came along?

A.   They were the dominant company, yes.

Q.   Until you came along?

A.   Until I came along? Sure.

Q.   Now, wasn't it NBS' policy to set its prices lower than its competitors' prices, if it could still maintain a reasonable profit?

A.   It was NBS' policy --

Q.   Was that your policy or not?

A.   Yes.

(Transcript, April 23, 1986, pp. 620-621). NBS was a copy-cat company:

Q.   Am I not correct that anything that NBS designed or developed was done in response to a demand in the marketplace; isn't that the case?

A.   Not entirely true.

Q.   Is that correct or not?

A.   No, it isn't.

Q.   Mr. Raymond, on June 16, 1981, you were asked again by Mr. Cook at page 30 of that deposition:

Q.   Can you describe any other additions to the product line?

A.   All right, anything we designed or developed was in response to a demand in the marketplace. The conventional suppliers, the Addressograph Multigraph Company had been selling flatbed data recorders at prices the market no longer wished to pay, and hence, the 170.

Did you give that answer to that question at that time?

A. Yes.

Q. Mr. Raymond, when you decided to enter this business, this infringing business, you made a business decision, not an emotional one, isn't that right?

A. That's right.

Q. You don't make emotional decisions in your business, isn't that right?

A. Not often.

Q. And your decision was such that you wanted to maximize the income of your company, isn't that right?

A. That's correct.

Q. Now, you had this dual stroke imprinter being made by an outside company, Stahle, isn't that right?

A. That's correct.

Q. And they manufactured it and you sold it, correct?

A. Correct.

Q. You bought it from them?

A. Yes.

Q. And you only had to spend about 17 or $18,000 in order to get into this business, isn't that right?

A. Correct.

Q. You didn't have to spend a great deal of money or a great deal of effort to enter this infringing business, correct?

A. Correct.

Q. And the goal was to increase the profitability of your company, right?

A. Correct.

Q. To make more money?

A. Yes.

Q. As you put it, to get a better or different mousetrap, right?

A. Yes.

Q. Now, your company has grown from the point in time that you introduced this infringing product from approximately $5 million a year in sales Canadian in 1978 to about $85 million or so this year, if the projections are right; is that right?

A. Correct.

Q. You're a successful company?

A. Yes.

Q. Now, you said, as I understood it, that there were advantages to both machines, the infringing machine and the non-infringing machine, right?

A. Yes.

Q. It was Twiddle-Dee or Twiddle-Dum; it didn't make much difference to you which one you sold, correct?

A.   Correct.

Q.   You didn't need this product?

A.   We didn't.

Q.   And you would have just switched back to the non-infringing product if you didn't have it, is that right?

A.   Correct, in time.

Q.   Customers didn't prefer it, is that right?

A.   Not generally. There were customers that preferred both models.

Q.   There was no customer demand for it, is that correct?

A.   I think the customer demand came about when they said, well, let's join in the club.

(Transcript, April 23, 1986, pp. 622-625). Look what NBS spent to defend its ability to sell a product it didn't need:

Q.   Now, you spent $2 million in this litigation in order to protect your ability to sell that product, isn't that right?

A.   Well, in hindsight --

Q.   Did you do it or not?

A.   Yes, we did.

Q.   You did that for a product you didn't care about; you were willing to spend $2 million to protect it, is that right?

A.   Well, we weren't prepared to spend $2 million to start with. We didn't know it was going to cost that much.

Q. Mr. Raymond, do you recall that I took your deposition about a month ago?

A. Yes.

Q. Do you recall that?

A. Yes.

Q. Page 42 of the transcript of that deposition taken on March -- Mach 19, 1986, I asked you this question:

Q. So, for a product that you really didn't care so much about, you were at least willing to spend $2 million on it to protect it, is that right?

A. In light of history.

Did you give that answer to that question?

THE COURT: I'm sorry, I didn't hear the answer.

THE WITNESS: What did I say?

BY MR. NIRO:

Q. (Laughing). "In light of history."

A. Yes.

Q. Did you give that answer to that question at that time?

A. I think I just said it again.

Q. You could have saved $2 million just by dropping the product, is that correct?

A. Had I known I was spending $2 million, yes.

(Transcript, April 23, 1986, pp. 622-627). Judge Bua later told me that once he heard NBS had spent $2 million fighting to keep a product it said was not important, his mind was made up -- $3 million was reasonable for a settlement.

Q. Is it not a fact, sir, that the dual roller/dual stroke imprinter, infringing imprinter, was significant to your business? Yes or no?

A. I just testified it was not.

Q. Didn't you want to keep it?

A. We were -- we wanted to keep it.

Q. And didn't it help launch your company?

A. That's a pretty loose word.

Q. Did it help launch your company? Yes or no.

A. Launch in the sense of being one product, yes, that helped other products.

Q. So, it did help launch your company, did it not?

A. It helped launch the company. Any product in a new company helps launch it.'

Q. Sir, could you just answer my question? Did it help launch your company? Yes or no.

A. I can only answer in light of my answer I just gave you.

Q. Well, when I asked you that question in your deposition, at page 48:

Q. Would you agree the dual roller/dual stroke machines helped launch your company?

And the answer is "Yes."

Did you give that answer at that time?

A.   Yes. I've just clarified it.

(Transcript, April 23, 1986, pp. 627-628).

Q.   Now, what happened, in fact, after you introduced the dual roller/dual stroke machine is that you replaced the single stroke machine in terms of what was happening in the marketplace; isn't that correct?

A.   In the United States, yes.

Q.   We have a chart, Exhibit 201, that shows your sales in the United States of infringing imprinters in red going up and your sales beginning in 1977 of the non-infringing imprinter, the single stroke imprinters, going down.

      Do you see that?

A.   Yes.

      MR. STOUT: Your Honor, may I note an objection? I would just like the record to reflect that I object to the accuracy of the chart in depicting what happened in 1977. It's contrary to our stipulation.

      MR. R. NIRO: I don't think it shows any --

      THE COURT: I beg your pardon? I can't hear you.

      MR. R. NIRO: I think it shows zero sales of non-infringing -- or infringing products in 1977.

      MR. STOUT: This area here is certainly between 1977 and 1978.

      THE COURT: You're talking about half the year.

      MR. R. NIRO: Right.

      THE COURT: Your objection is noted for the record.

MR. STOUT: Thank you.

BY MR. NIRO:

Q. Mr. Raymond, does this chart, as best you can determine, accurately reflect what was happening in the marketplace in terms of your sales of the infringing imprinters versus the non-infringing imprinters in the United States?

A. I can't say how accurate it is, but the trend was certainly to dual stroke machines in the United States.

Q. That's what the customer wanted, isn't that right?

A. That's what the salesmen decided the customer wanted, as well.

Q. That's what you were selling, isn't that right?

A. We were selling both.

Q. So, the answer is yes?

A. Yes.

(Transcript, April 23, 1986, pp. 628-630). By pricing low, NBS took the market away from AM (who created the invention):

Q. Now, you sold, from a pricing standpoint, at the low end of the market in terms of price, isn't that right?

A. Yes.

Q. Your prices were low?

A. Yes.

Q. And one of the things you were trying to do was to buy market share, isn't that right?

A. Wasn't everybody else?

Q. Is that what you were trying to do?

A. Yes.

＊ ＊ ＊ ＊ ＊

Q. All right, and you were willing to accept lower margins to increase that market share, isn't that right?

A. That's the reality of the world, yes.

Q. And your objective was to give the customer your product at the lowest possible price, isn't that right?

A. That's what the customer wanted.

Q. Isn't that what you were trying to do?

A. Yes, we were trying to meet the customers' needs.

Q. All right, your strategy was to build your market share quickly, is that correct?

A. Our strategy was to get as much market as we could, yes.

Q. Your strategy was to build your market share quicker, correct?

A. Yes.

Q. And you wanted to build product recognition quickly?

A. Yes.

Q. And you wanted to establish market presence quickly, isn't that correct?

A. Yes.

Q. And you wanted to develop market share sometimes at the expense even of margins, isn't that right?

A.   Yes.

Q.   And this gave you an opportunity to get credibility in the marketplace, isn't that right?

A.   We already had the credibility.

Q.   Didn't this provide you with an opportunity to get credibility, building this market share?

A.   It aided it.

Q.   All right, and it gave you an opportunity to do repeat business, is that correct?

A.   That's the name of the game.

Q.   And it gave you an opportunity to reduce your costs, isn't that right?

A.   Yes, hopefully.

(Transcript, April 23, 1986, pp. 630-632). I got him to disagree with other witnesses' testimony:

Q.   Now, you took business away from Security, did you not, solely on the basis of price?

A.   I'm sure we did, and I'm sure they took business from us.

Q.   Did you take business away from them solely on the basis of price?

A.   I'm not aware of it. I don't know.

Q.   Mr. Heasly -- you know Mr. Heasly, don't you?

A.   Oh, yes, I know him.

Q.   He's the president of Security?

A.   Yes.

Q. One of your competitors?

A. Yes.

Q. He testified in this case earlier in the week. I'll read you a portion of his testimony at Page 59 and -- Pages 59 and 60 of the proceedings in this case:

> "Q. Do you have knowledge of the circumstances or reasons why Security lost sales where it was competing with NBS for a particular sale?
>
> A. Yes.
>
> Q. Would you relate what those reasons are?
>
> A. Usually the information we get is that price is lower.
>
> Q. Than NBS'?
>
> A. Than NBS' price, yes."

Now, do you have any reason to believe that Mr. Heasly was not telling the truth when he gave this testimony?

A. No, I think Mr. Heasly is very biased in his testimony, as he ought to be.

Q. Didn't you lead the prices downward?

A. No, we did not. I told you Bartizan was already way down before anybody else came into the market with low prices.

Q. So your answer is no?

A. No.

Q. Mr. Heasly testified at Page 108:

"Q. Did any of those companies use price, lower price, as its chief strategy?

A. By companies, you are talking about competitors?

Q. Your competitors.

A. Yes, I believe so.

Q. Who?

A. NBS."

Do you believe that Mr. Heasly was not telling the truth when he gave this testimony?

A. I think Mr. Heasly was giving his distorted version of the truth?

Q. His distorted version of the truth?

A. Yes.

Q. So, he wasn't telling the truth, is that right?

A. He was telling it as he -- as it suited him.

Q. Now, you took business away from Bartizan solely on the basis of price, did you not?

A. I don't know.

Q. I will read to you from the testimony of Mr. Hoff. you know him, don't you?

A. Oh, yes, I do.

Q. He gave testimony in this case, as follows:

"Q. To what extent, if at all -- "

This is at page 129 of the record.

> "Q. To what extent, if at all, did you lose business to NBS and other accounts because of price?
>
> A. In my opinion, each and every time we lost business to NBS it was solely because of price.
>
> Q. Did you lose the business to NBS because of any other reason?
>
> A. I don't believe so."

Now, do you think Mr. Hoff was not telling the truth when he gave that testimony?

A. Another self-serving answer.

Q. Was he telling the truth in your opinion, or not?

A. He was presenting it as he wanted it.

Q. He was telling something that was self-serving, but not the truth?

A. Absolutely.

Q. All right, sir.

A. And he's part of this litigation.

Q. Mr. Hoff also testified, as follows, and this is at Page 127.

> "Q. To what extent did you observe the pricing patterns, if any, of NBS in the course of this competition?
>
> A. I would say in every instance, their prices were lower than ours, and in my viewpoint, pricing was central to their marketing strategy.

> Q. Did you observe their pricing?
>
> A. I observed it in the sense that I got feedback from our customers or prospects."

Now do you believe again that Mr. Hoff was using some self-serving version of the truth here?

A. Absolutely. The pot calling the kettle black.

Q. Now, you took business away from AM on the basis of price, did you not?

A. Yes.

(Transcript, April 23, 1986, pp. 632-636). The patented invention was better:

Q. Well, didn't the customers, the people that were buying your imprinters, the banking and financial institutions, didn't they perceive the dual stroke machines, the infringing machines to give a better imprint rate?

A. I'm not sure. There were quite acceptable imprint rates for the Bank of America on a single stroke machine. I do know that.

Q. You don't know whether or not there is a perception on the part of the customers that a two-stroke machine is more readable and gives better quality?

A. There may be a perception, yes. I am talking about the reality.

Q. So the answer is that as far as you know, there is a perception among the customers that the dual roller/ dual stroke machine, the infringing machine, gives a more reasonable and better quality. Is that right?

A. Yes.

Q.   And your salesmen helped sell on that basis. Isn't that right?

A.   Yes, they joined the gang.

(Transcript, April 23, 1986, pp. 639-640). ***End of story. End of case.*** We had our first million-dollar contingent-fee case.

THE OTHER SIDE'S EXPERT
WINS THE CASE FOR US

**In The Matter Of Mahurkar Double
Lumen Hemodialysis Catheter Patent Litigation,**
Civil Action No. MDL-853 (N.D. Ill., Aug. 1993)

In 1992, I had the privilege (if you want to call it that) of trying a patent infringement case before Frank Easterbrook, now the Chief Judge of the Seventh Circuit. Judge Easterbrook was sitting by designation as a district judge and, without a doubt, is one of the smartest individuals I have ever met -- he remembered everything he read, saw or heard. Amazing. He reminded me of my friend, Jeff Brinck, the number one student in our law school class. Amazing.

Our client, Dr. Sakharam Mahurkar, had patents on a hemodialysis catheter for treating acute kidney failure. Judge Easterbrook had previously held on summary judgment that because Dr. Mahurkar's utility patent was based upon an earlier design patent application (which had no words, only drawings), according to Judge Easterbrook, it contained no written description of the invention. The Federal Circuit reversed (Vas-Cath, Inc. v. Mahurkar, 935 F.2d 1555 (Fed. Cir. 1991)), holding the issue of whether a design drawing could provide a written description of a utility invention was a question of fact that could only be resolved by determining what a person of ordinary skill in the art would understand. Thus, the issue was, "Could a person skilled in catheter design look at the design drawings and see and comprehend the utility invention?"

The Mahurkar patent was held invalid because, if the utility patent was not entitled to the design application's earlier filing date, a corresponding Canadian Patent 50089 that had the identical drawings as the design application anticipated the utility patent's claims. It sounds confusing. What made the case a challenge was that Judge Easterbrook was waiting to get the evidence he needed to vindicate his view that the Mahurkar patent was invalid. All he needed was a witness to say the earlier design application drawings were insufficient to provide a written description of the utility invention.

I knew this as I began my cross-examination of the defendant's (IMPRA) expert, Gary Smith. I pretty much wrecked Smith on the issue of obviousness -- he used the wrong legal standard and impermissible hindsight:

Q.   Do you know anything about music?

A.   Some, yes.

Q.   Do you know how many notes there are in the musical scale?

A.   Yes, there's eight.

Q.   Some would say there are twelve, but whether it's eight or twelve, there are a limited number of notes that one can use to write new music, correct?

A.   Correct.

Q.   You'd agree that new music is written every day?

A.   Oh, I would agree [with] that, yes.

(Transcript, August 19, 1992, pp. 931-932). Smith used impermissible hindsight to reconstruct the Mahurkar invention:

Q.   I was intrigued by your analysis on this question of what's old and what's obvious. By my count in your narrative, you broke the Mahurkar inventions down into 25 separate pieces, is that about right?

A.   I haven't counted, but --

Q.   You didn't count the number of pieces you broke it into?

A.   Not specifically, no.

Q.   In the 35 pages between pages 10 and 45 of your narrative, I believe you said that there were 25 -- somewhere in that neighborhood -- 25 separate parts, and that each and every one of those parts was old and well known, is that about right?

A.   That's about right, yes.

Q.   Am I correct, though, that there is no single item of prior art that you are aware of, that you were relying upon, that shows the entire combination of 25 parts all put together in one place, isn't that right?

A.   That's correct.

Q.   Nothing shows the entire combination except the Mahurkar patents, correct?

A.   The entire combination?

Q.   Correct.

A.   I have seen nothing to that extent, correct.

(Transcript, August 19, 1992, pp. 932-933). He admitted he had used an impermissible legal analysis -- breaking an invention into pieces and then reconstructing it:

Q.   What you have done in your analysis is to break the invention down into its parts and then go out into the prior art and find the parts, isn't that right?

A.   It appears as though the --

Q.   Did you do that or not?

A.   Yes, I did.

Q.   And going through that analysis, you first looked at the Mahurkar invention ... the patent. You broke it down into the parts that you saw, and then you went out and looked at the prior art, isn't that right?

A.   Correct.

Q.   Then you put it back together [again, a] little like Humpty Dumpty ... fell off the wall[, right]?

A.   It was put back together.

Q.   Now, you didn't select any of this prior art, isn't that right?

A.   That's correct.

Q.   That was all done for you?

A.   Yes.

Q.   It was given to you by [IMPRA's counsel] Mr. Glazer?

A.   Yes.

(Transcript, August 19, 1992, pp. 933-934). Smith had no basis to combine the prior art:

> Q. And in your narrative, you didn't make a judgment as to whether or not the individual elements that you had itemized, that 25 or so components, you didn't make a judgment in your narrative as to whether or not they could be combined, isn't that right?
>
> A. That's correct.
>
> Q. You expressed no opinion that the prior art itself suggested any combination of that kind, isn't that right?
>
> A. Could you repeat the question?
>
> Q. You expressed no opinion in your narrative that the prior art itself suggested the combination set forth in the Mahurkar patents, isn't that right?
>
> A. Correct.
>
> Q. And you've agreed with me that there is no single item of prior art that has the entire combination, right?
>
> A. None that I've seen, that's correct.
>
> Q. When your deposition was taken, I think you said that you had spent somewhere in the neighborhood of three days of work, 24 hours or thereabouts working on this particular assignment, is that right?
>
> A. That's correct.
>
> Q. And in that time, you discussed the patents and other prior art and prepared your narrative, is that right?
>
> A. That's correct.

Q. And you didn't do the search, I think you established that, to find this prior art, correct?

A. Correct.

Q. And you didn't draw on your specific personal experience in selecting it, correct?

A. Correct.

Q. And you didn't have any opinions concerning the significance of any of that [prior] art from a legal standpoint, at least at the time of your deposition, correct?

A. That's correct.

Q. And you didn't talk to any IMPRA technical personnel to get their input on this subject, isn't that right?

A. That is also correct.

Q. You talked only to Mr. Glazer, right?

A. Correct.

Q. And then he wrote your narrative, and you signed it, right?

A. We reviewed it and [collaborated] on it extensively.

Q. Did you write it or [did] he write it?

A. I didn't specifically put pen to paper.

(Transcript, In re Mahurkar, Civil Action No. MDL-853 (N.D. Ill.), August 19, 1992, pp. 937-938).

But how could I get him to admit he could see everything in the Canadian patent (which was identical to the design patent that was the basis for the utility patent claims)? I had to get him moving in that direction because he wanted to prove the patent invalid because it was all there. What he didn't realize (until it was too late) is that by saying it was all there and he could see it, he actually was supporting the validity of Dr. Mahurkar's patent. It was late in the day, but I sensed an important moment and the judge gave me 10 minutes. It turned out to be the ten minutes that won the case:

> MR. NIRO: If your Honor would allow me ten minutes to cover one line, I can't finish him tonight and I leave it to the Court as to whether you would like to break now. There is one line that is fairly short. I think I could cover if your Honor thinks it's appropriate. If not, we can start in the morning.

> THE COURT: If you want to do it in ten minutes, we'll take ten minutes and then break and come back tomorrow morning.

> MR. NIRO: All right. Thank you.

> BY MR. NIRO:

> Q. You were shown the Canadian design patent -- maybe Mr. Glazer can help me find that particular patent -- and you were asked some questions about it.

❖ ❖ ❖ ❖ ❖

> Q. Okay. I'm going to use MMDL-425, which are the design drawings for the application 356,081 and ask you a few questions about it.

> I think in response to Mr. Glazer, you identified some of the things that were in the Canadian design. I'd like to go through those with you. You recognize there's a Double-D cross-section?

A.   Yes.

Q.   And it's a one-piece construction, I think you said?

A.   Yes, I did.

Q.   And a dual lumen --

A.   Dual lumen.

Q.   -- catheter? Has a conical tapered tip, correct?

A.   Correct.

Q.   And you even testified that the element in green was a strain relief?

A.   Yes.

Q.   That's immediately below the section 3 in figure 1. It has a septum; you can see that, correct?

A.   Correct.

Q.   And that septum is longitudinal, isn't that right?

A.   That's correct.

Q.   And planar, is that correct?

A.   Planar.

Q.   It divides the interior of the two lumens?

A.   Yes.

Q.   Separates the tube into two lumens?

A.   Separates the tube.

Q.   There's a longer lumen and a shorter lumen, correct?

A.   Correct.

Q.   You can see that in the drawings?

A.   Yes, I can.

Q.   You can understand that, correct?

A.   Yes.

Q.   And the openings are axially spaced, is that correct; the longer lumen and the shorter lumen, is that right?

A.   Yes.

Q.   And you can see that in the drawing?

A.   I can see that.

Q.   It has a smooth, conical tapered tip again, correct?

A.   Correct.

Q.   And the longer lumen goes the length of the catheter, correct, end to end.

A.   End to end.

Q.   And its inside wall; that is, the wall of that lumen, the longer lumen, extends the length of the catheter, correct?

A.   The longer lumen from the drawing, I can see extends -- yes.

Q.   You see the longer lumen has a septum --

A.   That's correct.

Q.   -- and it forms a wall?

A.   An outer wall.

Q.   And that wall then extends the length of the catheter to define the passageway, correct?

A.   Correct.

Q. And you can see that in the drawings and understand that, correct?

A. Yes.

Q. And the diameter at this point I'll call A is greater than the diameter B, isn't that right; that is --

A. Is that arrow pointing to the septum there?

Q. Yes. Diameter A I have is the diameter of the catheter --

A. The diameter.

Q. -- below the end of the shorter lumen.

A. I'm referring to the diameter B that you put on, is that --

Q. That's the diameter of the lumen itself.

A. Okay. Your pencil mark is extending to the inner wall. Yes.

Q. Okay. And the cross-section, figure 5, shows that; namely, that the diameter of this catheter at the point below the -- at that point below the shorter lumen, the end of the shorter lumen is of a larger diameter than the point above it; namely, that point B.

A. Yes.

Q. Correct?

A. Correct.

Q. It shows that the tip is part of the catheter, this drawing?

A. It's uniform, yes.

Q. And it's integral, is that correct?

A.   Correct.

Q.   And you can see all of this?

A.   On this drawing, yeah.

Q.   And you can understand that?

A.   Yes.

Q.   You have no problem doing that, correct?

A.   Correct.

Q.   *Using your limited skills in this field as a non-hemodialysis catheter expert, someone not skilled in the catheter design in that area, you had no problem putting that together and understanding that, correct?*

A.   *Correct.*

Q.   *You could see it all in combination, correct, that entire combination?*

A.   *Correct.*

Q.   *And you didn't have any trouble getting to those words, Double-D, relative diameters, and so forth, correct?*

A.   *Yes.*

MR. NIRO: *I think my ten minutes are up.*

THE COURT: Thank you very much, Mr. Niro. We will see you tomorrow morning at 9:30.

(Transcript, <u>In re Mahurkar</u>, Civil Action No. MDL-853 (N.D. Ill.), August 18, 1992, pp. 920-926; emphasis added). After that testimony, Judge Easterbrook nodded at me as if to say, "You did it!" Incredibly,

IMPRA's expert had admitted the design application did show everything claimed in the utility patent. *We had won*.

As Judge Easterbrook explained in his opinion, I had gotten IMPRA's expert to admit that all the elements of the claims of the '141 utility patent were shown in the Canadian design patent drawings and, thus, in the U.S. design application as well. The design drawings provided a written description of the invention:

> Resolving a tension in its own cases, the Federal Circuit concluded on an earlier appeal that diagrams may satisfy the "written description" requirement of § 112 when they "clearly allow persons of ordinary skill in the art to recognize that [he or she] invented what is claimed."

⊩ ⊪ ⊪ ⊪ ⊪

> But of course judges and other amateurs in this technical field are not the right audience. During the trial each of Mahurkar's three experts in catheter design stepped through each of the elements in each claim of the '968 and '141 patents. *Each expert was asked whether the claim could be seen in the design drawings. Each answered yes.* Mahurkar's lawyers produced charts relating each element of each independent claim to a specific part of the drawings. The experts stated that this correspondence was accurate. *I credit those answers*, which when combined with the Federal Circuit's legal standard means that the design applications satisfy the written description requirement of § 112.

⊩ ⊪ ⊪ ⊪ ⊪

> ... Still, the leaders of a field understand something about how the median members of the discipline think, and each of the three witnesses testified that not

only he but also a "normal" catheter designer could see the correspondence. *I credit those statements, too -- especially given what happened when IMPRA's expert Smith took the stand. Mahurkar's lawyer took Mr. Smith through exactly the same charts and questions. Could Smith see the correspondence between the design drawings and the claims of the utility patents? Yes, Smith answered, he could, at least for the '141 patent (in which the link between the drawings and the utility claims is harder to establish).*

In the Matter of Mahurkar Double Lumen Hemodialysis Catheter Patent Litigation, 831 F. Supp. 1354, 1362-63 (N.D. Ill. 1993) (bracketed material in original; emphasis added).

And this is what Judge Easterbook had to say on the issue of obviousness in his post-trial opinion:

> All of this is just another way of making a staple proposition in patent law: decomposing an invention into its constituent elements, finding each element in the prior art, and then claiming that it is easy to reassemble these elements into the invention, is a forbidden ex post analysis. E.g., *In re Fritch*, 972 F.2d 1260, 1265-66 (Fed. Cir. 1992). With hindsight the transistor is obvious; but devising the transistor was still a work of genius. An invention lies in a combination of elements that are themselves mundane. "Virtually all inventions are combinations and virtually all are combinations of old elements." *Environmental Designs, Ltd. v. Union Oil Co.*, 713 F.2d 693, 698 (Fed. Cir. 1983).

⚜ ⚜ ⚜ ⚜ ⚜

> Certainly IMPRA has not established anticipation or obviousness by clear and convincing evidence. Its technical witness, Gary Smith, is not an expert in either

kidney disease or catheter design. His job is managing quality control at a firm making arterial catheters (which carry wires to pacemakers); he did not design any of these devices. He knows nothing of the *objectives* of the designs he analyzed for purposes of this case, and although he can see the menu of options he cannot enlighten on how a person skilled in the art in 1981-83 would have chosen among them for optimal results. He explicitly followed the forbidden strategy of decomposing the patented device into elements and seeing whether he could find each in some other catheter. He found 25 such elements, and testified that each of the 25 appears in some other device. Smith added that *he* thought it obvious how to reassemble them to get the '968 catheter. This is much like testifying that because Shakespeare used only 26 letters, each of which had been used many times before, his plays are obvious.

◦ ◦ ◦ ◦ ◦

Perhaps turning to the secondary evidence is an occasion for a 15-yard piling-on penalty. Doing so, however, removes the last vestiges of doubt.

The existence of an enduring, unmet need is strong evidence that the invention is novel, not obvious, and not anticipated. If people are clamoring for a solution, and the best minds do not find it for years, that is practical evidence -- the kind that can't be bought from a hired expert, the kind that does not depend on fallible memories or doubtful inferences -- of the state of knowledge.

In the Matter of Mahurkar Double Lumen Hemodialysis Catheter Patent Litigation, 831 F. Supp. 1354, 1374-75, 1377-78 (N.D. Ill. 1993; emphasis added).

We had won over the toughest juror of all -- the trial judge -- who had earlier held the Mahurkar patent invalid, but in the end (because of the cross-examination of the defendant's expert) found the patent valid and infringed. It was a great victory, as though I was getting up off the canvas with the referee counting 5, 6, 7, 8.... And winning through the opposing side's expert is the best thrill of all.

THE FINAL WORD

In reflecting on the cases discussed in this book, a couple of thoughts occur to me. First, so much, it seems, is centered on cross-examination of the opposition's expert. I have often wondered why use experts at all when their testimony can be so harmful. We had experts implode on us in the MuniAuction and USM cases and had to drop our technical experts in the TFD and Westinghouse cases. The C&F, Bosch, Southwestern, Porter-Cable, Mahurkar and USM cases were likely won on expert cross. In Calabrese, we did just fine without any experts.

Then, of course, there is the exception: Joe McAlexander in the Grail Semiconductor v. Mitsubishi case (which resulted in a $124 million verdict in May 2012) carried the day for us with his incredible technical skills, Texas charm and ability to explain complex technology (semiconductor memory chips) to a jury. Having good witnesses (often the inventors themselves) and a good story also really helps. In the Polaris case, our client had retained the world's most renowned expert on two-cycle engines. But we refused to use him because we felt the best witness on the technology was our own inventor, Ron Chasteen, and he had to testify anyway. Worse, the technical expert retained by our client was a disaster waiting to happen. So we used Ron and the result was the then-largest collected verdict ever in Colorado -- $75 million.

We had hats made in the IMS v. Haas case that said "Speed Kills." People at the hotel thought we were DEA agents. But the speed we were referring to was the speed with which we were forced to finish the trial in the Eastern District of Virginia ("the rocket docket"). I believe it is always a good idea to put your case on in three days or less. Be efficient. Don't be repetitive (Judy accuses me of this all the time). Make your point and get on with it. And always respect the jury's time and commitment. The string of witnesses we destroyed in one day in the Black & Decker v. Coleman case shows what can happen when you use speed to your advantage. The night before the cross-examination of the defendant's parade of witnesses, the entire team sat in my room to plan our cross. I sat on the floor with a folder for each witness and everyone contributed ideas. My son, Raymond, found the mistake in the declaration and the hole in the damage expert's report that let me go into the prior jury verdict in our favor. The speed and focus we used the next day won the case.

I have always believed that no one has a monopoly on good ideas. My closings in C&F, TCS and MuniAuction were inspired by my family, my personal experiences and the insight of my wife, Judy. My son, Dean, was critical in the IRS, Porter-Cable and Bosch cases. Brady Fulton noticed the verbatim testimony in the witness declarations that undermined the key defense witness in the TCS case. Countless others helped in all the cases and I remained open to all suggestions. (I do not adopt them all, but I do listen.)

Maybe the very best example of mining an idea occurred in the Flow-Rite of Tennessee v. Sears Roebuck & Co., et al. case. I make a point of putting enlargements of the patent before the jury during my opening. There is a blue ribbon along the side and, in this case, the defendant's lawyer told the jury in his opening to remember that, "Blue ribbons don't make heroes." One of our secretaries, Barb Zylman, who was in the back of the courtroom during openings told me afterward that she really didn't like the comment about blue ribbons not making heroes. I put that thought away to use later. And defense counsel did it again in closing. It became the cornerstone of my closing remarks to the jury:

> You know, we have heard twice now about the blue ribbon. And I want to show you the blue ribbon again. It's right on the cover of the patent. The blue ribbon with the seal, little red bow at the bottom. Mr. Grumley said in his opening "That a blue ribbon does not a hero make. Don't judge this case on the basis of blue ribbons." And he said it in closing too. "Don't be impressed by the blue ribbon."
>
> And for two weeks that's been ringing in my ears. The blue ribbon does not a hero make. You know, I grew up in a family with a mom and dad who were immigrants and came to this country with no education and who gave [me] the opportunity to -- to be here with you today. And I remember the story that my dad would tell me about becoming a citizen and how he learned about our [C]onstitution and our laws. And he showed me his citizenship papers. He was proud of that. He had become an American. It had a little blue ribbon on it. And it showed that he was accepted. He had paid his dues. ... [H]e was a hero to me.
>
> Well, that blue ribbon means something to David Bethshears. Blue ribbons do make heroes. It shows that somebody recognized his invention, somebody believed it was patentable. And these defendants that come in here with their parade of defenses saying, "It's simple, it's obvious, it's easy, it doesn't work, take it away from

him," they don't care about blue ribbons, but David Bethshears does care about blue ribbons.

Thank you.

(Transcript, Flow-Rite of Tennessee v. Sears Roebuck & Co., et al, Civil Action No. 89 C 4035, October 28, 1991). The jury was out only 20 minutes -- our client's patent was held valid and willfully infringed and there was an award of treble damages which exceeded $4 million. That award eventually increased to $20 million, since we were paid in Wisconsin Pharmacal stock.

Of course, there are many other cases and other cross-examinations and closings that could be in this book. They include the Spencer case involving two physicians fighting over who invented a rod to prevent spinal curvature. And the Black & Decker v. ProTech case concerning the DeWalt yellow and black trademark (where the defendant's expert admitted the DeWalt yellow and black color trademark was as recognizable to tradesmen as the McDonald's golden arches). We did more than 20 lawsuits for B&J Manufacturing Company on rasp blades for preparing tire surfaces for retreading. We have the delayed impeachment in the Matrix (Ray Wenk case), where Tom Scavone asked a witness when another witness was telling the truth -- yesterday or in his deposition (see p. 228). In the Jackson v. Glenayre case, we had to prove a hard-wired circuit was the equivalent of a microprocessor. And the toughest case of all was Flow-Rite, where we had to make fish attractant particles go up (not down). I could write a book on that case alone.

When I started as a trial lawyer, I did some criminal cases which I tried with Bob Cummins -- a charming Irishman who looked like

Robert Redford and, with minimal preparation, could stand on his feet in front of a jury and do the impossible. We actually got "not guilty" verdicts in two successive murder cases. I also won an appeal for Jim Doherty, the Cook County Public Defender, which reversed a guilty verdict in a third murder case. While it was fun at the time, I much prefer intellectual property cases.

The cases in this book are what I recall as the very best. Most cases were won. Each win resulted in a multi-million dollar verdict. Each had an electrifying moment.

I urge trial lawyers who read this book to take the next step and create even better stories from their own cases. Those who read the book because they know me or just wanted to have some fun, take this thought away with you: no giant is so big or bully so overwhelming that they cannot be brought to their knees by someone willing to stand-up to them. That's what cross-examinations and closings are all about.

GO FOR IT!w